Claire Tomalin has worked in publishing and journalism all her life. She was literary editor first of the *New Statesman* and then of the *Sunday Times*, which she left in 1986. She is the author of *The Life and Death of Mary Wollstonecraft*, which won the Whitbread First Book Prize for 1974; *Shelley and His World* (reissued by Penguin in 1992); *Katherine Mansfield: A Secret Life* (1988), a biography of the modernist writer on whom she also based her 1991 play *The Winter Wife*; the highly acclaimed *The Invisible Woman: The Story of Nelly Ternan and Charles Dickens*, which won the 1990 James Tait Black Memorial Prize for Biography, the NCR Book Award in 1991, as well as the Hawthornden Prize; *Mrs Jordan's Profession* (1995), a study of the Regency actress; *Jane Austen: A Life* (1998); a collection of her literary journalism entitled *Several Strangers: Writing from Three Decades* (1999); and *Samuel Pepys: The Unequalled Self*, which won the Whitbread Biography Award and which went on to win the Whitbread Book of the Year Award for 2002. All her books are published by Penguin.

CLAIRE TOMALIN

KATHERINE MANSFIELD
A SECRET
· LIFE ·

PENGUIN BOOKS

PENGUIN BOOKS

Published by the Penguin Group
Penguin Books Ltd, 80 Strand, London WC2R 0RL, England
Penguin Putnam Inc., 375 Hudson Street, New York, New York 10014, USA
Penguin Books Australia Ltd, 250 Camberwell Road, Camberwell, Victoria 3124, Australia
Penguin Books Canada Ltd, 10 Alcorn Avenue, Toronto, Ontario, Canada M4V 3B2
Penguin Books India (P) Ltd, 11 Community Centre, Panchsheel Park, New Delhi – 110 017, India
Penguin Books (NZ) Ltd, Cnr Rosedale and Airborne Roads, Albany, Auckland, New Zealand
Penguin Books (South Africa) (Pty) Ltd, 24 Sturdee Avenue, Rosebank 2196, South Africa

Penguin Books Ltd, Registered Offices: 80 Strand, London WC2R 0RL, England

www.penguin.com

First published by Viking 1987
Published in Penguin Books 1988

9

Printed in England by Clays Ltd, St Ives plc
Filmset in Lasercomp Ehrhardt

www.greenpenguin.co.uk

Penguin Books is committed to a sustainable future
for our business, our readers and our planet.
The book in your hands is made from paper
certified by the Forest Stewardship Council.

This book is dedicated with love
to my father and stepmother
Emile and Katharine Delavenay,
who lent me a sunny Mediterranean terrace
on which to work
and gave me help, advice and encouragement
over many years

'I am a secretive creature to my last bones'
– Katherine Mansfield to Ida Baker, 22 March 1922

CONTENTS

∎

LIST OF PLATES

∎

FOREWORD

∎

Research for this book was begun in the mid 1970s and laid aside for various reasons, one of them being the appearance of biographies of Katherine Mansfield by both Jeffrey Meyers (in 1978) and Antony Alpers (in 1980). Inevitably, there was a wide overlap of research. It could hardly have been otherwise. Mr Alpers has devoted many decades to interviewing and researching – he published an earlier biography in 1953 – and must be the greatest living authority on his subject. Professor Meyers is also prodigiously widely read and vigorous in pursuit of his subject. I read both of their books with admiration, and have profited from both of them.

My own notes, correspondence and draft chapters were put to gather dust and I turned to other work. After some years, however, I began to think that there might be something else to say about Katherine Mansfield after all, some fresh material to be considered, a different perspective from which to view her. Mr Alpers had certainly produced the epic version, with Katherine as playful genius, undervalued and misunderstood on the whole by her contemporaries; he was cautious of J. M. Murry's powers of recall, but inclined to accept his version of those events in which he was involved. Professor Meyers, altogether more cynical in his approach, drew what he called a 'darker' Katherine without, I thought, fully exploring the nature of this darkness.

Both seem to me to have underestimated the importance of certain aspects of her life, in particular the chain of events leading from her first foray into sexual freedom in 1908, and the various long-term results of her association with Floryan Sobieniowski in 1909. I felt that her medical history required more careful study, and the result of this has been a reinterpretation of certain key questions in her life. I have also looked afresh at the blackmail in 1920, and suggested a new approach to that.

Katherine's relations with D. H. Lawrence have been generally underplayed. I have, I hope, shown just how close and important the links between them were, and in particular the use Lawrence made of her experience in some of his most controversial writing. The impress of Katherine's personality on two of the greatest of her contemporaries, Lawrence and Virginia Woolf, produced some very remarkable results.

The fact that I have been able to use the recently published letters of J. M. Murry to Katherine (as well as having access to the unpublished ones) has added a new dimension to the picture of their relationship. I have also had the benefit of many talks with the only daughter of the late Edith Robison (née Bendall) about her mother's character and feelings for Katherine; and Mrs Robison herself kindly taped a long interview for me before she died.

Neither the Oxford University Press *Collected Letters of Katherine Mansfield* (vols. I and II) nor the Cambridge University Press *Letters of D. H. Lawrence* (vols. I, II, III and IV) were available to earlier biographers. Both have enriched and facilitated my work.

One final point is that I am of the same sex as my subject. It may be nonsense to believe that this gives me any advantage over a male biographer. Yet I can't help feeling that any woman who fights her way through life on two fronts – taking a traditional female role, but also seeking male privileges – may have a special sympathy for such a pioneer as Katherine, and find some of her actions and attitudes less baffling than even the most understanding of men.

Virginia Woolf said that women think back through their mothers. As I worked on Katherine Mansfield's story, I often thought of my mother-in-law, herself a wild colonial girl from Canada who brushed the fringes of Bloomsbury; and of my mother, who came to London from Liverpool in 1917 with a music scholarship. They are both dead now, but they were both gallant and gifted outsiders, and through what they told me of their adventures, ambitions and terrors I felt I approached Katherine Mansfield's experience at certain points. Hers was a painful life, and it has been a painful task to write about it; but I am glad to have done it, and to have had the chance to salute a character in whom recklessness and scrupulousness combined in so extraordinary a fashion.

Claire Tomalin
London, 1987

ACKNOWLEDGEMENTS

■

Research for this book was begun in the 1970s and interrupted. I should like to express gratitude to the following people who gave me their time, answered my letters, searched their memories or files and in other ways gave me assistance. To some my thanks are, sadly, posthumous.

Antony Alpers; David Arkelli; Neal Ascherson; Enid Bagnold; Ida Constance Baker; Barbara Barr; Anne Oliver Bell; Professor Quentin Bell; David Blow; Gill Boddy; Professor J. T. Boulton; Margaret Budden; Dr William Bynum; Carmen Callil; John Carswell; Dan Davin; Peter Day; Professor Emile Delavenay; Christopher Edwards; Mrs Valerie Eliot; Faith Evans; Hans Fellner; Michael Frayn; Angelica Garnett; David Garnett; Richard Garnett; Dr A. S. Grimble; Michael Holroyd; Dr and Mrs John Hopkins; Juliette Huxley; Dr Jagodzinski; Professor Frank Kermode; Professor Mark Kinkead-Weekes; Eric Korn; Moira Lynd; Bruce Mason; James Moore; Colin Middleton Murry; Mary Middleton Murry; Rollo Myers; Nigel Nicolson; Mrs J. Nowak; Vincent O'Sullivan; Donna Poppy; Jeanne Renshaw; Susan Rose-Smith; Dorothy Richards (née Trowell); Edith Robison (née Bendall); Margaret Scott; Jackie Simms; Navin Sullivan; Frank Swinnerton; Sophie Tomlin; Professor Joseph Trapp; Douglas Trowell; Dr Trevor Turner; Karen Usborne; Julian Vinogradoff; Christopher Wade; Professor John Waterlow; and Barbara Webber.

I should also like to thank the following libraries or institutions: the Alexander Turnbull Library, Wellington; the British Library; the London Library; the Humanities Research Center, University of Texas at Austin; the Senate House Library, London; the Library of the University of Reading; the University of North Carolina Library at

Chapel Hill; the Library of the Royal College of Obstetricians and Gynaecologists; the Wellcome Library; the Swiss Cottage Public Library; the Polish Cultural Centre Library; the Society of Authors; the Cambridge University Press; and the Oxford University Press.

Grateful acknowledgement is made to the following for permission to reproduce copyright extracts: The literary estates of Virginia Woolf and Leonard Woolf, the Hogarth Press and Harcourt Brace Jovanovich, Inc.; A.D. Peters & Co. Ltd (as the literary representative of A.E. Coppard); Laurence Pollinger Ltd and the Estate of Mrs Frieda Lawrence Ravagli (for *The Letters of D.H. Lawrence*, edited by James T. Boulton, published by Cambridge University Press); the Society of Authors as the literary representative of the Estate of John Middleton Murry, the Estate of Katherine Mansfield (where it applies) and the Bernard Shaw Estate, and King's College, Cambridge, and the Estate of E.M. Forster.

Cambridge University Press; Jonathan Cape Ltd; Constable Publishers; Alfred A. Knopf, Inc.; Oxford University Press (for The *Collected Letters of Katherine Mansfield*, vol. I, 1984, vol. II, 1987, edited by Vincent O'Sullivan and Margaret Scott, copyright © the Estate of Katherine Mansfield, 1984, 1987).

Every effort has been made to trace copyright holders. The publishers would be interested to hear from any copyright holders not here acknowledged.

1

'THE FAVOURITE OF THE GODS'

■

Katherine Mansfield was born a century ago and died in 1923, but there is still something tantalizing about the 'faint ghost with the steady eyes, the mocking lips and, at the end, the wreath set on her hair.'[1] She has been praised and attacked in memoirs, biographies, critical essays, even fiction and drama, and appeared in different guises as the tragic cult figure; the sharp-tongued comedienne; the true modernist who changed the rules for the English-language short story; the pioneering 'New Woman'; the sentimentalist and miniaturist, overpraised and with bad morals – there are many variants of K.M. Readers all over the world have responded to the letters and diaries that record her illness, loneliness and exile and her yearning for husband and a home; at the same time there has been criticism of the way in which her husband, John Middleton Murry, exploited the image of his dead wife by publishing her private papers, and doubts as to the truth of his version of her as 'a perfectly exquisite, perfectly simple human being'.[2] Seen through different eyes, her image trembles and blurs: now ambitious and reckless, now vulnerable and wounded; now a simple seeker after purity and truth in life and art, now tarnished and false.

The very names her parents gave her – Kathleen Mansfield Beauchamp – she transformed into multiple alternative versions to suit different moods, different friends, different facets of her personality: Kass, Katie, K.M., Mansfield, Katherine, Julian Mark, Katherine Schönfeld, Matilda Berry, Katharina, Katiushka, Kissienka, Elizabeth Stanley, Tig, and of course the name by which she became known to the world as a writer, and which, for convenience, this book will stick to.

Her face was often described as being like a mask. She was pale and dark, innocent and decadent, first too fat and then too thin. She was sexually ambiguous, with a husband and a wife, and lovers of both sexes. In her lifetime she was disliked both as a person and as a writer, and also revered as both. Not many people took a stance between these two attitudes, although some – Virginia Woolf was one, D. H. Lawrence another – alternated. The testimony left by these two friends, each outstandingly gifted and sensitive to other people, is of the greatest importance in trying to understand Katherine. She herself cared a great deal for friendship. Her letters went out in convoys, seeking reassurance and making offerings; but she was also manipulative and treacherous. The letters and journals are dizzying switchbacks of love and hate as well as vivid records of work, travel and suffering.

Her life was essentially a lonely one. She travelled too far outside the boundaries of accepted behaviour for her family to feel she was one of them, but she did not find herself at home in any other group, nor did she make a family of her own. The particular stamp of her fiction is also the isolation in which each character dwells. Failure to understand or to be understood is endemic in Mansfield. Foreigners misinterpret one another, adults and children are at cross purposes, gulfs of incomprehension separate wives from husbands. Neither happiness nor pain is shared very much, or for very long. Family life may have a complacent surface, but beneath it fear and cruelty stalk. In one of her most memorable images a good wife imagines giving her husband little packets with her feelings in them, and his surprise as he opens the last packet to find it full of hatred. Hatred was her favourite emotion.

Couples are like cannibals; a man like a python invites a friend like a rabbit to share his flat, and the rabbit agrees meekly. Kindly old men turn into ogres, friendly women into rats, a man wanting a kiss shows teeth like a dog's. The oddities of human appearance and behaviour are relished – Lawrence noted her affinity with Dickens[3] – but there is no history in these stories, and no exploration of motive. The most brilliant of them are post-impressionist (and post-Maupassant) works, grotesquely peopled and alight with colour and movement. For Mansfield, the indifferent beauty of the natural world was a force as strong as any human emotion, giving her a pleasure so keen that it breathes through her sentences today as freshly as when she set them on the page.

Not that she lacked an interested and admiring circle. Many of its members were famous in their own right, and there are patches of her life that look like a literary Piccadilly Circus, as Frank Harris, Rupert

Brooke, Lady Ottoline Morrell, Bertrand Russell, Aldous Huxley, the Lawrences and the whole of the Bloomsbury group crowd past. The convolutions of her relations with them, and the diverse testimony they offer of her kaleidoscopic nature, provide some rather welcome comic relief to a story whose main theme is undoubtedly a black one. For Katherine's early and reckless pursuit of experience brought atrocious punishments. She lived, worked and died with the Furies on her heels.

It could even be said that her story hinges on a single physical fact. By becoming pregnant during the first months of her passionately sought freedom in London, she set in motion a sequence of events which ran to her death fourteen years later, events which darkened her relations with her family most unfortunately; which profoundly affected both her marriages; which involved her reputation as a writer; and which destroyed the foundations of her bodily health. It is a bleak, inescapable, cautionary tale, reading more like one of George Eliot's plots of nemesis than any of the modernist works of Katherine herself or her contemporaries, and involving her in exactly those desperate, secret stratagems into which the heroines of Victorian fiction – Mrs Transome, Lady Dedlock, Lydia Glasher, Gwendolen Harleth – were so often forced.

*   *   *

To become a writer, Katherine felt she had to begin by escaping from her family and country. She changed her name, and she fled from her native New Zealand; and although much of her best writing returns to both family and country, and she herself wondered at the end whether she had been done more harm than good by transplanting herself,[4] the relationship was profoundly uneasy. To understand her, it is necessary to understand her background, the mixture of adventurousness and anxiety she felt as a colonial coming to England, and, not least, the curious attitude displayed by the English towards colonials. Her friend Virginia Woolf allows one of her characters, Louis in *The Waves*, to go through his entire life burdened with a sense of inadequacy because his father is an Australian banker; he can never quite forgive himself this solecism.

Katherine's father was also a banker and born in Australia, although he made his fortune in Wellington, New Zealand. Her mother too was born in Australia, and both were children of men and women who had, for one reason or another, found that they were not wanted, or could not make their way in England. In the nineteenth century, New Zealand was for many a colony of Australia as much as Australia was a colony of England; it was the very last place, the furthest you could go, the end of the line. Perhaps for that very reason the people ('the most provincial on earth', according to Beatrice Webb in the 1890s) yearned towards 'Home' 12,000 miles away all the more, trying to overlay the alien landscapes, plants, beasts and seasons with whatever could lend an illusion of what many had never seen. The wooden bungalows, the municipal buildings, the schools and shops were built to match English mid-Victorian buildings. The pleasant country house in which Katherine spent part of her childhood was named 'Chesney Wold' after the Dedlock mansion in Dickens's *Bleak House*, a name determinedly expressive of cultural loyalty, but less than appropriate to the actual wooden building.

Anthony Trollope, visiting New Zealand in the 1870s when Katherine's father, Harold Beauchamp, was a lad, noticed the New Zealander's 'confidence that England is the best place in the world and he is more English than any Englishman'.[5] As soon as Beauchamp achieved a position which permitted it, he travelled to England. He repeated the journey as often as he could and, by the time he came to write his memoirs, he was able to boast that he had 'crossed the line' twenty-four times. The first of these trips was made in 1889, a year after the birth of his third daughter, Kathleen.

Katherine's childhood was never penurious, and her father made money fast and in large quantities from 1890 onwards; but he had a severe initial struggle. His own father had left London for Australia in the middle of the century to make his fortune with gold or sheep or salesmanship, succeeding at nothing, though always a lively and amusing man, and blessed in his wife, Elizabeth, a Lancashire orphan despatched like a parcel to the antipodes by an aunt, as young women often were at the time. She bore him nine sons and a daughter, all delivered by a Maori midwife once they had moved to New Zealand. When Harold was eleven, his father, in Dickensian style, wanted him to leave school, but the boy pleaded to stay on until he was fourteen. He helped his mother with all the housework, and swept and clerked and auctioned for his father, often working until eleven at night, travelling through the bush on horseback. Sir Harold Beauchamp's *Reminiscences and Recollections* is a discreetly worded book throughout, but it is clear that, while he considered his mother an 'earthly saint', he saw his father as the principal drain on her saintly patience.

All this had a decisive effect on his attitude towards his own wife and daughters. They were shaped, deliberately and determinedly, into the mould of late Victorian ladies whose activities are confined to giving orders to servants, flower-arranging, party-giving, travel, tennis, a little music, a little reading, a little French and German, a little hypochondria and much choosing of hats and camisole ribbons. It gave him evident pride and pleasure to toil first at his insurance business, then as he prospered at the Wellington Harbour Board, and at the boards of frozen meat and chemical and gas companies and banks, in order that these women for whom he was responsible should never go through what he had seen his mother endure.

His insistence on decorous and conventional behaviour may have had a further spur. If his own father was a trial, his first cousin Fred was another, for he settled in New Zealand also, and there begot at least five sons upon a Maori 'wife', giving them the family names of George, Sam, John, Henry and Arthur. Katherine, fascinated by the exoticism of the Maoris and happy to pretend to Maori blood herself on occasion, seems never to have been told of these cousins, who are not recorded in her father's memoirs, despite its elaborate genealogical charts.[6]

Beauchamp's choice of wife was very different from Fred's. Annie Burnell Dyer was the sister of a clerk in the insurance firm in which young Harold, once he had resolved to part from his father, began his climb to affluence. Annie was always considered delicate, although this did not stop her from bearing children or travelling round the world time and time again; so perhaps her 'weak heart' was a version of the invalidism of so many Victorian ladies with reasons of their own for wishing to be spared domestic demands.

Joseph Dyer, Annie's father, had come to Australia in the 1840s, married a Sydney girl, Margaret Isabella Mansfield, and in 1871 was sent to Wellington to be the first resident-secretary of the Australian Mutual Provident Society. Six years later he died; but his widow was a capable woman, his children prospered, and when Harold Beauchamp married Annie in 1884 they were pleased to have Mrs Dyer to live with them, together with her two youngest daughters. Granny Dyer, who was only in her forties, took over the running of the house and much of the care of the children; Katherine's youngest sister, Mrs Jeanne Renshaw, recalled that most of her childhood meals were eaten with Granny and not with her parents.[7]

Harold prospered steadily. He made himself indispensable to his firm, so that by 1889 he was a partner, and five years later in sole charge. In the 1890s he began to be offered directorships, and joined the Wellington Harbour Board and the board of the Bank of New Zealand. He revelled in his own success and was thoroughly confident in the world of business. His wife is a more elusive character altogether. We can see from photographs that she was beautiful. She is also described as fastidious and delicate, and what we know of her behaviour suggests that she was cool – or possibly cold – and could be formidable. Appearances were very important to her. She knew she had married well, and that New Zealand was a snobbish place in which the families of businessmen, however successful, were not accepted as the social equals of professional people and that, however rich they became, the old settler families would continue to look down their noses at them as *arriviste*. Katherine noted early in her journal how her mother told her father 'what he must do and not do' in a social setting.[8] In her home, Mrs Beauchamp lavished money on clothes for herself and her daughters, on flowers, on entertaining, but she was not a housewife. She was good at giving orders to her servants; her pleasures were reading, letter-writing and travel.

Whenever she could, she accompanied her husband on his journeys, and she was perfectly happy to travel alone, given the chance. Another note in Katherine's journal (made after her mother's death, in 1921) describes Mrs Beauchamp most arrestingly, sitting down to button her boots, wearing short frilled knickers, with her fine, springy hair standing out round her head, and saying she wished she had never married. If her own father had not died, Katherine remembered her saying, she would have liked to have become a traveller, an explorer even.[9] The key to Annie Beauchamp was, perhaps, that she craved and felt herself capable of independence; but since the world was organized along lines that made such independence impossible, she determined at least to order her life as efficiently as possible. She was not a natural mother, but she was good at organizing and commanding her children. Her youngest daughter, Jeanne, told the author that her mother never spoke to any of them about their bodies and advised her eldest daughter, Vera, to bring *her* children up by 'teaching them to control themselves'.

Emotionally, Annie appears to have held herself aloof from her family, and, if we allow ourselves to judge by Katherine's fictionalized versions of her parents (particularly in 'Prelude' and 'The Stranger'), her attitude towards her husband's sexual needs was that she satisfied them out of pity tinged with resentment, and a sense of what was due to the master of the house: not much more.

These were the parents to whom, on 14 October 1888, Katherine was born. The birth took place at home, at 11 Tinakori Road, a long, high, winding street with a view over the sea, for Wellington Harbour is set amid hills. Her two elder sisters, aged three and one, were Vera and Charlotte, or 'Chaddie' (all the Beauchamps were passionate for nicknames). When Katherine was just one, her parents set off for their first visit to England. Her mother was away for six months, returning alone to give birth to a fourth daughter, who died. Then there was a fifth, Jeanne; and in 1893 the family moved to Karori, outside the city, to give the children the experience of country life. This move is recorded in Katherine's story 'Prelude'; the Karori house was Chesney Wold and here the last Beauchamp child was conceived, a boy, Leslie (or Boy, or Chummie, or Bogey). Mrs Beauchamp had borne six children in nine years, and now that she had provided a son she stopped and bore no more, although she was only thirty. Here, too, she was clearly an efficient organizer.

The parents set off for England again early in 1898. Again, Granny took charge. Katherine remembered her mother bringing her back a tie-pin from Switzerland, 'made like a violet, and one shut one's eye and looked through it at the "Lion of Lucerne"'.[10] Evidently they had taken in a Continental tour, and they also spent several weeks in America on their way back – a total absence of nine months, which must have seemed an eternity to the children. They brought back with them a newly published book by Harold's cousin 'Elizabeth' (née Mary Annette Beauchamp, now von Arnim): *Elizabeth and Her German Garden*, which was already on its way to becoming a best-seller. Ten-year-old Katherine was hugely impressed. According to family legend, it inspired her with the wish to become a writer also.

The family now moved back into Wellington. Their new house, again in Tinakori Road, had a billiard room and a tennis court in the garden: 'a big, white-painted square house with a slender-pillared verandah and balcony running all the way round it'.[11] We are entering the world of Edwardian middle-class luxury, and it is the setting for Katherine's story 'The Garden Party', one of the best evocations ever written of that phenomenon. As in 'The Garden Party', the small, shabby houses of the poor – half-castes with too many children, washerwomen – were only a step away; but, 'as Father said ... there was no doubt that land there would become extremely valuable ... if one bought enough and hung on'.[12]

Beauchamp's success made him an increasingly important, if not much loved, figure in the small community: Wellington's population was about 40,000, the equivalent of Tunbridge Wells or Scarborough today. A childhood friend of Katherine's remembered spending Christmas with the Beauchamps in the 1890s and described how the socialist Prime Minister, Richard Seddon, visited them, impressing the little girls with his frock coat and top hat – despite the heat – and above all the diamond stud on his shirt front. Beauchamp too was a stickler for correct appearances; it is said that when he went ashore at Honolulu under a burning tropical sun, on his way to England, he invariably kept his bowler hat on his head and carried an umbrella. His children were obliged to take a cold bath every day, and he himself, with his prominent blue eyes and ruddy complexion, 'had the fresh look of a man who, having recently emerged from a cold bath, had anointed himself liberally with Eau de Cologne'.[13] Katherine herself described him as 'thoroughly commonplace and commercial', but in a more affectionate moment she wrote:

Father's a Tolstoy character. He has just the point of vision of a Tolstoy character. I always felt that Stepan in *Anna Karenina* reminded me of someone – and his well-nourished, fresh body was always curiously familiar to me – of course – it is my Papa's ... the smile and the whiskers.[14]

The ambivalence about her father remained throughout her life. He might be vulgar, crass, tight-fisted, but he was also strong, reliable and magically rich. In fantasy, at any rate, whenever she felt like a small child herself, he appeared as glamorous and omnipotent.

The children did not lack for fresh air, exercise, good food and kindly care; Granny Dyer was a much loved figure in their lives. The girls were often dressed alike, but in character they were markedly different. Vera took her position as eldest seriously and had a strong sense of decorum and responsibility; Chaddie was merry and easy-going; Katherine (always known in the family as Kathleen or Kass) was difficult, the odd one out, intense in her feelings, given to outbursts of rage, jealous of the success or friendships of others, and humiliated by being fat. Her Canadian friend, Marion Ruddick, who travelled with the Beauchamp parents in 1898 and heard about the girls from Mrs Beauchamp before she met them, said that she, 'in her decisive manner, completely overlooking Kathleen, decided that Chaddie was the one I would like best.'[15] She went on to describe how, as the girls came out to the boat to greet their long-absent mother,

she gazed down in a detached way at the group and to my mind didn't seem overjoyed as I thought she would be after such a long absence. Finally it was to Kathleen she spoke first, for everyone to hear. 'Well, Kathleen,' she said, 'I see that you are as fat as ever.' And in my first glimpse of Kathleen I saw her eyes flash, and her face flush with anger as she turned away with a toss of her ringlets.[16]

Marion became Katherine's best friend; and both she and her sister Jeanne stressed her separateness from the rest of the family. 'Kathleen was silent as she so often was when her sisters were present,'[17] wrote Marion. Jeanne talked of 'old' and 'young' souls to explain the undoubted difference between Katherine and the others, and said that her mother did not talk about her at all after she left for England in 1908 except to say with a sigh, 'My poor child.'*[18]

Whatever gulfs and rifts there were below, it was a family with a good deal of surface manner. The girls called their parents 'father dear' and 'mother dear'; their grandmother was 'gran dear', and 'darlings' and 'dearests' flew around animatedly. Even in her eighties Jeanne still spoke with tremendous verve, articulating as distinctly and beautifully as an actress. She also sprinkled French and German phrases very freely in her conversation, just as Katherine did in her letters. The habit belongs to a generation of women with leisure to dabble in languages for fun, the leisure supplied by an enormous servant class. Katherine was quick to identify with servants in her writing, and to offer them special imaginative sympathy, although she grew up in a society in which the social division between maids and masters seemed absolute.

The luxury of her upbringing, with visiting sewing maids as well as house parlour maids, gardeners and people to do the washing and ironing, had its drawbacks later. Katherine virtually never saw her mother labour with her hands – either make a meal or sew a garment – and she herself was not expected to learn how to clean or cook anything: she was Miss Kathleen. She did know how to handle and charm servants, and was always served very willingly, but when she suffered from poverty as a grown woman, the practical deficiencies in her education made

---

* Antony Alpers spoke to another witness of Beauchamp family life, Rose Ridler, in 1947, who said Mrs Beauchamp did not appear to like her third daughter.[19]

things more difficult for her, and at the end of her life she turned to the idea of manual work as salvation.

Katherine saw herself as 'the odd man out of the family – the ugly duckling'.[20] But to be the odd one, the difficult one, not understood, separate, the 'thundercloud',[21] is also a privileged position, the position of Cinderella. 'She had vague notions that it was always, would always be the third who was the favourite of the gods. The fairy-tales that she devoured voraciously during her childhood helped to stimulate the thought,'[22] she wrote in one of her adolescent notebooks. Vera and Chaddie, both from general testimony good-natured enough girls, never gave their version of childhood in the Beauchamp family – publicly at any rate – and were reluctant to speak of their sister; if they partly disliked or feared her, they did not say so. 'The family was very conventional, Kass was the outlaw,' said one of her teachers.[23] Part of the convention of such a family is that all its members love one another; but the convention is denied, of course, in fairy-tales, which allow for all the other feelings of hatred and jealousy. No wonder they appealed so strongly to Katherine.

There was something else at work too. Katherine was always a performer. She needed to enchant an audience, but there was no one in her family on whom she could successfully cast a spell. They simply did not see her as she wished to be seen.

Katherine attended three schools in New Zealand. First, Karori primary school, where all the local children went, and where she learned to read, to write with a slate and to enjoy memorizing poetry. She also began to divide the world into people she liked, 'her' people, those who knew she understood and responded, and all the others. Much of her life was spent in sorting people in this way, seeking 'her' people, reviling the rest.

Reading quickly grew into a passion. When she was eight she was put into steel-framed spectacles, of which she was rather proud; but whatever they were meant to do for her sight, she soon outgrew any need for them, and she was never myopic. Quite the contrary: her observation was as acute as though she had trained herself to examine and retain everything she saw. She called herself a squirrel, storing up her impressions. 'Nothing has happened until it has been described,' said Virginia Woolf, but Katherine's capacity to take in visual detail was exceptional, to be drawn on, sorted and selected later, as if from a box of prints.

The next school was Wellington Girls' High School, where she went in 1898, and where she met Marion Ruddick. She proclaimed Marion one of her people, and loved her with a dominating and possessive love. In the mornings the girls did formal work, while the afternoons were given to drawing, poetry and sewing; the little girls worked on chemises for the Maori mission. Katherine had a brief moment of enthusiasm for the idea of becoming a missionary among the Maoris, but she detested sewing. She chose whenever possible to read aloud instead and claimed later that she could always make the other girls cry when she read Dickens to the sewing class.[24] Swimming was another afternoon activity – in New Zealand it was compulsory for all children to learn to swim – and it was at the swimming pool that Marion discovered the degree of jealousy of which Katherine was capable, receiving a covert but memorable thump when she talked too much to another girl. It was by no means the last such thump Katherine was to give.

Marion's parents were moved to another posting, and Katherine lost her friend; and in June 1900 Harold Beauchamp moved his daughters to their first fee-paying school, Miss Swainson's. Like most girls' schools of the period, Miss Swainson's aimed to turn out young ladies who fitted in, not combatants: 'It was one of those snobby semidiocesan schools where the dear Vicar was always hanging around. Education was not so much of a feature but you didn't eat peas with a knife or dip your bread in the gravy,' explained Katherine's cousin Burney Trapp later.[25] She was not popular there, and the teachers disapproved of her. At the high school she had been praised for her contributions to the school magazine, stories of children's holiday amusements and Christmas; but at Swainson's she was told her essays were too long, too untidy, badly spelled (her spelling was never good) and too self-centred. With some spirit, she produced her own 'school magazine', full of jokes and stories. She was imaginative, but 'imaginative to the point of untruth', according to the headmistress.[26]

Miss Swainson's had another unusual pupil in Martha Grace, or Maata Mahupuku, a few years older than Katherine, whose forebears were Maori chiefs and uncle a friend of the Prime Minister, Richard Seddon. Through her uncle she was heiress to a considerable fortune. She was dark-skinned and exotically beautiful, and she was sometimes called Princess Martha, to emphasize just how little she had in common with the 'half-castes' in the squalid houses in Tinakori Road, with their gardens full of empty jam tins and old saucepans.

Martha was constantly at the Beauchamps' house. The girls who were not allowed much money were pop eyed with the amount Maata always had to spend. All the same she was very pretty, bright and generous and nothing of a snob herself. She and Kathleen were particularly friendly.[27]

If a later entry in Katherine's journal is to be believed, she had some experience with Maata during their schooldays that was sexually disturbing; it seems to have been more than a matter of a schoolgirl crush, and it became the germ of her awareness of her own bisexuality.

Still the Beauchamps prospered. In 1901, when the Duke and Duchess of Cornwall visited New Zealand, Harold helped to entertain them and Jeanne presented a bouquet to the future Queen Mary. The elder girls were beginning to 'appear with their parents in public and were all busy with their music and other accomplishments'.[28] Vera and Katherine took piano lessons. Chaddie sang, and all three were prepared to entertain guests around the ebony piano on its dais.

Katherine's interest in music took a new turn. When she was thirteen, the family met a good-humoured, attractive music teacher named Thomas Trowell, who had come from England in the 1880s. The elder of his twelve-year-old twin sons, Arnold, showed remarkable talent with the cello; the shy twin, Garnet, also played the fiddle well. There was a pretty ten-year-old daughter, Dolly. Katherine became speedily infatuated with the whole family, calling Dolly 'little sister' and going for long, confiding chats with the parents. Mr Trowell agreed to give her cello lessons. She became so obsessed that she took to wearing brown to match her instrument. Mr Beauchamp humoured this adolescent passion and the Trowell boys were invited to Tinakori Road to perform.

Katherine, who had already caused a stir by questioning a schoolteacher about the meaning of free love, decided to be in love with Arnold, whom she renamed 'Caesar'. In a sense, she was in love with the whole family, whose priorities and values were so fascinatingly different from those of the Beauchamps. They had no money, but were outstandingly gifted; they lived in a thoroughly informal, easy way, but were utterly dedicated when it came to the art of music. It was obvious to her that the Trowells, not the Beauchamps, were her soul-mates.

Katherine was not alone in appreciating the musical gifts of the family.

The twins – and particularly Arnold – were generally considered in Wellington to possess such outstanding talent that they deserved to be sent to study in Europe. The Trowells were in no position to pay for this, but a group of Wellington families agreed to raise the money, and it was settled that Arnold and Garnet should be sent to study in Germany in 1903. Among the benefactors was Harold Beauchamp.

It may well have been this act of generous patronage that set him thinking about his own children's education; at all events, even before Arnold and Garnct could leave, Mɪ and Mrs Beauchamp had taken a momentous decision about their family. Vera, Chaddie and Katherine were also to go to Europe. They would be completing their education at Queen's College, Harley Street, London. It was an extraordinarily bold plan.

2

QUEEN'S: 'MY *WASTED,*
WASTED EARLY GIRLHOOD'

■

They embarked in January 1903. Harold Beauchamp, with one of his
pleasant, princely gestures, booked the entire passenger accommodation
of a small cargo ship, the *Niwaru*, sailing via the Pacific and Cape Horn.
There were nine in the party: the five Beauchamp children, both parents,
and Annie's younger brother Sydney and sister Belle, a favourite with
her brother-in-law. She had volunteered to remain in England to keep
an eye on her three nieces, a position of authority that would not endear
her to Katherine. Perhaps Belle had some thoughts that this was her
last 'chance', for no suitable husband had appeared in Wellington, and
she was nearly thirty; she had attempted a career in nursing, but been
warned off with the threat of tuberculosis. Now, however, she was in
stout health. Katherine was fourteen and physically mature; like many
third daughters who grow up alongside their elder sisters, she took for
granted the right to the same freedoms and privileges they had acquired.

The voyage lasted for seven weeks. Katherine has left no account
of what she thought of it beyond one brief, nostalgic reference in a
letter written to her father during the last year of her life, when her
mother was dead and her glances into the past had become gentle and
regretful:

> I have a very soft corner in my heart for the *Niwaru* ... Do you remember
> how Mother used to enjoy the triangular-shaped pieces of toast for tea? Awfully
> good they were, too, on a cold afternoon in the vicinity of the Horn. How I
> should love to make a long sea voyage again one of these days. But I always
> connect such experiences with a vision of Mother in her little seal-skin jacket
> with the collar turned up.[1]

For Beauchamp himself, the proud and generous leader of his own troupe, this was the most enjoyable voyage of his life. It was also the last time he was in control of his entire family. Edwardian ocean-going ships could be very domestic; the *Niwaru* provided the ladies with a clavichord and a sewing-machine as well as a caged canary.

A photograph taken at Las Palmas shows a remarkably handsome and well turned out family. Mrs Beauchamp and Belle display huge, pancake-like straw hats adorned with flowers and feathers, little Leslie is in a sailor suit and the girls are in high-buttoned boots, gloves and straw boaters; their hair is up and they are wearing ankle-length skirts and high-necked blouses. The men are in dark suits with stiff collars. Belle has two roses pinned to the front of her dress. It is a formally posed picture: everyone stares out at the camera, Mr Beauchamp with a pleased and confident air, his hair and beard white, sideburns still sandy. Mrs Beauchamp has her detached, correct, unruffled look; Vera, her anxious eldest daughter's face. Belle's expression is as well arranged as her costume, and Katherine's has a blank intensity: oval face, wide brow, neatly turned features, dark eyes that look as though they could be attentive if only they could alight on something worth attending to. Incongruously, her blouse is the most unkempt-looking garment of the party and the waistband of her skirt is visibly under strain; she was to be a fat girl for several years more, and even into her twenties was described as 'square' or 'dumpy' by non-admirers.

The first month in England was taken up with cultural touring – Stratford was one of their first objectives – and with visits to the complicated sets of relatives who were, with Belle, to assume some responsibility for the three girls when the Beauchamp parents returned to New Zealand with their youngest children.

'The Retreat' at Bexley in Kent was where Harold's much older cousin, Henry Beauchamp, had settled in the 1860s after making a fortune in Australia. The most spectacular of his children was the youngest, 'Elizabeth', a source of anxiety in her wilful girlhood but now the pride of the whole family: not only had she captured a German nobleman as her husband, it was she who had produced *Elizabeth and Her German Garden*. She was, of course, no longer at Bexley, but in Pomerania, where she kept her typewriter in a summerhouse with *Procul Este Profani* inscribed over the door, and quarrelled with her husband. Her sister Charlotte had married a City merchant, and *her* son Sydney Waterlow (Katherine's second cousin) was now in the Foreign Office, but yearning towards a more intellectual and artistic life; later he hovered on the periphery of Bloomsbury and introduced Katherine into that circle.

Two other Beauchamp cousins were Sydney, a doctor, and Henry, who was musical – he played the cello and sang – and perhaps for that reason was pressed into being made the girls' legal guardian. They instantly named him 'Guardy', and Katherine enthused about his poetical tenor voice.[2]

It was to the Retreat that the girls went for most of their school holidays. The school itself was both unusual and unusually good: Queen's College, at 45 Harley Street, in the very heart of London, within walking distance of Regent's Park, Piccadilly Circus and Hyde Park. There was a family reason for the choice of school. Annie Beauchamp's father had left behind him, when he emigrated to Australia in the 1840s, a sister Eliza, an able and energetic woman who ran her own school in London and married another schoolteacher, Joseph Payne. Payne was self-taught and developed strong views on educational reform; he was particularly interested in the education of girls and helped to establish the Girls' Public Day School Trust. His son, Joseph Frank Payne, Annie's cousin, became a physician; his practice was in Wimpole Street and, sharing his father's views on the importance of girls' education, sent his three daughters round the corner to Queen's College. It was natural enough, since the school took boarders, to recommend it to Annie for her girls too.

The flavour of Queen's was a special one. It resembled neither the big, rather militaristic girls' public schools modelled on their male counterparts nor the high schools of the London suburbs and provincial cities, which were also given to well-organized and standardized academic forcing. Queen's had been founded in 1848 with the aim of cultivating individuality and free intellectual endeavour in its pupils rather than cramming them with facts or moulding them into preordained shapes. It was quite small, and still uncertain of its status, somewhere between boarding school and college; about forty boarders were tucked into little upstairs rooms and attics in neighbouring Harley Street houses, all built as private dwellings in the eighteenth century and so quite lacking in institutional atmosphere. Discipline was not strict: there was no uniform, and girls were allowed out in pairs to explore London – an adventurous policy in 1903, when the poor were considered an alien and possibly dangerous breed apart by most people.

The curriculum was also very freely organized. From Katherine's records it is clear that girls were allowed to concentrate on favourite subjects and drop others altogether. She soon gave up theology, chemistry, geography, ancient history, drawing and arithmetic (for which she received o out of 150 in a scholarship paper) and kept only German, French, English, singing and cello. A minimum of ten hours a week in class was expected, with an hour of private study in preparation for each class. Much of the girls' work was done comfortably and informally in the library, which Katherine described to a friend as 'thick Turkey carpeted, great armchairs everywhere, neat little tables, rugs, and charming pictures. Even Latin would be interesting in this room.'[3] Girls were encouraged to make their own choice of books and a special arrangement with the London Library in St James's Square widened the possible range.

Pupils did not sit for outside examinations; they were taught by visiting professors, many of them men, whose method was to lecture and set essays. Some of the lectures were so attractive that members of the public attended them. This free and flexible system had been set up by the founder, F.D. Maurice, the Christian Socialist and friend of Tennyson and Kingsley, a gentle, idealistic man who also founded a working-men's college.

Girls tended to come from the merchant and professional middle classes, and a good many went on to enter professions themselves, although the school was by no means a forcing house for Oxford and Cambridge. The historian Gertrude Bell was a Queen's girl. So was Florence Farr, the feminist writer and actress admired by Bernard Shaw and Yeats. Sophia Jex-Blake, another fighter for women's rights and pioneer in medical training for her sex, had also been a pupil there. Among Katherine's classmates was the daughter of a Yorkshire mill-owner, a granddaughter of the founder, the daughters of a journalist and, of course, many doctors' daughters like the Payne cousins.

The fees for Queen's were twenty-two guineas a term for boarding and nine for tuition, with a reduction for three daughters from one family, which must have appealed to Mr Beauchamp. Still, it was a handsome investment for a father to make in his daughters' futures. When the time came to part from them, he noted that it was 'a wrench'. Katherine saw things differently, or so one of her fictionalized accounts suggests:

She was to meet total strangers. She could be just as she liked. They had never known her before – oh, what a comfort to know that every minute saw the others farther away from her! 'I suppose I am preposterously unnatural,' she thought and smiled.[4]

The sisters' room was at the top of 41 Harley Street, and they were taken up by another pupil, the aptly named Ida Constance Baker, who was to become the most devoted and remain the most faithful of Katherine's friends throughout her life. She was nine months older than Katherine, and neither quick-witted nor beautiful; but she had a thoughtful, gentle face framed in heavy, long hair. Where Katherine was elated at the adventurousness of her new life, Ida was melancholy at this first meeting. Her mother had just died and her difficult father had taken the younger brother and sister to the country, leaving her alone to board at Queen's for the first time. She was in desperate need of something to fill the gap in her life, which had been partly spent in Burma, where her father served as an Army doctor, although the family came from Suffolk. Like Katherine, she had been around the world, but her response was stoic rather than excited.

On the first day she noticed Katherine's dark eyes observing everything about her. Then she found they shared a taste for poetry. Later, walking in Regent's Park, Katherine turned to her and asked commandingly, 'Shall we be friends?' Almost from that moment, Ida saw herself as devoted to Katherine's service; she would spend hours sitting with her in her room, while Vera and Chaddie were out, listening as she practised her cello, or talking about Katherine's plans, Katherine's future, Katherine's life. To Ida, Katherine seemed extraordinary in her dark beauty and her intensity.

Katherine loved the bedroom, with its view over the lead roofs and the mews where the horses and the coachmen lived; she also loved the whole atmosphere of the school, and felt more at home there than at the Retreat. She wrote to her favourite cousin, Sylvia Payne, during a school holiday about how she thought constantly of Queen's and its 'strange fascination'; in another letter written from school she described herself watching 'the lamp in the mews below ... flickering and moving about restlessly, and my flowers in my window ... nodding and talking to me at a great rate.'[5] A long section of her journal, written in February 1916 when she was living happily in Bandol, shows the remarkable detail of her memory:

I was thinking yesterday of my *wasted, wasted* early girlhood. My college life, which is such a vivid and detailed memory in one way, might never have contained a book or a lecture. I lived in the girls, the professors, the big, lovely building, the leaping fires in winter, all the pattern that was – weaving. Nobody saw it, I felt, as I did. My mind was just like a squirrel. I gathered and gathered and hid away, for that long 'winter' when I should discover all this treasure ... why didn't I listen to the old Principal who lectured on Bible History twice a week instead of staring at his face that was very round, a dark red colour with a kind of bloom in it and covered all over with little red veins with endless tiny tributaries that ran even up his forehead and were lost in his bushy white hair. He had tiny hands, too, puffed up, purplish, shining under the stained flesh. I used to think, looking at his hands – he will have a stroke and die of paralysis ... I never came into contact with him but once, when he asked any young lady in the room to hold up her hand if she had been chased by a wild bull, and as nobody else did I held up mine (though of course I hadn't). 'Ah,' he said, 'I am afraid you do not count. You are a little savage from New Zealand.' ... And why didn't I learn French with M. Huguenot? What an opportunity missed! What has it not cost me! He lectured in a big narrow room that was painted all over – the walls, door, and window-frames, a grey shade of mignonette green. The ceiling was white, and just below it there was a frieze of long looped chains of white flowers. On either side of the marble mantelpiece a naked small boy staggered under a big platter of grapes that he held above his head. Below the windows, far below there was a stable court paved in cobble stones, and one could hear the faint clatter of carriages coming out or in, the noise of water gushing out of a pump into a big pail – some youth, clumping about and whistling. The room was never very light, and in summer M.H. liked the blinds to be drawn half-way down the window ... He was a little fat man.[6]

The precision of the recall is astonishing in itself, as is the way she builds fancifully upon it. No doubt her self-reproach about academic failure was justified – Queen's was often accused of letting its students idle away their time – but in 1916 she was judging herself against Murry, who had been educated to the standards of Christ's Hospital; there can have been no comparison between the levels of achievement aimed at by the two schools. And, in fact, her French and German, though ungrammatical, were fluent and effective. Ruth Herrick, a fellow New Zealander who was Katherine's contemporary at Queen's, recalled her insistence on trying to converse in French when neither of them knew more than a handful of words. Miss Herrick thought it was affectation, but it was evidence of spirit and intelligence as well. She also linked it with Katherine's general interest in mimicry and drama – helpful to a linguist – and added that she made up wild stories to impress, including one of rape and pregnancy.[7] Since these themes crop up in early note-books, the obvious thought is that she was trying out her plots on her friends, as well as enjoying shocking them. Katherine told lies all her life, but usually more for effect than advantage.

For her, as for many precocious girls, an early interest in sexual adventure may have been partly a refusal of the feminine role required by family and other authorities, a defiance of their decrees. To be wilful, to be assertive, to be overtly interested in sex, was the prerogative of young men; but why should it be? Why not refuse the reticences and timidities expected of girls? If this boldness drew disapproval, it also gave her an exceptional appeal, because she was adopting the role of a young male in a predominantly female establishment. Katherine was unpopular with many of the girls at Queen's: 'Those who were not her particular friends on the whole disliked her,' a history of the school says diplomatically.[8] A recent headmistress said quite flatly that a number of her contemporaries said they hated her because she showed off so much. But she had her group of admirers to balance the dislike of the majority, as anybody with superabundant vitality will.

Miss Herrick was obviously irritated by the memory of the slavish devotion displayed by Ida Baker, and by Katherine's willingness to exploit it. But Miss Baker, who spoke with abiding tolerance and love of Katherine's temperament and needs, was critical in her turn of Miss Herrick's old intense attachment to Katherine. Each implied something 'unwholesome' – a word once favoured in girls' schools – about the other. The emotions and rivalries, persisting over so many decades, kept the hothouse hot; the two quiet and correct old ladies discovered, to their bewilderment, something called lesbianism, and began to tie this tag gingerly on one another while preserving their own intensities as blameless.

Miss Baker remembered herself as a friend apart from Katherine's group, one who listened and, in her own phrase, began to 'see' Katherine as one sees only a truly loved person. To some extent, she did suffer from feeling excluded from a good deal of her friend's life, partly because the Beauchamp girls were rich and able to go on many outings, to concerts and theatres and to buy new clothes with their aunt Belle, and also because there were other girls who enjoyed a different sort of intimacy. The most forceful and congenial was Vere Bartrick-Baker (no relation of Ida); she was a few months older than Katherine, shared her intellectual tastes and encouraged her in sophisticated reading and conversation quite beyond Ida. Vere and Katherine were in the same class, and were both dazzled by the young German professor, Walter Rippmann.

> I am *ashamed* at the way in which I long for German. I simply can't help it. It is dreadful. And when I go into class I feel I must just stare at him the whole time. I never liked anyone so much. Every day I like him more and more. Yet on Thursday he was like *ice*![9]

wrote the fifteen-year-old Katherine. Rippmann became their mentor, and it was he who encouraged them to read modern writers, the Symbolists and Decadents and social reformers: Bernard Shaw, Maeterlinck, Ibsen and Tolstoy, Arthur Symons and Oscar Wilde, whose prose Katherine soon began to imitate. Rippmann himself enjoyed some Wildean posing, and would advise the girls on the necessity of selfishness and avoidance of the Seven Deadly Virtues.

Vere is described in the only story Katherine ever published about Queen's, 'Carnation', an evocation of a hot afternoon in a schoolroom full of girls, written in 1918, in which 'Eve', who is given thin red lips and a cruel little laugh, brings a red carnation into a French lesson and drops it down 'Katie's' shirt-front with a murmur of *'souvenir tendre'*, after the French master has done his best and Katie has allowed her thoughts to wander to the bare-chested man splashing the horses with water from the pump in the mews below the window. As a tribute to the school it is equivocal, but as a piece of atmospheric writing it is disconcertingly effective, rather as though Colette and D. H. Lawrence had come face to face in Harley Street.

Vere's background was an unusual one. Her mother wrote poetry under her maiden name, lived alone in Surrey and proclaimed herself a widow, although she was, in fact, divorced – almost unheard of then. Both parents had been Plymouth Brethren when young, but had broken away from the movement, and the father, without much formal education, had managed to become a journalist on the *Financial Times*. All this was naturally intriguing to Katherine, who took a favourable view of unconventional families as well as literary aspirations; and Vere was possessed of advanced, even cynical, views on life. The two girls would meet in the school's dark lower corridor before lessons began, to discuss the ideas of their favourite writers, and were apparently suspected of 'immorality' of a kind unspecified.[10]

The tone of their conversation may be guessed from the fragmentary draft of a novel Katherine began to scribble in her notebook towards the end of her schooldays, and in which the characters of the two girls are clearly based on Katherine and Vere (whose name sometimes appears by mistake for 'Pearl', that of the character). In one passage the girls, who are imagined sharing lodgings in London, agree to a permanent alliance, abjuring matrimony. It is, reflects 'Juliet' (Katherine), 'death to a woman's personality. She must drop the theme and begin playing the accompaniment. For me there is *no* attraction.'[11] In another, Pearl begins the conversation:

Got a mood? she said.

Yes, said Juliet. It's the very Devil. While it lasts I think it's going to be eternal and I'm contemplating suicide.

It's sure to be something physical. Why don't you sleep better Juliet? Are you – you're not – expecting?

Good heavens, no. The truth is, my dear girl – well I hardly like to own it to myself even, you understand. Bernard Shaw would be gratified.

You feel sexual.

Horribly – and in need of a physical shock or violence. Perhaps a good smacking would be beneficial.[12]

Perhaps it is understandable that the good ladies of Queen's were a shade nervous about the friendship between the two girls; Pearl, 'with her pale eager face and smiling ripe mouth, crying to Juliet "Here I am, here we both are. Trust me, dear, live with me, you and I to reach for things together, you and I to live and prove our new Philosophy." '[13] In a vignette Katherine wrote later and sent to Vere, she describes how they climbed to the top of the towers of Westminster Cathedral and looked down on to the distant house where they once exchanged kisses. Vere continued to haunt Katherine's imagination. Many years after her death, Murry (who proposed to Vere and then backed out) told her that Katherine

once confessed to me that she was *afraid* of you, and that she felt that one day you would 'strike back at her'. (I don't vouch for the actual phrase: but the sense of it is accurate enough.) I came (I don't know why) to the conclusion that there were some 'incriminating' letters. Possibly, because I knew that at one period Katherine was rather addicted to such letters. But I never had the faintest doubt of the reality of her fear of you.[14]

If there were any such letters – and Katherine mentions them in her journal too – Vere destroyed them.

Katherine's official writing during her three years at Queen's appeared in the school magazine, in which Rippmann took a particular interest. She became first assistant and then editor. Four of her stories are almost unbearably coy accounts of charming children getting up to mischief, but the fifth, 'About Pat', is quite different, a spare reminiscence of the Karori handyman Patrick Sheehan, told without a trace of sentimentality.

But while Karori existed in her head, the three homeless years at Queen's effectively detached Katherine from her parents' world. She was always busy, working intensely at her cello and taking lessons at the London Academy of Music, where her cousin Henry worked, as well as at school. She dreamed of becoming a professional musician; she also kept a photograph of Arnold Trowell beside her bed, and saw him and his brother Garnet when they came to London, introducing both Vere and Ida to them. They had left New Zealand a few months after the Beauchamps, and studied in Frankfurt for a year. They were narrow-faced, thin, pale boys, Arnold with red hair and Garnet, always over-shadowed, merely brown, not good-looking but impressive by virtue of their Continental student ways. They wore big black hats and smoked cigarettes in long holders, observed by Katherine with passionate admiration.

At Easter 1906 Aunt Belle took the girls to Paris and then Brussels, where the boys were currently studying. Katherine and her sisters, entering into the spirit of the *vie de Bohème* of the Brussels music students, boasted of going for a swim naked. But *Bohème* was not all larks. Another music student, a friend of the Trowells called Rudolf, shot himself in a despairing moment soon after this visit. It was a real enactment of the *fin de siècle* melancholy that Walter Rippmann had encouraged Katherine to admire. Rudolf's passionate dedication to aesthetic living and his equally passionate rejection of life impressed and disturbed her.

Rippmann himself actually married one of the Queen's girls in 1905. He invited several favourite pupils, Katherine included, to visit his Kensington house with its Japanese prints and aesthete's decor. The gulf between Ladbroke Grove and Tinakori Road was wide and probably unbridgeable.

Nevertheless, in the spring of 1906 Mr and Mrs Beauchamp were there to escort their three daughters back to New Zealand. It was difficult to accept that 'Home' was not after all home. None of them was enthusiastic about leaving England, although the matter was not officially under discussion; their father was already upset about losing his sister-in-law, for Belle had found herself a husband, a shipowner, and embarked on a life devoted to tennis and golf. Harold the patriarch wanted no more tribal losses and began to lay down the law. Katherine was not to become a professional musician as she begged; and, while this upset her, she decided

it is no earthly use warring with the inevitable – so in future I shall give *all* my time to writing. There are great opportunities for a girl in New Zealand – she has so much time and quiet – and we have an ideal little 'cottage by the sea' where I mean to spend a good deal of my time.[15]

But Katherine's initial docility and pleasure at seeing her parents again wore off during the summer. Harold busied himself with the congress of Chambers of Commerce of the British Empire, was received at Buckingham Palace by King Edward, and took Vera to France while the younger girls stayed in London. Katherine, still at school, clung to her friendships with Vere and Ida, who 'believed in' her, and took to solitary cello practice up in the French classroom in the evening. Some of the feminist tradition of Queen's had taken hold of her. She told Sylvia:

I am so keen upon all women having a *definite* future – are not you? The idea of sitting and waiting for a husband is absolutely revolting – and it really is the attitude of a great many girls ... It rather made me smile to read of your wishing you could create your fate – O how many times I have ... felt just the same. I just long for power over circumstances.[16]

But the only power she had for the moment was in her imagination: the power to impersonate characters in her notebook, where Juliet's adventures included a visit to a worldly-wise older man, Walter.

'How about those complications?' 'O they're quite gone thank you. I ... I took your advice.' 'That's fine, that's fine. I knew you would, my dear girl. I always said you had the grit in you.' O the fearful paternal conceit.[17]

She also sketched an encounter with the decadent Rudolf, who apostrophizes from his piano stool:

Live this life, Juliet. Did Chopin fear to satisfy the cravings of his nature, his natural desires? No, that is how he is so great. Why do you push away just that which you need – because of convention? Why do you dwarf your nature, spoil your life? ... You are blind, and far worse, you are deaf to all that is worth living for.[18]

At some point during this year, Maata, who was being 'finished' in Europe, appeared in London; according to Katherine's cousin, 'she took with her an introduction to a Madame Louise who made the Beauchamps' clothes . . . Maata . . . was mad on dress and went in donkey deep with Louise and left England without squaring up. Madame claimed the amount from the Beauchamps and if you Knew Uncle Harold you could imagine the commotion. I think the upshot was that the friendship was compulsorily cut short.'[19]

Katherine and her family sailed for New Zealand in mid October. Aboard the *Corinthic* her life continued to be as drama-filled as her notebooks. There was an MCC cricket team aboard, and she embarked on a flirtation with an Adonis-like creature:

> He taught me piquet . . . It was intensely hot . . . The more hearts you have the better, he said, leaning over my hand. I felt his coat sleeve against my bare arm. If one heart is a very primitive affair, I answered, in these days one must possess many. We exchanged a long look and his glance inflamed me like the scent of gardenia.*[20]

It was not quite Oscar Wilde, whose aphorisms she was busy copying out, supplemented by her own ('No life is spoiled but one whose growth is arrested.' – O.W. 'Happy people are never brilliant. It implies friction.' – K.M.), but it ministered to her desire to appear worldly-wise and prepared for adventure. Privately, she indulged in some masochistic fantasy, congratulated herself on the beauty of her dancing and speculated as to whether she could make a conquest of him, or whether she might become *une jeune fille entretenue*. This, she decided, would be better than being the child of her parents, who were now watchful, quarrelsome, too interested in shipboard meals, and vulgar. Like many fathers who channel their pride into hopes for their daughters, Beauchamp found he had educated Katherine to despise him for having 'an undeniable *trade* atmosphere'.[21] She might be indulging in high-flown erotic fantasies, but her father called it 'fooling around in dark corners with fellows' and her mother was 'constantly suspicious, constantly overbearingly tyrannous'.[22] In truth, Katherine's interest in the idea that sex was a commodity which could earn money – and she was always fascinated by prostitution – was evidence less of vice than of her being

---

* Katherine's Adonis has been tentatively identified by David Kynaston in *Archie's Last Stand* as R. H. ('Ronny') Fox, a New Zealand-born amateur. He appeared as a Maori chief at the ship's fancy-dress ball.

her father's daughter, with a keen eye for business opportunities.

'Would you not like to try *all* sorts of lives – one is so very small?' had been her cry before leaving England, but long before the *Corinthic* docked at Wellington she was in rebellion against the prospect of her life there, the life she outlined satirically as

The Suitable Appropriate Existence, the days full of perpetual Society functions, the hours full of clothes discussions, the waste of life. 'The stifling atmosphere would kill me' she thought. The days, weeks, months, years of it all. Her father, with his successful characteristic respectable face, crying, 'Now is the time. What have I got for my money? Come along, deck yourself out, show the world that you are expensive.'[22]

There is a sharp note here which may go nearer to the heart of the situation in the Beauchamp family in 1906 than any of Katherine's later, softened accounts of her family.

She had been in England for nearly four crucially formative years – from fourteen to seventeen – living in a girls' school that allowed her a much greater degree of independence, physical and emotional, than she would have found at home, and that was situated in the heart of London, with immediate access to the life of the streets and parks as well as shops, galleries and concert halls. She had stayed in London and provincial hotels with her family, and visited relatives in various parts of the country, from Surrey to Sheffield. She had been to Paris and Brussels, and made friends among music students who spoke as familiarly of Germany as of England. Since all her dreams were of becoming a musician or a writer, and all her cultural heroes and heroines were European, it was natural for her to wish to remain. But something more than the sense of being at home in Europe was stamped on her by this period: this was the habit of impermanence. The hotel room, the temporary lodging, the sense of being about to move on, of living where you do not quite belong, observing with a stranger's eye – all these became second nature to her between 1903 and 1906. With this impermanence went the sudden forming of intimacies, the swiftly decisive declarations of friendship that so characterized her. She took up impressions with wonderful speed; she also took up people fast, sometimes too fast for judgement or safety; but then safety was never her concern.

3

NEW ZEALAND 1907:
'THE SUITABLE APPROPRIATE EXISTENCE'

■

Harold Beauchamp may well have felt mocked by all the good things he had done for his daughters: education, travel, the experience of Europe, independence. All three were disposed to mope over their loss and condescend towards what they were being brought back to, but Katherine was the fiercest. It is normal enough for an eighteen-year-old, weighed down by puppy fat and spurred on by huge ambitions, to rebel against the constrictions of family and home; in her case there was also some justification in the claim that she would find what she was looking for far more easily in London than in Wellington. Meanwhile, she faced what was on offer with less than delight: the city over the deep, crater-shaped harbour with its painted wooden buildings, leafy gardens and red tin roofs, surrounded by empty beaches and summer-flowering landscape; the comfortable house in Tinakori Road; the company of her generally affectionate sisters; and even the rediscovery of her little brother, Leslie, when he came home from boarding school. On a bad day, her *Heimweh*, as she chose to call it to her cousin Sylvia, was almost unendurable: 'I feel absolutely ill with grief and sadness ... How people ever wish to live here I cannot think ... But I shall come back because here I should die.'[1]

A real death had, in fact, faced her almost on arrival: that of her grandmother Dyer, the central figure in her childhood home. She died on New Year's Eve. Katherine had been too 'busy' to visit her, but she felt the drama of the loss: 'Death never seemed revolting before – This place – steals your Youth ... I feel years and years older and sadder.'[2] Later she mourned and commemorated her grandmother in poems and stories, but she was too absorbed in her own life to do so now. The deaths in her notebook jottings are suicides or tragic illnesses of the young, the price paid for free and risky living – a price imagined easily and cheerfully enough by a young and healthy woman.

Within weeks of Granny Dyer's end, another death brushed the family when a young workman living in a lane behind Tinakori Road was killed on the day the Beauchamps were giving a summer party. The eldest daughter, Vera, was sent down to the bereaved family with some food, still wearing her party dress and hat. Katherine observed and listened. When she wrote 'The Garden Party' fourteen years later, she made the story centre round the emotions of the 'artistic' daughter, Laura, who feels divided from most of her family by her sensitive, grieving response to the death. She sees them as crassly materialistic and snobbish and thinks she prefers the workmen who come to put up the marquee to the silly boys she has to dance with. At the same time, Laura does enjoy the party, and shares in the womanly life of the household with pleasure.

The story is plainly not autobiographical, but the fluctuation between cold hostility to the family and warm enjoyment of some aspects of its luxurious way of life was part of Katherine's experience in 1907. There was pleasure to be had in concerts and parties, dances and new clothes. All the sisters turned up their noses when they re-encountered the New Zealand boys they had known as children (and none married a New Zealander). The departure of the English cricket team was deeply mourned. Chaddie insisted that all colonial men were inferior, and, although Katherine boasted about her own popularity as a dance partner and the five proposals of marriage she received from local men, she took none of them seriously and assured Vera that 'living here you will certainly not marry'.[3] Their Wellington cousins found them 'frightfully English. Nothing in NZ was good enough for them ... [They were] breaking their necks to get back to England'.[4] Katherine in particular kept her family fully informed about her dissatisfaction; 'the dear old thing I hate to feel she is so unhappy here isn't it a horrid state to be in so early in life?' inquired Chaddie sagely of cousin Sylvia.[5]

The one young man she did take seriously, and who remained her dream of sophistication and achievement, was Arnold Trowell, who combined the work of an artist with a successful career as a concert violinist in London. While Ida sent news and press cuttings of his appearances, Katherine drafted love letters (whether she posted them or not is another matter) and visited his parents and sister to talk about him. They were planning to join Arnold and Garnet in London, but for the moment she continued her cello studies with Mr Trowell and embarked on a strenuous regime of practice. Although Arnold wrote occasionally, he made no pretence of returning Katherine's feelings; clearly, he was the model for the elusive beloved, teasing, superior and finally indifferent, who appears in fragments of fiction written at this time. The faithful and loving correspondent was always Ida, to whom Katherine could pour out her grumbles about the family and her situation. 'I hear, constantly, from Ida ... You know how I love her very much indeed,' she told her cousin Sylvia.[6] She also kept in touch with Vere Bartrick-Baker, and mused about their reunion in her journal.

Ida was still living with her family in their Baker Street flat, a sheltered life as she called it later, in which serving and placating their short-tempered and tyrannical father was the chief employment of the daughters. Vere's education and ambitions had taken her no further than a job as a theatre usherette, which she found so humiliating that she soon gave it up to work in a country bank and live with her mother. Yet, from Katherine's perspective, they inhabited a promised land. What was there for her and her sisters to do, beside the social round and whatever their own wits could devise, now that they had left school and Europe behind? Leslie would follow Papa into the business, of course; there was no question of the girls doing so. In principle they had their 'interests': music and painting for Vera, singing for Chaddie, cello and literature for Katherine – all strictly ladylike and amateur occupations. But if Arnold could earn money and fame with his music in London, why should class and sex bar Katherine from following the same path? It was not as though she had any duties; she did not even make her own dresses, although, judging from many items in the social columns of the Wellington press, the Beauchamps kept squads of dressmakers busy with their tussores and laces, pipings, silks and matching hats.

And still they prospered.

> Harold Beauchamp's a man of some rank,
> Why, doesn't he manage a bank?
> Oh, he cuts a fine figure,
> And grafts like a nigger,
> He'd swim if Customs Street sank![7]

announced the New Zealand *Freelance*. For, in April 1907, he was elected chairman of the board of the Bank of New Zealand. He chose this moment to sell up 75 Tinakori Road and move his family into a more splendid house at 4 Fitzherbert Terrace.

There was a ballroom, a croquet lawn and a smoking room, where Katherine was frequently to be found with a cigarette, a habit which became a lifelong addiction. Her bedroom was arranged with the aesthetics of Ladbroke Grove in mind: the curtains were kept symbolically shut against the world outside, producing a 'fascinating twilight', a Velázquez Venus presided on the wall; in one corner stood the cello, and the scent of flowers, artistically arranged in low bowls, filled the air. Behind the curtains she worked at her sketches and stories, wrote her moody letters and read with furious energy. She borrowed books from the excellent library attached to Parliament House; at this time she read Balzac, Flaubert and Maupassant in French; Ruskin, Browning, Pater, De Morgan, Rossetti, William Morris, Stevenson, the Brontës and Meredith; and the American writers Hawthorne and Whitman. She was also interested in thoroughly up-to-date English writers preaching social reform: Bernard Shaw, Granville-Barker and Edward Carpenter. Few of their ideas can have fitted in very happily with the way of life at Fitzherbert Terrace, but Katherine's view was that their influence was urgently needed in New Zealand: 'These people have not learned their alphabet yet.'[8]

Her passionate curiosity did not allow her to stay behind her drawn curtains for too long, however. She looked up her old school friend Maata, still fascinatingly beautiful, flirted with her and flattered her; Maata was pleased, but she was busy with her own marriage plans.* Then Katherine found something more serious. She learnt that the daughter of some old family acquaintances, the Bendalls, had a studio in Fitzherbert Terrace. Katherine called on her and asked if she could 'be her friend'. Edith Kathleen Bendall was strikingly beautiful, twenty-seven years old (nine years older than Katherine), and had shown remarkable talent and initiative in her life. She was the eighth child of

---

* Maata married twice. She had two daughters of the second marriage, and spent her fortune lavishly until it was gone: she had 'plenty of charm a clever talker and in her adult years a distinct disinclination to sleep by herself. Quite irresponsible about money . . . On a small scale she was a kind of Amber. I think that is the best way to describe her. I have lost count of how many times she was married.'[9] (Amber was the heroine of a bestselling soft-porn novel, *Forever Amber*.)

Maata was well aware of the interest her association with K.M. aroused, and claimed to have sent her money, although there is no evidence of any contact after Katherine's return to Europe in 1908. A fragment of a diary kept by Maata was acquired by Ruth Mantz and is in Texas, and there was talk of a further manuscript, which she encouraged; even after her death in 1952 her daughter made mysterious references to it, but nobody has ever produced it and it is almost certainly a piece of pure invention.

a sea captain turned marine surveyor who had been born in Bristol in the 1830s. The family were not well off, and Edith, who loved drawing, had paid her own way through art school by taking a job in the library. In 1904 she had earned enough from an exhibition of her work to pay her fare to Sydney, where she continued to study and was introduced to various magazine publishers; she was immediately given commissions, for her highly stylized drawings of children in particular. Frances Hodgkins, who became New Zealand's most famous painter, gave her some lessons and, although she had to return to Wellington when her mother became ill, she was now a fully fledged professional artist, selling her drawings regularly in Australia and New Zealand.

Edith was attractive, graceful and sweet-natured, but more important,

I was a worker and that's why she liked me. I was working all day in my studio and at 5 o'clock I went for a walk and she used to come with me. Kathleen asked if she could walk with me every night. I said, 'I'd love you to, Kathleen ...' I was her real friend in Wellington ... I was completely taken with her ... She liked me and she let me know it.[10]

Katherine was deeply fascinated by this discovery of a true artist on her very doorstep. They planned to produce a book together: poems about children by Katherine, drawings by Edith. The poems were written, and survive; they are essentially a pastiche of Robert Louis Stevenson's *A Child's Garden of Verses*, with touches of Hans Christian Andersen. While they are on the sweet side for modern tastes, they are charming and skilfully written, and certainly publishable. Unfortunately, no publisher was found; but the friendship blossomed.

'She wrote me these lovely little letters every night – perfect letters, absolutely beautiful';[11] and she invited Edith to go with her to the seaside bungalow her father had built among the rocks at Day's Bay, away from Wellington. There was nothing but a beach, a scattering of houses and the hills all around. The Beauchamps had built a very simple wooden structure on a point where the waves almost reached it, with just one main room and one bedroom furnished with bunks.

Here, alone with Edith, Katherine felt, according to her journal entries,

more powerfully all those so-termed sexual impulses with her than I have with any man. She enthrals me, enslaves me – and her personal self – her body absolute – is my worship. I feel that to lie with my head on her breast is to feel what life can hold ... pillowed against her, clinging to her hands, her face against mine, I am a child, a woman, and more than half a man.[12]

Another passage describes her joy when Edith came silently to her and took her in her arms, to comfort her when she found her crying:

We lay down together, still silently, she every now and then pressing me to her, kissing me, my head on her breasts, her hands round my body, stroking me, lovingly – warming me ... Then her voice, whispering 'Better now, darling?' I could not answer with words. And again 'I suppose you could not tell me.' I drew close to her warm sweet body, happier than I had ever been, than I could ever have imagined being.[13]

Edith recalled the bungalow and its bunks clearly and without embarrassment in her old age. To one of her generation and upbringing it was out of the question even to consider, let alone discuss, the possibility of an erotic relationship between two women. 'I was completely taken with her,' were her words at the age of ninety-eight, speaking of Katherine's incipient beauty, her plumpness, her lovely voice when she read aloud to her, and her fascination. At an earlier time, when she felt she had had enough of intrusive questioning about the relationship, she said she thought Katherine had simply misinterpreted her motherly gestures. No one can say with any certainty now whether Katherine was working up the incidents at the beach in her notebooks, dramatizing them to make literature, or recording a true experience; but despite the slightly comic invocation to Wilde, there does seem to be a genuine note here:

Here by a thousand delicate suggestions I can absorb her – for the time. What an experience! And when we returned to town, small wonder that I could not sleep, but tossed to and fro, and yearned, and realized a thousand things which had been obscure ... O Oscar! Am I peculiarly susceptible to sexual impulse? I must be, I suppose – but I rejoice. Now, each time I see her to put her arms round me and hold me against her [sic]. I think she wanted to, too; but she is afraid and custom hedges her in, I feel. We shall go away again.[14]

She was probably right about Edith's respect for custom; and she had already met her future husband, Gerald Robison, a housemaster at Wellington College and ten years her senior. At all events, Katherine soon decided Edith was too passive, and 'she will never be great'. Yet Edith did treasure Katherine's letters. She kept them in her bedroom, in a drawer. While she was on her honeymoon in 1908, a maid removed and destroyed them, or so she was told (or so she said). Evidently, they were disapproved of by someone; but 'fancy taking letters out of a drawer in your bedroom!'[15]

Katherine seems to have retreated into more 'normal' love. Some unnamed men appear in a brief, torrid flurry in her journal. Arnold's distant magic still cast a spell at times, and Ida half remembered a piece of scandalous behaviour with a sailor at a dance, which annoyed the Beauchamps. Yet it was not as simple as that. Later in the year Katherine wrote a story called 'Leves Amores' which is undisguisedly lesbian, and sent a copy of it, together with a few of her other vignettes, to Vere Bartrick-Baker, who kept it among her papers until her death.* Kàtherine had learned that there was something in her nature that would not quite fit in with the accepted pattern of behaviour required by society, at the same time, she never wanted to reject that pattern entirely. She wanted marriage and children and the outward manifestations of a conventional arrangement. She feared Vere all her life, because she felt she had some sort of hold over her: doubtless it was this knowledge of the other side of her nature.

She accepted without reciprocating Ida's worship, mocking it to the world while privately relying on it; it did not cause a problem, because there was no physical attraction on Katherine's side. None of her sexual relations with men appears to have given her happiness or even satisfaction, and she said that her relationship with her husband, Murry, was more like that between two men or two children than between a man and a woman – and even that she was the man, Murry the woman. Throughout her work, men appear as clumsy, emotionally inept, cruel, treacherous, foolish, pompous, tyrannous, greedy, self-deluding, insensitive and disappointing; and the theme of women conspiring against and excluding men is a recurring one, as in 'The Lady's Maid', in which a servant sends away the man she is about to marry because she cannot bear to leave her mistress, or 'At the Bay', where all the women rejoice when the master of the house leaves for work, allowing them to get on with their real lives unimpeded.

Katherine does not appear to have written about her love for Edith Bendall beyond the journal entries, but it may have made its way into English fiction by a circuitous route. When Katherine was living near D. H. Lawrence and Frieda in the winter of 1914, they were on very intimate terms, and she was particularly dissatisfied with Murry. Frieda said later that Katherine 'told me many things from her life',[16] and, indeed, this was one of the ways in which Katherine established intimacy, with her women friends especially. Frieda, with her interest in Freudian theories, was no doubt an enthusiastic audience for anything unusual

* The story is reproduced in Appendix 1.

Katherine had to tell, and it is very likely that Lawrence listened too, or that Frieda repeated her friend's stories to him. At this time he was reworking the manuscript of the book that was to become *The Rainbow*, in which the character of the young 'New Woman' struggling for emancipation, Ursula, is generally thought to be drawn from both Frieda and a former fiancée of Lawrence's, Louie Burrows, with episodes in the schoolroom taken from Lawrence's own experience as a teacher for good measure. The book was substantially finished, but at some point during the winter Lawrence suddenly introduced an entirely new and startling element into Ursula's story. In a chapter called 'Shame' he describes her lesbian passion for a schoolmistress called Winifred Inger. Ursula is meant to be about seventeen, Miss Inger twenty-eight, 'clever, and expert in what she did, accurate, quick, commanding'. Ursula begins by admiring Winifred for her cleverness and then becomes obsessively interested in her body, especially after she sees her swimming in the school pool. Later Winifred, reciprocating Ursula's passion, invites her to a small bungalow beside the river, 'a tiny, two-roomed shanty set on a steep bank'. After a discussion of feminist subjects such as death in childbirth and prostitution – both favourite Mansfield topics – the two girls go swimming naked in the dark summer night. As they go towards the water, Winifred takes Ursula in her arms and carries her into it, kissing and caressing her. Later Ursula suffers a revulsion (much as Katherine did, and recorded in her notebook), but then writes a 'burning, passionate love-letter'.

This is not, of course, in any sense a factual account of Katherine's passion for Edith Bendall. Winifred is a different type of person, and Lawrence weaves her into the plot further by marrying her to Ursula's uncle. But Ursula (like Katherine) reverts to heterosexuality, resumes an unsatisfactory love-affair, becomes pregnant (as Katherine did in 1909) and loses her baby, again as Katherine did. The points of coincidence are striking enough, and the timing of the insertion of the lesbian episode into the manuscript of the novel is such that it is hard to resist the idea that Lawrence was doing what he so often did: using a portion of a friend's reported experience as the basis for his work.*

Ironically, it became one of the chief reasons for the banning of *The*

---

* Comparable episodes are the use of Helen Corke's experiences in *The Trespasser* and the use of Jessie Chambers' in *Sons and Lovers*. Lawrence also asked Mabel Dodge Luhan to give him notes on her life, which he planned to turn into a novel, in 1922, and he used Frieda's reminiscences in his work also. Had Lawrence and Katherine agreed on a collaborative work, we might have had something very startling indeed.

Rainbow, which reduced Lawrence to desperate poverty for several years. Katherine made no comment on the book beyond an expression of dislike, according to Murry, at any rate. He certainly disliked it and found its sexual explicitness troubling. On the other hand, it caused no breach in her friendship with Lawrence. Perhaps she thought privately that he had caught something true in his treatment, or perhaps she was embarrassed at the possibility of Murry finding out that she had told other people things she had not told him.

In real life, the most characteristic part of the Edith affair is that Katherine did the courting, the letter-writing and the jilting, as she did in almost every affair she had. Edith bore no grudge, but went up to Napier, in the north of the island, for a holiday, where the two young women had a friendly meeting in December. Shortly afterwards Edith married; she and her husband were very happy, and had a daughter. Contact was never re-established between the two after they had become Mrs Robison and Katherine Mansfield, but when Mrs Robison wheeled her baby out in Wellington, Harold Beauchamp made a habit of stopping to look approvingly into the pram. Edith remained a cheerful, sweet-natured and maternal woman. She continued to paint into her old age, selling and exhibiting her work successfully. But she grew weary of Mansfield researchers pestering her with indiscreet questions. She lived to be 107 years old, clear in her mind to the last, dying in 1986.

When Katherine and Edith were planning their book, Katherine needed to have her poems typed; she turned to her father's secretary, who obliged out of friendliness. Soon Katherine was sending her prose pieces too. When Miss 'Matty' Putnam commented on the glumness of her work, Katherine responded with confident cheek: 'Soon I shall write Poems full of cheerfulness – though to tell you a secret I prefer the others – the tragic pessimism of Youth – you see – it's as inevitable as measles!'[17] She continued to produce morbid and decadent pieces, and to boast of her own sophistication. Katherine could be absurd, but there was never any doubt of her capacity for hard work and her passionate determination. Now, through her father, she met a journalist called Tom Mills and showed him some of her vignettes. He was impressed, if a bit taken aback by their tone, and advised her to submit them to a Melbourne literary monthly magazine, the *Native Companion*, which promptly took some. The first three appeared in the issue of October 1907. They were about girls dreaming of future fame, music students and London, and alternated between purplish description and a cynical, world-weary tone. Brady, the editor, wrote to Katherine, querying whether the author was really the novice she claimed to be. She answered boldly that she was indeed an obscure eighteen-year-old with a hatred of plagiarism, 'a rapacious appetite for everything and principles as light as my purse'[18] whereupon Brady sent her a cheque for £2. The Beauchamps were delighted and proud, and her father wrote privately to Brady, praising his daughter's originality; he did not know that she was writing at the same time to insist on the importance of her pseudonym. She could be 'K.M.' or 'K. Mansfield' but not K. M. Beauchamp; another name she suggested was 'Julian Mark', which she fancied enough to use when writing to her sister Vera, on holiday in Sydney.

The *Native Companion* took two more contributions. One was a description of the Botanical Gardens in Wellington; the other, 'In a Café' set in London, has a girl of advanced views – she has read all the modern European authors – discussing Art and the Ten Deadly Conventions with a Trowell-like music student,

slightly taller than she, with the regulation 'stoop' and heavy walk, and the regulation wide hat and soft tie. But to her he walked in a great light, and she knew that genius had traced the laurel wreath around his brows.[19]

She steers the conversation to the subject of marriage and he teases her lightly; she gives him the violets she is carrying, and later finds them carelessly dropped outside the café. She grows 'white to the lips' but then starts to laugh. For all its juvenile posturing, there is something striking about the story and its heroine, who woos, is rejected and refuses to be broken-hearted. She is a much tougher girl than the later rejected women such as Vera in 'A Dill Pickle' or Mouse, with her soaked handkerchief, in '*Je ne parle pas français*' a decade later.

Brady was asking for more, and Katherine was growing in confidence. She also believed she had wrested permission from her parents to return to London and wrote jubilantly to the Trowells – all now settled in St John's Wood – to tell them to expect her in the new year: 'Kiss London for me – and tell it – that when I come back I shall live in a tent in Trafalgar Square – and only leave it for Bayreuth.'[20]

In the meantime she accepted an invitation from another musical friend of her own age, Millie Parker, to join her on a very different sort of expedition. This was a month's camping holiday in the northern wilderness, organized by Millie's Maori-speaking cousin. Work was set aside, although Katherine intended to take notes to be used as raw material for vignettes. It was to be a real adventure.

Katherine and Millie set off together by train for Hastings, 200 miles north of Wellington, where they were to join the rest of the party, all older people unknown to Katherine. They included a farmer and a chemist with his young wife; she described them in her notebook as 'ultra-colonial but kind-hearted and generous'. The plan was to travel with two large, horse-drawn wagons, carrying tents; their route would take them across some very difficult terrain, including mountains, scrub and pumice plain where the road sometimes disappeared altogether, and places where the Maoris were evidently hostile (it was only twelve years since the most recent fighting between Maoris and white settlers). Although they would occasionally camp near hotels, the intention was that they should prepare most of their meals and generally look after themselves. Katherine soon revealed that she did not know how to peel potatoes, but set to willingly enough when instructed.

It was midsummer heat, and she was soon bitten and burnt, despite a large hat and the tight thick clothes that she, like all the women of the party, felt obliged to wear. Her laundry list, written out in the same notebook in which she mentions the pleasure of feeling the sun on her skin through her blouse, is heartbreaking: petticoat, bodices, drawers, stockings, vests and dress shields (worn under the arms against sweat). No wonder she sometimes felt ill in the sultry heat.

Even from the wildest parts she sent letters home as well as keeping a journal, and her account of the long, rough rides, the walking and camping – the whole party shared an enormous tent – the spectacular landscape with its rivers, waterfalls and springs, and the many encounters with Maori families and groups, gives a vivid impression of the state of the country at the time. Casually and often almost illegibly scrawled, with dashes for punctuation, it has the true Mansfield voice, whether she is describing a storm in which they are lost and benighted in wet clothes in the 'utter back blocks', or her joy in the lily of the valley, clover and breast-high manuka, or bird-song at dawn, or a 'wonderful huge horsefly' by the Galatea River. She was interested in the Maoris, and sympathetic in particular to the young girls with their babies. Their guide was himself the son of a Maori mother and an English father; but this did not prevent signs of marked hostility from some groups of Maoris, which she also recorded.

So there were some bad moments; but it was too interesting and arduous for Katherine to do anything but enjoy herself and gather copy just as she had intended. Her final description of camping in a pine forest near Lake Taupo, with lush grass, mimosa, honeysuckle, and splashes of light falling through the trees, is entirely idyllic.

A few days later she and Millie were back in Napier. Katherine visited Edith, and treated her to satirical imitations of her travelling companions and the Maoris encountered on the trip; Edith was amused, and found her altogether much more 'down to earth'. Then Katherine and Millie took the train for Wellington.

In the train – December 17th – Has there ever been a hotter day – the land is parched – golden with the heat – The sheep are sheltering in the shadow of the rocks – in the distance the hills are shimmering in the heat – M. and I sitting opposite each other – I look *perfectly charming*.[21]

Now she proposed to herself a programme of six hours' work daily with her cello, followed by three hours' writing; evidently she still thought of a musical career as a possibility. But her parents' agreement to let her go to London was rescinded, to her intense exasperation. One reason may have been the contents of her story 'Leves Amores' (mentioned on p. 37), which she had asked Miss Putnam to type for her in December. She apologized for it in advance, saying, 'I'm afraid you won't like Leves Amores – I can't think how I wrote it – it's partly a sort of dream'.[22] Dream or not, it is set in Wellington and names a local hotel. Miss Putnam may well have let her employer, Mr Beauchamp, see it, and it must have suggested to him either that his daughter was a practising lesbian or at least that she had an unhealthy interest in sex and squalor. He must have been appalled at the thought of her publishing, or even trying to publish, such a story, or even letting Miss Putnam see it.

Miss Putnam's reaction to the story is not known. Later she described Katherine as a girl with a 'fine proud bearing, magnificent dark eyes ... and distinction'.[23] But she also said that she never laughed and spoke 'without inflection or vivacity', which sorts rather oddly with Katherine's coyly flirtatious letters to her: 'Well – I must go to bed – Shall I build a castle with a spare room for you – Yes I will – so please return the compliment'.[24] And later: 'Am just off to Island Bay for a long day & maybe an evening – I am going to write – and have to go to the sea for "Copy" – Do bring a book and come – too – dear – and we shall "paddle" and "bake". Don't you *love* the two processes?'[25] But whether Miss Putnam went for her paddle and bake, she never told.

In January 1908 the *Native Companion* ceased publication and, although Tom Mills had decided she was a genius and wished to publish her work in his up-country local paper, it was not quite the same thing. Besides, he was making a nuisance of himself; she complained to Vera, 'he likes me far too much'.[26] Another admirer, a teacher from her old school, Miss Swainson's, advised her simply to go to Europe steerage, 'with your genius and your future'. 'That is gratifying,' reflected the young genius, 'but not feasible.'[27] Her mother was meditating a plan whereby all three girls should return to London together for a limited time, sharing a flat and an allowance of £300 a year, but evidently Vera and Chaddie were more reconciled to life in New Zealand than Katherine, and more enthusiastic about the available young men.

Still Harold hesitated, while Katherine grumbled and lamented in her journal; she also did more sensible things, such as enrolling for a typing and book-keeping course at the local technical college. She was attempting to write a novel about a Maori girl, amassing notes for stories and reading as voraciously as ever; Elinor Glyn and Elizabeth Robins* were discovered at this time, the last earning Katherine's particular tribute: 'I like to think she is only the first of a great never ending procession of splendid, strong woman writers – all this suffragist movement is *excellent* for our sex – kicked policemen or not kicked policemen'.[28] (She did not stay to ponder the fact that women had had the vote in New Zealand for several years already, without producing any discernible effect on the quality of life there.)

Another woman writer who made an indelible impression on Katherine at this time was the Russian diarist Marie Bashkirtseff, whose posthumously published journal became a worldwide bestseller. Bashkirtseff, born about 1860 (the year of Chekhov's birth) was an aristocrat who determined to become a painter rather than a society beauty, studied in Paris in the care of an adoring mother who was separated from her father, and travelled in Italy, Germany, Austria and Russia as well as France. She became a friend of Maupassant, among other eminent men; and she kept a remarkably frank journal in which she recorded her wildly fluctuating moods, her feminist ideas and her artistic aspirations; but she developed tuberculosis and died at the age of twenty-four. Her mother had the journal published; and, though some discreet excisions were made, it is none the less a remarkable piece of self-revelation. It is

---

* Elizabeth Robins (1862–1952) became President of the Women Writers' Suffrage League, founded in 1908, and author of a successful play, *Votes for Women*, produced in 1907.

easy to see how it would have spoken to Katherine: both women possessed a temperament in which despair and elation, love and jealousy, alternated; both had a passion for travel and the determination to pursue an artistic vocation rather than a social life.

But Bashkirtseff lived her brief life at the centres of European culture, cherished by her mother and able to pursue her studies with the best masters. Fitzherbert Terrace, Wellington, New Zealand and the Technical College and General Assembly Library were no equivalent. In due course, the Beauchamps understood this and realized they must let Katherine go. 'There was no question of standing in her light,'[29] declared her father retrospectively; probably there was a certain amount of trepidation as to what she might get up to next if she remained in Wellington. Years later there would be a buzz about her name at tea-parties, and a sudden hush if a schoolgirl daughter came into the room.[30]

None of her English relatives was willing to take her on; but a respectable lodging was arranged in a hostel for music students in Paddington. It was called, by coincidence, Beauchamp Lodge. Katherine was to have an allowance of £100 a year, not very much for a banker's daughter, but more than the annual earnings of a young schoolteacher at the time. She sailed in July 1908, after a farewell party given for her at the house of the Prime Minister. The New Zealand *Freelance* reported:

A great number of the guest of honour's girl friends came to wish her good luck. There was a pig-drawing competition during the afternoon, which was won by Miss Esme Dean, and afterwards the book was presented to Miss Beauchamp as a souvenir. In the billiard room some beautiful records of Melba and Tettrezini [*sic*] were heard, and a fortune-teller was kept busy in another room. The tea table looked very pretty with bright-coloured lights in the centre, and little bowls of violets and primroses scattered about, and great bunches of myrtle and holly adorned the mantelpiece ... Miss K. Beauchamp wore a dark brown coat and skirt, and black fox furs.[31]

A few weeks before she left, Katherine wrote in her journal a very straightforward assertion of feminist independence, which must have sustained her through the pig-drawing and fortune-telling of that afternoon:

Here then is a little summary of what I need -- power, wealth and freedom. It is the hopelessly insipid doctrine that love is the only thing in the world, taught, hammered into women, from generation to generation, which hampers us so cruelly. We must get rid of that bogey -- and then, then comes the opportunity of happiness and freedom.[32]

Fine, fighting words which would always be in conflict with her rival desire to live out a perfect, loving relationship. Yet the claim on power and wealth as well as freedom shows that she knew herself, the banker's daughter, never drawn to the indignities and discomforts of poverty, and clear-sighted enough to see that her father's money had given her a London education that could be used to get her back to London, and not in the steerage class. She was always prepared to ask him and her friends for money, although she was also extremely proud of what she earned for herself and insistent in her wish to work for money; she was also notably generous and supersensitive to meanness in others.

What she wanted was the power to control her own life without being held in any web of convention. Her instinct to return to London was just; the coolly independent Katherine could not exist in the context of her family, whom she felt to be stifling and intellectually uncongenial. She told Tom Mills that her father was interested only in money and her mother in social climbing, a judgement that may have been unfair and does not entirely sort with what she said later, but certainly had an element of truth to it. Little Leslie, sensitive and artistic as he might be, was not a strong enough ally; the example of Edith Bendall suggested a path to independence, but it did not go far enough. Katherine was right to doubt whether she could command power or wealth by her own efforts in the antipodes in 1908, whereas London was set like a stage for the entrance of a young woman of independent mind and talent.

4

LONDON 1908: NEW WOMEN

■

Katherine sailed towards London in the summer of 1908 in the joyous mood of the successful rebel, confident that an exciting destiny must be awaiting her there. The time was well chosen; she was travelling to a country in which the patterns of Victorian life were being thoroughly shaken about, and none more vigorously than the pattern of Victorian womanhood.

In New Zealand women had been given the vote in 1893 and had already declared that they hardly noticed the difference. In New Zealand too the Boer War had increased prosperity; Harold Beauchamp's fortune was considerably enlarged by it; but in England it had divided people and unsettled the old imperial confidence. Ideas which had merely hung subversively in the air until now began to take on body and strength, and behaviour which would have been unthinkable a generation earlier began to appear openly, at least in intellectual circles. Changes were of many kinds: in politics, over fifty Labour Members of Parliament reached the House of Commons in the 1906 election, and the Liberal Government had an unprecedented majority. The suffragette movement was approaching its militant zenith; in 1907 the first candidate of the National Union of Women's Suffrage Societies, standing at a by-election in Wimbledon, was Bertrand Russell, member of the political aristocracy, Fellow of Trinity College, Cambridge, and distinguished as a philosopher and mathematician. A newspaper commented sagely that 'the mere fact that a thinker of his intellectual distinction should stand primarily to promote women's suffrage marks an immense advance in the fortunes of the cause'.[1] In the same year a pamphlet called 'The Endowment of Motherhood', the work of an early Freudian, Dr David Eder, was published, presenting the first written case for state provision to women who bear children as an alternative to financial dependence on men. The issue was hotly debated in the Fabian Society, where there were also violent arguments on the question of marriage reform in general, with H. G. Wells in favour and Beatrice and Sidney Webb against – Wells a feminist and great lover of women, the Webbs childless by choice and highly suspicious of any sexual irregularity.

The arts were in a similar state of eruption. Galsworthy's novel attacking bourgeois and patriarchal marriage, *The Man of Property*, had appeared in 1906, its indignant revelations producing *frissons* of horror mixed with pleasure; even within marriage, it announced, a man might be said to rape his wife. A young Croydon schoolmistress of this period, whose cousin died in childbirth, said she regarded the bereaved husband as guilty of manslaughter.[2] In the theatre the plays of Harley Granville-Barker and Bernard Shaw were critical of all the values of the governing classes, not least their view of women. Granville-Barker's *Waste*, in which two outsiders, one a sexually unconventional woman, the other an incautious politician, destroy one another, was banned in 1906. In response to this and other similar infringements of freedom, a Society for the Abolition of Censorship was set up and enthusiastically supported by the writing community; and its secretary, a young and much-admired writer called Gilbert Cannan, extended his own freedom to such a degree that he was soon cited by one of its leading members, the playwright J. M. Barrie, as co-respondent in a divorce case.

New magazines, edited and written by new men and women, and read by an intelligentsia no longer confined to the middle classes, were appearing. The *English Review* started in 1908, with a declared policy of seeking working-class writers. Its editor, Ford Madox Hueffer, chose the year of its foundation to leave his wife for an outspoken feminist writer, Violet Hunt. Editorial advice was given by two other writers of advanced views, Wells and Edward Garnett, who was also busy writing plays with social themes such as unmarried mothers and women's suffrage at this time. In the pages of the *English Review* a young elementary schoolmaster with literary ambitions, David Herbert Lawrence, read Wells's serialized *Tono-Bungay* with passionate relish.

Another essentially new magazine which Lawrence also read and recommended to his friends was the *New Age*, edited by an eccentric Nietzschean ex-schoolmaster called A. R. Orage; he too, following what looks like a pattern, was separated from his wife and living with a dashing woman writer, Beatrice Hastings. The pages of the *New Age* were crammed with eugenics, marriage reform, socialism, free love, protests against sweated labour and capital punishment, women's questions from abortion to the vote, psychoanalysis, foreign affairs, philosophy and theatre criticism, together with drawings by Augustus John and Walter Sickert, sometimes candid studies of nudes. The *New Age* had its own press, on which Eder's pamphlet, among others, was printed; Eder was a frequent contributor (he also married a divorced woman in 1908, Edith Haden Guest, née Low, a friend of Wells and a believer in 'open' marriage).

The society that Katherine Mansfield was about to encounter in London was set to welcome a young woman scared of nothing and ready to pioneer social changes, to become, in fact, their heroic embodiment. The moment seemed made for her, and she for the moment. This was an adventurous and unorthodox society, open to new ideas, determinedly rejecting the values of its parents. If we pause to trace the experiences of some of Katherine's contemporaries who were later to become her friends, a clear pattern emerges of women crossing the barriers of class and defying the sexual conventions.

The woman who most demands to be considered in relation to Katherine as friend, rival and *semblable* was Virginia Stephen, twenty-six in 1908 and so six years her senior. By the time they met in 1916, she was Virginia Woolf, her reputation as a writer attached to the name of her husband; but in 1908 she was still the unmarried, orphaned, shy daughter of Leslie Stephen, the great Victorian man of letters, with no achievements of her own. She had lost not only her mother and father but also a much-loved elder brother and step-sister. To trauma were added two episodes of madness, most recently in 1904. The personality that appears in her letters is a rigorous one; she may be playful, but she is not fluid like Katherine. Where Katherine lets her pen run on, trailing emotion, Virginia's phrases shine like thin ice over dark water.

Virginia had received less formal education than Katherine – she never went to school – but she had more book knowledge. Her father, every bit as much the patriarch as Harold Beauchamp (and with the same habit of bullying his women over the household accounts), was, at any rate, a scholar-patriarch. Although he never considered sending his clever daughter to a university alongside her brothers, she had the use of his library. Almost through her skin she imbibed the habit of study and took to hard work early; after her mother's death, when Virginia was thirteen, her father taught her himself and arranged for her to have Greek lessons. She struggled with and mastered the grammar, not content simply to pick up the sense of a passage.

Unlike the pleasure-seeking Beauchamp women, the Stephens considered that service to the community was an obligation. Virginia was not expected to have a career, but for three years, from 1904 to 1907, she gave adult-education classes in history and literature to milkmen and typists at Morley College, London (albeit with rather mixed success). Later she joined the women's suffrage movement and did the dreary work of addressing envelopes and sitting on platforms with the suffragettes.

Her ambitions were, from the start, purely literary, and she was born into the literary establishment: Henry James and Thomas Hardy were among Leslie Stephen's friends, and his first wife was the daughter of Thackeray. Accordingly, Virginia began to review books early, for the old-established *Cornhill* magazine and the newly created *Times Literary Supplement*. She took the work seriously – not being a churchgoer, she often chose to write her reviews on Sunday – and did it very well.

In 1907, following the marriage of her elder sister Vanessa to Clive Bell, she set up house with her brother Adrian at 29 Fitzroy Square in Bloomsbury. The eighteenth-century Adam houses, once grand, were now shabby offices, lodgings and workshops; the Stephens' was the only one inhabited by a single family. The noise from traffic and working people distracted her, and her conventional relatives thought it a bad address, but she delighted in the freedom. No chaperone, no lady's maid; and in the summer of 1908 she wandered off quite alone to stay in rooms, first in Wells and then Pembrokeshire, in order to concentrate on the novel she was writing. At that time it was called *Melymbrosia* and was peopled with heroines with Meredithian names, Cynthia, Letitia; the names were changed in later drafts, the traces of Meredith expunged, and the novel finally appeared in 1915 as *The Voyage Out*.

Virginia complained that in London she had to contend with

obscene old women, and young women too with beaks dripping with gore, who advise you to marry. That is my daily penance ... 'I think you should keep a maid Virginia – to do your hair – it makes such a difference – Men notice these things – not of course' – and so on and so on.[3]

Vanessa supported her in defying this sort of advice, and provided other amusements: trips to France and Italy, play-readings in her house, with Virginia taking the parts of Miss Hoyden in Vanbrugh's *The Relapse* or

Rebecca West, the adulterous and suicidal heroine of Ibsen's *Rosmersholm*. It was also in Vanessa's drawing-room in the summer of 1908 that a conversation took place between the two sisters and Lytton Strachey which has been described (though possibly with tongue in cheek) as a key moment in the history of British culture.[4] Finding the ladies sitting in white dresses under Augustus John's huge painting of Pyramus, and noticing a stain on Vanessa's skirt, Strachey pointed to it and squeaked 'Semen?' – thus, according to Virginia, bringing down with one word all the barriers of reticence and reserve that had constrained their conversation until that point. From then on, she claimed later, 'we discussed copulation with the same excitement that we had discussed the nature of the good'.

Whether this was really so, or what it meant precisely, is not too clear. Whatever the freedom of her spoken word, her written word remained chaste, and when, in the pages of the *New Age* in 1910, Edward Carpenter called for relief from 'the stifling atmosphere of the drawing-room' in literature and a return to the use of 'a *whole group* of words – that group, namely, which represents the coarse, the concrete, the vulgar and the physiological side in human life and passion',[5] his response did not come from Bloomsbury. (It did not come from the *New Age*'s writers either; and when it did, from Lawrence, in the late 1920s, the results were hardly what Carpenter had hoped for.)

Despite Strachey's boldness, Virginia remained intensely virginal. She had passionate attachments to some older women – Madge Vaughan, Violet Dickinson – but they were chaste, innocent and quasi-filial. She knew she needed calm. Her childhood experiences with a fumbling stepbrother had given her a deep distrust of sex and her precarious mental balance seemed to require the protection which her sister and then her husband (and, indeed, all those who loved her) offered. Despite this difference, both Virginia and Katherine had natures which set them at a definite distance from the established female modes of passivity or resignation.

Not far from Virginia, but in a distinctly grander part of Bloomsbury, at 44 Bedford Square, another woman at odds with her background and determined to establish her own style of living had also set up house recently. Lady Ottoline Morrell, in appearance wonderful, in character generous, enthusiastic and sometimes absurd, passionately devoted to the idea of the arts and artistic living, used and abused by the many writers and artists to whom she offered copious hospitality, was just embarking, at the age of thirty-five, on her career as a hostess.

Ottoline Cavendish-Bentinck had been born into the most blinkered section of the aristocracy. Her father was in the Army, her half brother left the Army on becoming Duke of Portland, and her other brothers were all in the Army; they spent their spare time in shooting and other field sports, not infrequently in the company of royalty. Ottoline, the only girl, brought up by her widowed mother and governesses, was taught very little beyond riding and dancing – she was not expected to dress herself or brush her own hair – and it was supposed that she would make a suitable marriage to one of her brothers' friends after a Season or two. The fact that she grew to nearly six foot, with a decidedly commanding face, did not prevent her from being considered a good match: she was handsome, impeccably aristocratic and also rich, her allowance in 1900 being £1,500 a year. She was not, however, interested in any of the young men on offer. Her mother, who died when she was twenty, had given her a taste for foreign travel; and her grief at losing her mother inclined her towards religion for a time. After a flirtation with the sixty-nine-year-old Archbishop of York, she decided to tour the Continent with a woman friend, a companion and a maid; her brothers were persuaded to give permission with some difficulty.

Between 1896 and 1901 she travelled in France, Italy, Germany and Switzerland, Ruskin in pocket, and also put in a spell of study at the University of St Andrews, where she found logic did not come easily to her, and at Oxford, which she attended as a 'home student'. Her relations with her family grew gradually more distant; two of her brothers were wounded in the Boer War, one dying of his injuries later. Ottoline fell in love with Axel Munthe, the fashionable Swedish doctor who practised in Italy, but was jilted by him. Another elderly admirer appeared in the shape of the Home Secretary (and future Prime Minister), Asquith; then in 1902 she agreed to marry a young solicitor she had met in Oxford, Philip Morrell. He seems to have had little in common with her beyond an interest in literature, but he was content to let her be the dominant partner.

Ottoline found the early years of her marriage unexciting. She relieved the boredom by continuing to flirt with other men, one of them being the same John Cramb who taught Katherine history at Queen's (he fell deeply in love with Ottoline, and later wrote a pseudonymous novel about the episode). Morrell, meanwhile, had been persuaded to take an interest in politics and indeed to campaign for the Liberal Party in Oxfordshire; unlikely as his election in this deeply conservative part of the world seemed, he won a seat in the Liberal landslide in January 1906. In May of the same year Ottoline gave birth to twins. She was a reluctant mother. One twin died; the survivor was cherished but remained her only child, for within a year she decided to have an operation which effectively prevented her from bearing more children.

She was now free to embark on her chosen life as hostess and patron of the arts, pursuing it with single-minded zeal; and she was extraordinarily successful in capturing the lions she sought. Her Thursday At Homes in Bedford Square were soon famous. Augustus John became her portraitist and her lover and, when he had determinedly disentangled himself from intimacy, remained her friend; through him she met Clive and Vanessa Bell and the whole of Bloomsbury. Virginia, who first met her in 1908, described her as having 'the head of Medusa; but she is very simple and innocent in spite of it, and worships the arts';[6] and the two became friends.

A few years later Ottoline embarked on a celebrated and lengthy love-affair with Bertrand Russell; she was flattered by his passionate love, but found his physical demands on her overwhelming, and his arrogance infuriating. When she wanted to be left in peace to read, 'he told me that I could never accomplish anything important in my life by *my* reading, while I could help him by being with him'.[7] Since Katherine also drew back from an affair with Russell later, it may be that she felt nervous of him for somewhat similar reasons.

Ottoline shared with Katherine a determined rejection of the values and pursuits of her own family, and an intense wish to set up a life in which the arts, friendships and pleasure should all play their part; both women contrived their personal appearances very consciously to produce a dramatic effect, and both cared deeply for the idea of a beautiful house and garden, the difference between them being that Ottoline could afford to carry out her plans, while Katherine rarely got further than dreams. Both Ottoline and Katherine took a fairly elastic view of their own sexual fidelity, while reacting strongly to 'betrayal' by others; both sought to establish ardent intimacies with chosen friends; and both learnt to be suspicious of mockery and malice, two flourishing growths in Bloomsbury, although this did not prevent them from being thoroughly malicious about one another at times.

Another woman who was to become a close friend to Katherine was the Hon. Dorothy Brett. In 1908 she was twenty-five and preparing to study painting at the Slade School, where she changed her name to an androgynous and classless 'Brett'. Like Ottoline Morrell, she was in flight from her aristocratic family and their way of life, which she disliked, the more so on account of her lack of qualifications to lead it, for she was very deaf, rather plain and possessed of a certain artistic talent. With slow persistence she made her way out of the circle into which she had been born and arrived in one she found congenial, among artists and writers. Her family continued, like Katherine's, to hand out money when she needed it, enabling her to behave generously towards her new friends such as Mark Gertler, a penniless young East End painter whom she befriended at the Slade, and Dora Carrington, a younger woman painter also in determined flight from her narrow, provincial background. Brett was always more loving than loved. Lawrence later called her a born 'sister' and Katherine described her as a 'clinging vine', because she attached herself to couples and fell in love with her cultural heroes, who often abused her affection and trust, as they did Ottoline's.

Brett had a streak of pure silliness, and she made disappointingly little of her gift as a painter, but she did at least contrive to live the life she chose rather than the one laid out for her, and that was in itself a remarkable feat.

One more woman of importance in Katherine's English life must be mentioned: Frieda Weekley, living quietly in Nottingham in the summer of 1908, in the home of her husband Professor Ernest Weekley, a staid and industrious modern-languages teacher and author of many successful text books, fourteen years her senior. Frieda was twenty-nine and had three small children, born between 1900 and 1904.

The daughter of an aristocratic and military German family, the von Richthofens, Frieda had grown up in the garrison town of Metz on the French border. The von Richthofens were not rich; the Baron was a hero of the 1870 war, but also a compulsive gambler, and this soured his marriage. Of the three daughters, the eldest was brilliantly clever – one of the first women to attend Heidelberg University – and the youngest a beauty; Frieda, in the middle, was the tomboy, and her convent school education did not eradicate her wild spirits.

In 1899 she made her surprising marriage. She was intelligent, a good musician and well read in English and German – she produced two small teaching editions of German classics – but she was quickly dissatisfied with her dull life in the Midlands and her dull, good husband, and she had taken to deceiving him. Her most serious love-affair had begun during a visit to her elder sister in Munich in 1907; her lover was a young follower of Freud, Dr Otto Gross. Gross was also a fervent apostle of free love; his relationship with Frieda was thrilling and passionate, but never intended to be binding on either side (and, in any case, both lovers were married). She kept his letters and continued to believe in his ideas for the rest of her life; but for the moment she was simmering in Nottingham.

These women shared a common determination to escape from the worlds they had been born into, to reject the moral, social and cultural rules inculcated into them in their childhood, however diverse those childhoods were. Each came to love and admire Katherine, and to feel that she had formed a specially intimate bond with her. She must have seemed blessedly fortunate and free, appearing from the far side of the world unfettered by the restrictions they had had to break through. Yet, as we shall see, her initiation into English life was such that she sacrificed this enviable freedom almost before she could seize and exploit it.

5

'MY WONDERFUL, SPLENDID HUSBAND'

■

Katherine's future lay with these friends; but for the present, as she stepped off the boat-train at the end of August 1908, there was Ida waiting on the dusty platform: Ida, faithful and almost overcome with emotion, with a hansom cab waiting to bear her off to the Baker family flat in Montagu Mansions, to be acclimatized to London again, the familiar and exciting London of Baker Street and Regent Street, the National Gallery and the concert halls – the Aeolian, Queen's, the Bechstein in Wigmore Street – Covent Garden and the Palace Music Hall, the Serpentine for rowing parties, the Vienna Café and the Blenheim Café in Bond Street, the tea shops and flower shops Katherine loved. Ida was officially a music student, a violinist like the Trowell boys; but it was clear to her, and to Katherine, that the first object in Ida's life was friendship.

'You're the only one who believes in me,'[1] Katherine had told her before leaving Queen's in 1906; the idea had become something like a sacred trust to Ida, and Katherine, fascinated by this degree of devotion, did not hesitate to avail herself of it. Just how interesting she found Ida's feelings she made clear in the opening chapter of a novel started some years later, in which Ida was shown preparing for the return of her adored friend by addressing her photograph in a whisper, 'rocking to and fro on heavy unbreaking waves of love':

You are perfection ... It is my destiny to serve you. I was dead when you found me and without you I am nothing. Let me serve ... I am here, waiting. Let me serve ... There is only one thing left that has any terror for me ... it is that you have grown too strong to need me. You are so terribly strong ... I cannot follow you on to the heights. Stoop sometimes to me. I know you cannot belong wholly to me – the great world needs you – but I am all yours.[2]

In this fragment Ida was given half Edith's name – she is 'Rhoda Bendall' – but whereas beautiful Edith had given Katherine quasi-maternal love, plain Ida gave the docile adoration of a subject. It did not thrill but it did intrigue, and Katherine never sought seriously to discourage it.

Ida went with her to help settle her into her room at Beauchamp Lodge, a very large, square, handsome house in Warwick Crescent, Paddington, overlooking the Grand Union canal basin (and today marooned in the spaghetti of the motorway junction). The existence of such a hostel for young women, and the way in which it was run with the very minimum supervision by the two professional women musicians in charge, were signs of the times. With her own key, Katherine was free to come and go at whatever hours she chose; this was more freedom than she had yet known. The residents, mostly music students dependent on parental handouts, but with a sprinkling of genuine working women, actresses among them, met in the communal dining-room; the rest of the establishment consisted of bed-sitting rooms. Katherine's was on the first floor, with a balcony overlooking the canal, from which she could watch the barges below: the Grand Union was still a working canal.

Once a month she would have to collect her allowance from her father's banker in the City, Mr Kay. Over half of it – 25s a week – was for her room and meals; but she wasn't always there to take the meals, because Beauchamp Lodge was within easy walking distance of the Trowells in Carlton Hill, and they gave Katherine an enthusiastic welcome as a dear, adoptive daughter, often inviting her to stay for tea, or supper, or even the night. Mrs Trowell must have been lonely in London, and glad of a familiar face from Wellington. She and her husband were quarrelling, and he was not finding it easy to make ends meet. But Katherine still thought of the Trowells as her other, truer family; she called Mrs Trowell 'little mother' and enjoyed her company as she baked pies and scolded the servant-girl in the kitchen, or sat darning her sons' socks by the dining-room fire. Sixteen-year-old Dolly, with her pretty face and head of red curls, was 'little sister', teasing and affectionate with Katherine as none of her real sisters were. A letter from Vera informed her that at home in Fitzherbert Terrace, 'We have never been such a happy united family.' 'I *ought* to rejoice, I suppose,' commented Katherine, bitterly offended.[3]

Ida was introduced to all the Trowells and the two young women took Dolly out for teas and shopping trips, to concerts and the British Museum; Dolly thought Ida nice but wet. On other occasions Arnold and Garnet made up a foursome with Ida and Katherine. She was no longer in love with Arnold, but when he put an arm round Ida in the train one evening, she scolded him sharply: 'She doesn't like that sort of thing.'[4]

It was easier to control friends if they were kept apart from one another, and this on the whole Katherine did. Looking back forty years later when Antony Alpers spoke to them, her Beauchamp Lodge girl-friends felt she had established intimacy with each of them separately, confiding different secrets and giving different versions of her experience. Some were hurt or baffled when they found that there were other facets; others dismissed her angrily as someone who had lied for fun.

Katherine was a liar all her life – there is no getting around this – and her lies went quite beyond conventional social lying. Whereas Murry 'forgot' things or distorted subtly, she was a bold and elaborate inventor of false versions. A charitable view of the origin of this habit could be that it was a bid for attention, a response to feeling obscured and overlooked in a large family with an inattentive mother; this may then have developed into a pleasure in dramatizing for its own sake, making herself into the heroine of a story. If the truth was dull, it could be artistically embroidered; and if she was the heroine of her own life story, lies became not lies but fiction, a perfectly respectable thing.

That autumn she told two friends at Beauchamp Lodge that she had been taken ashore from the *Papanui* at Montevideo and drugged, and now feared she might be pregnant. Ida heard nothing of this, and, in any case, there was no pregnancy; but it was the sort of danger young girls used to be solemnly warned against, and it is easy to see how a shipboard romance (and a late period) might have been worked up into something half terrifying and half enjoyably dramatic. Had she been in real trouble, there was a whole posse of relations to turn to: Aunt Belle, her Payne cousins, who were doctors' daughters, and her Beauchamp cousins, one of whom was also a doctor. It would not have been the first time the family had dealt with such a problem; Charlotte Beauchamp had borne an illegitimate child at the age of fifteen, discreetly disposed of in Switzerland.[5] But Katherine did not know about that, and she had not crossed the world to throw herself into the family's arms.

One weekend was sacrificed to a visit to Aunt Belle in Surrey. Katherine duly cooed over the baby, lead-paned windows and old oak chests, and enjoyed a ramble in Ashdown Forest while her sporting aunt played golf, but the visit was not repeated. More exciting invitations came from the family of Margaret Wishart, a new Beauchamp Lodge friend, who invited Katherine to go to Paris with them in October. They toured all the traditional sights, but she was most pleased by the Latin Quarter and fantasized about living in two small rooms, high up, with a wood fire, coffee and cigarettes, closed shutters, the lamp on the table 'like the sun on a green world'. She was magnetized by Paris throughout her life, and the account of this trip is the first of her letters in which the characteristic Mansfield appears, intoxicated by the pleasures of travel. This is the embarkation at Newhaven:

I have a confused impression of rain and dancing lights and sailors in great coats & boots like Flying Dutchman mariners. We go aft to the Ladies Cabin where a little French woman is in attendance, her white face peering curiously at us over billows and billows of apron. Such wide blue velvet couches, such hard bolsters for tired heads. We slip off boots and skirts & coats, wash, and wrapped round in my big coat & a rug tucked round my toes I settled down for the night. It was amusing, you know, all round these same huddled figures, in the same little brown rugs, like patients in a hospital ward. And the little French woman sits in the middle knitting a stocking. Beside her on a red table a lamp throws a fantastic wavering light. All through the hours, half sleeping, half waking I would open my eyes and see this little bowed figure & the wavering light seemed to play fantastic tricks with her & the stocking in my fancy grew – gigantic – enormous.[6]

Her writing is alive, her observation acute, and her imagination has a touch of nightmare intensity: Katherine's characteristic talent is already formed, and showing its affinity with Dickens.

Other glimpses of Katherine that autumn show her going along alone to a suffragette meeting in Baker Street, intending to write it up for a New Zealand paper. The mixture of solemnity and shabbiness was too much for her, and she was not turned into a supporter of the Cause:

Immediately I entered the hall two women who looked like very badly upholstered chairs pounced upon me, and begged me to become a voluntary worker. There were over two hundred present – all strange looking, in deadly earnest – all looking, especially the older ones, particularly 'run to seed'. And they got up and talked and argued until they were hoarse, and thumped on the floor and applauded – The room grew hot and in the air some spirit of agitation or revolt, stirred & grew. It was over at 10.30. I ran into the street – cool air and starlight – I had not eaten any dinner, so bought a 2d sandwitch at a fearful looking café, jumped into a hansom, & drove home here, eating my sandwitch all the way – it was a tremendous two pen'north – almost too big to hold with both hands – & decided I could not be a suffragette – the world was too full of laughter.[7]

A deplorable response, perhaps, but at least an honest one; Katherine was, in general, on the side of the suffragettes, but had not the temperament for the dreary, necessary political work of meetings, discussions and fund-raising.

Other incarnations of Katherine appeared at dinner-parties given by Caleb Saleeby, the scientific journalist (and contributor to the *New Age*), and his wife, Monica, daughter of Alice Meynell. Saleeby was a keen amateur musician – it was probably through the Trowells that Katherine met him – and he liked nothing better than entertaining pianists and singers alongside his literary and newspaper friends in his house in Hamilton Terrace, St John's Wood; he and his wife took to Katherine and invited her often. Sometimes she appeared in demure dresses with a manner to match; sometimes she transformed herself dramatically by appearing in Maori costume (modified to suit British tastes) with a string of amber beads.

She knew how to make an impression, and she craved fame without knowing how best to approach it. One evening she went to a concert given by a Venezuelan pianist she had already heard in Wellington in 1907, Teresa Carreño, 'the Valkyrie of the piano', who was giving a programme of Liszt and Beethoven at the Bechstein Hall. Katherine praised her performance as 'the last word in tonal beauty and intensity', but was more interested by her subsequent visit to Carreño, who evidently remembered her with affection and invited her for an afternoon visit which was spent

talking in the half-dark – in a fascinating room full of flowers and photographs – fine pictures of her famous friends, and Russian cigarettes – and books and music and cushioned couches ... we talked ... of Music in Relation to Life – of the splendid artist calling – of all her journeys – a great deal besides. Truly she is one woman in a thousand.[8]

Carreño might well impress Katherine. She was in her fifties, had had four husbands, begun her public career in New York at the age of eight, composed a considerable amount of music for piano and strings while she toured the world, managed an opera company, conducted and even sung in various operas. The remarkable thing is that Katherine should have impressed her enough to be given so much of the Valkyrie's time; perhaps she was simply charmed by Katherine, or perhaps she mistook her enthusiasm for real musicianship.

The truth was that Katherine realized her own cello-playing could not pass muster in the professional musical world. She was, after all, surrounded by young women at Beauchamp Lodge who were wholly given up to becoming professionals, not to mention the Trowell family. In the course of the autumn she sold her instrument, and began to think of an entirely different plan. It began by reading aloud sketches and poetry she had written to selected friends, and practising in front of a mirror; and when this went well, she resolved 'to revolutionize and revive the art of elocution'[9] by writing and performing her works in public:

> Nothing offends me so much as the conventional reciter – stiff – affected – awkward – but there is another side to it – the side of *art*. A darkened stage – a great – high backed oak chair – flowers – shaded lights – a low table filled with curious books – and to wear a simple, beautifully coloured dress – You see what I mean. Then to study *tone* effects in the voice – never rely on gesture – though gesture is another art and should be linked irrevocably with it – and express in the voice and face and atmosphere all that you say ... Well, I should like to do this – and this is in my power because I know I possess the power of holding people ... I could then write just what I felt would suit me – and could popularize my work – and also I feel there's a big opening for something sensational and new in this direction.[10]

This striking project – with its obvious affinities with Dickens's public performances – did not get very far. For a while Katherine earned some pocket-money by appearing at drawing-room parties given by hostesses who liked to offer a little entertainment to their guests, and whom she would oblige with a song or a recitation. Later she performed similarly at a few small concerts, but whether she could have held a large audience with a full programme of her own was never put to the test.* Interestingly, her contemporary Ruth Draper, who also began with

---

* Both Vera Brittain and Rebecca West spoke of Katherine's appearance at a reputedly lesbian night club, The Cave of the Golden Calf, in 1913, where she is said to have either performed or introduced the acts.

private-party pieces written by herself, did succeed in making a lifelong and dazzling career in this way.*

We should have very little information about this period of Katherine's life were it not for a batch of letters she wrote during the autumn and winter of 1908, and which were carefully and secretly preserved by their recipient, Garnet Trowell. For Garnet, the sweet and shadowy second fiddle, nobody's favourite, less good looking and less gifted than Arnold, the gentle, shy and nervous Garnet had become the recipient of Katherine's passionate attentions.

Her love-affair with him resembles most of the affairs in her life in that she seems to have initiated, dominated and ended it. Whatever Garnet himself wrote, or thought, or said about it is unknown. His letters have not survived and he never explained his part to any member of his family; years later he promised Dolly that he would tell her the whole story, but he died without doing so. In 1908 Garnet was a tall, dreamy and bookish boy of nineteen; he had gone through the same musical education as his twin, living the student life in Frankfurt and Brussels from a very early age, but always lacking Arnold's total dedication and virtuosity. The best he could manage now was a job with the orchestra of a travelling opera company, the Moody-Manners. It was a thoroughly professional and thoroughly popular company; opera was not then regarded as an élite art form in Britain. The star singers, Fanny Moody and Charles Manners, toured all over the British Isles with an Italian conductor, chorus, principals and players ready to perform Verdi, Wagner, Puccini and Wallace (the now forgotten but once hugely popular Irish composer) evening after evening, in one provincial theatre after another. It was a demanding life, involving hours of uncomfortable train travel and all the uncertainties of theatrical lodging houses, but it was also exciting and enjoyable for both audiences and performers: Beatrice Campbell, a friend of Katherine's later, who came from a highly respectable Dublin family, said she was tempted to join the Moody-Manners with her sister when they were young, for the sheer fun of the experience.

For Garnet, it was a reasonable job – his family could not afford to keep him – and all through the autumn he was away touring in Birmingham,

---

* Ruth Draper was born in New York in 1889. Her success came in London in 1920, when she gave a public performance of her own sketches, very much in the manner described by Katherine in 1908.

Halifax, Liverpool, Newcastle, Glasgow, Edinburgh and Hull, playing under the artistic pseudonym of 'Carrington Garnet' (his full name was Garnet Carrington Trowell). Katherine's love for him seems to have begun within a month of her arrival in England, and almost from the start of her passionately worded correspondence she addressed him as 'my wonderful, splendid husband'[11] and fantasized about their future life together. In October he sent her a ring for her birthday, and the Trowells accepted that they were engaged. Dolly had a clear memory of a morning in Garnet's room in Carlton Hill – the room had crimson wallpaper, with a band of green all round the middle on which he had pinned reproductions of great paintings – when Garnet and 'Kass' came in to tell her they were engaged.

In December, when he was home for a short break from the tour, Katherine seems to have moved out of Beauchamp Lodge and into Carlton Hill. They were in love, and driven to all the time-honoured devices for being alone: late evening walks to Primrose Hill, where they could sit and kiss in the cold, staying up by the fire after the parents had been tactfully persuaded to go to bed. Arnold teased the couple amicably, Dolly was thrilled, and for a while all was well. Mr and Mrs Trowell had to go away for a few days. Garnet and Katherine became lovers. Then he had to return north to the Moody-Manners.

What seems to have happened next is that Katherine and the Trowell parents fell out. They were short of money, short enough to be forced to give notice to their servant. Katherine was equally unable to manage on her allowance. She could never resist buying flowers, clothes and books, or accepting presents from Ida; she had grown up in a family that was rich and growing richer all the time, and could not accommodate to scrimping poverty. She became disdainful of the Trowells' poverty, and they in turn suspicious of her 'fine ways'.[12] Mrs Trowell asked her to pay for her washing at Carlton Hill and she refused, probably because she couldn't. There was an explosion. Katherine foolishly blurted out the true nature of her relationship with the absent Garnet. At this the parents became 'violent, hysterical, half mad', and banished her from the house.

Nothing was explained to Dolly who found herself suddenly and inexplicably cut off from her big 'sister'. Katherine's name was quite simply never mentioned again. Dolly hid her photograph in the wardrobe. Later, she remembered, she felt obliged to cut her on the steps of Queen's Hall. The nearest Garnet came to any comment was to tell Dolly he could not go to his father for advice on personal matters.[13] He was younger than Katherine, still a minor, with no home but that of his parents, and no regular source of income. Garnet was in no position to make chivalrous or defiant gestures.

Katherine returned to Beauchamp Lodge, taking a cheaper room on the ground floor. Her situation, as far as her other friends and family knew, was unchanged, and she continued to go out to parties, dinners and shows. She had met at the Saleebys' a singing teacher and ex-choral scholar of King's College, Cambridge, a bachelor in his early thirties called George Bowden, who asked her out and showed signs of finding her fascinating. More invitations, little notes and flowers followed. They shared an interest in elocution – some of Bowden's pupils were clergymen wishing to improve their pulpit performances – and Bowden thought Katherine accomplished enough to do some of her sketches at his concerts:

> Both in the little work she did with me and in the public recital of some of her own sketches given at one or two of my concerts, the use of her voice was quite unselfconscious. Its charm lay in its clear embodiment of her subject lit up by the delicate prism of her mind. The effect was a unity which maintained her integrity intact.[14]

His responses at the time were probably less carefully phrased; she took to visiting him regularly at the flat he shared with a man friend, and when Bowden had to go into hospital to have his tonsils out, she offered to collect him in a taxi. He felt they shared a modern outlook and a sense of humour; presently he proposed to her, and was accepted. Marriage was to liberate Katherine from the tyranny of her family, it seemed, although she told him she was already over twenty-one. Apparently, money was not discussed.

Bowden's account of his courtship of Katherine, written many years later, is so determinedly gentlemanly, fair and cautious that it is impossible to see what his emotions really were at the time, or why a man of his age, just building a career which depended on being free to accept a great variety of engagements, many of a semi-social nature, a man comfortably installed in a small bachelor flat with a manservant, should have got himself abruptly married to a young woman he hardly knew after a few teas at Rumpelmayer's and a few evenings together chatting about music, life and the emancipation of women. From this distance, it looks like a case of rabbit and ferret. Katherine had decided to be married, and had lighted on this kindly, possibly rather weak, easily deceived man, clearly not a passionate lover, but equally in thrall to her. Having told him she was twenty-two, she introduced him briefly over tea to Henry Beauchamp (the cousin who had been her guardian) and his sister Elizabeth von Arnim, who happened to be in London but who had no reason to take any interest in the fate of this little cousin from New Zealand. Katherine insisted that they should not contact her parents, in case they should try to delay the marriage. She also wrote Bowden a note, warning him not to expect 'too much' of her.

Why was she in such a hurry to be married to a man she clearly neither loved nor respected? Bowden did not know it, but she was pregnant with Garnet's baby. Whether Garnet knew or not is uncertain; there are no letters extant for this period.

The wedding day was fixed for 2 March at Paddington Registry Office (Vera was to be married in September in the pro-cathedral in Wellington). The plan was that Katherine should move into Bowden's flat after a brief honeymoon in a London hotel. She told no one at Beauchamp Lodge. Cousin Henry had written to her parents dutifully, but the mail took six weeks. The Trowells were not informed, of course, although the Saleebys knew at least of the engagement, for which they had given a celebratory dinner.

Ida was invited to be Katherine's witness, although she and Bowden had not met previously. Katherine wore a black suit and hat which, in Ida's version, represented her sombre feelings, although Bowden considered it simply a smart and suitable get-up. According to her own and Bowden's recollections, Ida was upset, but Katherine appeared quite normal. She and Bowden went off to a musical show, and then dined in a restaurant. All went reasonably well, until they reached their hotel. In the bedroom, with its pink-shaded lights and satin furniture, she changed abruptly and made it obvious that she was not prepared to consummate the marriage. It seems unlikely that the note from Ida saying 'Bear up', inserted in her small suitcase, was responsible for this change of heart. As far as Bowden was concerned, her behaviour remained incomprehensible for the rest of his acquaintance with her, although in the immediate aftermath of the fiasco of the wedding he thought her frigidity towards him might be a sign of lesbianism.

Katherine herself offered no explanation and simply departed in the night. She went back to Beauchamp Lodge, but this was strictly for single women; so when she came down to breakfast and announced she was married – a tableau she could not resist – she knew she would have to leave. Even her closest 'friends' had no idea what she had been planning, and she departed in a cloud of mystery and a certain amount of bad feeling for her duplicity.

Ida helped her to find a room. It was not a nice one, above a nearby hairdresser's shop. Bowden called and was turned away. Katherine sat and wept. What had she intended? And what was she to do now? Never at a loss for long, she took a train north a few days later, arrived in Glasgow, where the Moody-Manners was in full spate, and joined Garnet in his lodgings.

Katherine was still in love, or half in love, with Garnet. A poem from this period suggests that they spent a day or two on their own, perhaps outside Glasgow, in moorland country that was still bleak and wintry. 'Sleeping Together' certainly evokes the mixture of emotions – young love and tenderness, a sense of adventure simply in being together, exhaustion and foreboding – that must have enveloped them:

> Sleeping together ... how tired you were! ...
> How warm our room ... how the firelight spread
> On walls and ceiling and great white bed!
> We spoke in whispers as children do,
> And now it was I – and then it was you
> Slept a moment, to wake – 'My dear,
> I'm not at all sleepy,' one of us said ...
>
> Was it a thousand years ago?
> I woke in your arms – you were sound asleep –
> And heard the pattering sound of sheep.
> Softly I slipped to the floor and crept
> To the curtained window, then, while you slept,
> I watched the sheep pass by in the snow.
>
> O flock of thoughts with their shepherd Fear
> Shivering, desolate, out in the cold,
> That entered into my heart to fold!
> A thousand years ... was it yesterday
> When we, two children of far away,
> Clinging close in the darkness, lay
> Sleeping together? ... How tired you were! ...[15]

Conventional as the tone is, real feeling and a real moment are created: Garnet, worn out with weeks of slogging in the orchestra, travel, tension and conflicting emotions; Katherine, knowing she had got herself into a hopeless position, however much she played different parts with different people.

Yet in Glasgow and then Liverpool, to which they travelled next, she could fancy herself for a while a professional woman among other professionals, sharing Garnet's theatrical digs and actually being paid to go on stage herself, for she was allowed to join the chorus of the Moody-Manners company. So it became partly an amusing adventure too; and parents and propriety were both being defied successfully, since neither the Beauchamps, nor the Trowells, and least of all Bowden, so much as knew where she was or what she was up to.

Still the main problem remained unsolved. We do not know whether she told Garnet of either her pregnancy or her wedding. An announcement of the marriage appeared in the *Morning Post* on 17 March, presumably placed there by the unfortunate Bowden. Then in April Katherine appeared in London again. The affair with Garnet was hopeless; they were both too young to sort things out. 'You're your mother's boy,' she made the heroine of her fragmentary novel accuse her lover,[16] but what could a boy of nineteen in his circumstances have done?

Ida and Katherine went flat-hunting and found a small place in Maida Vale, 'unpainted wood, bamboo furniture – the sort that tumbles over – and cotton curtains'.[17] Katherine now told Ida about her pregnancy, and seemed unhappy and frightened; she kept writing to Garnet, and did not like living alone. She also began to take veronal, sometimes dosing herself heavily in order to sleep. Meanwhile, Mrs Beauchamp, weak heart or no, was steaming full speed round the world, alone, to investigate her delinquent daughter's behaviour.

In late April, Katherine took a trip to Brussels, also alone, 'on the spur of the moment',[18] using the name 'Mrs K. Bendall' and writing notes which were possibly intended to be sent to 'Garnie'.* They spoke of her overpowering desire to be out of the country: 'I loathe England,' a sentiment that would have raised a wry smile in her parents. She was self-conscious enough to comment on the interest taken in her trip by one of her Beauchamp Lodge friends, and self-possessed enough to

---

* Katherine's notebooks contain many scraps of 'letters' which may have been drafts of letters actually sent, or simply notes in which she addressed a chosen person, as she did later her dead brother.

observe approvingly of her own appearance, 'I wear a green silk scarf & a dark-brown hat with a burst of dull pink velvet'.[19] She ordered a brandy and soda for herself before sleeping on the boat, washed her hair in the ladies' cabin in the morning and enjoyed noticing that her fellow passengers thought she was French.

What did she hope for in Brussels? Perhaps she intended to make arrangements to give birth to her baby there, though she also mentions New York, where she and Garnet had talked of going. She may have been considering seeking an abortion, or even had thoughts of suicide, remembering the Trowells' friend Rudolf, who had shot himself there. Another note, written in London and signed 'Katie Mansfield '09', apparently addressed to Ida, suggests that Katherine was worrying about her lesbian impulses also. She specifically excluded Ida from them, mentioned how strong they were in New Zealand, and related them to Rudolf's similarly aberrant behaviour, which caused him 'ruin and mental decay' and was the reason for his death. Katherine talked of the fear of becoming 'insane or paralytic' and finished, 'I think my mind is morally unhinged and that is the reason – I know it is a degradation so unspeakable that – one perceives the dignity in pistols'.[20] The note was apparently found by Bowden, with a paper round it inscribed 'Never to be read on your honour as my friend, while I am still alive. K. Mansfield'. Something about it does not ring quite true, and makes one wonder whether it was one of her histrionic gestures, or even a plant, intended to impress and mislead her husband.

Whatever she had gone to Brussels for, she was back within a few days, and settled down to wait rather nervously for her mother's arrival at the end of May. She met the boat-train in a newly bought large black straw hat; Mrs Beauchamp looked disdainfully at her, carried her off to her hotel in Manchester Street, and consigned the hat to the chamber-maid. She then went to consult with the hapless Bowden.

He had now decided that the trouble was due to Katherine's lesbian-ism, and since Mrs Beauchamp had come with this possibility in mind, she was happy to let him believe it. For good measure, she went to see Ida's father, Colonel Baker, about the 'unwise' friendship between the two young women. As summarily as the straw hat – for Mrs Beauchamp had no time to waste – the bewildered Ida, who had no idea what anyone was talking about, was dispatched on a cruise to the Canaries with her sister May: the two families, not normally lavish with their daughters, splashed out most generously on fares, cruises and hotels. Privately, Mrs

Beauchamp must have realized that perverted love was not the real problem at all, or at least not the main one now facing her.

Both Ida and Katherine's younger sister Jeanne suggested later that Mrs Beauchamp did not realize Katherine was pregnant at this time. It is not possible to believe this. The only reason Katherine had for her hasty marriage was her pregnancy. She must have conceived the baby in December, probably at Carlton Hill; she was still a plump girl, but even so her experienced mother cannot have failed to notice that her daughter was five months' pregnant. And what other reason would there have been for rushing her off to Bavaria? Another Channel crossing, another train across Europe, and the two women were installed in the Hotel Kreuzer, in Bad Wörishofen in the hills west of Munich, within one week of Mrs Beauchamp's arrival in London. Who recommended Wörishofen, and what her mother hoped Katherine would do there, nobody knows; to judge from her subsequent behaviour, she may well have hoped she had seen the last of her embarrassing child. Equally, she may have taken counsel with the English Beauchamps, and been told how Charlotte got away with her inconvenient baby by staying out of England. Mrs Beauchamp was back in London in time to sail on the *Tongariro* on 10 June, leaving Katherine alone in Germany.

In New Zealand Vera was preparing for her wedding to a rising young Canadian geologist, and the Beauchamps were furious to discover that evil tongues were warning him against marrying into a family with Katherine's bad blood. Fortunately, he took no notice, and when he and Vera were married in the autumn, every ship in Wellington Harbour flew its flags in celebration, so powerful and prominent the Beauchamps had become. But on her arrival in Wellington, Mrs Beauchamp sent for her lawyers and rewrote her will – the ultimate bourgeois gesture – cutting Katherine out completely. The gesture was never revoked.

6

BAVARIA 1909: 'KÄTHE BEAUCHAMP-
BOWDEN, *SCHRIFTSTELLERIN*'

∎

Katherine was not at all crushed by her mother's disposal of her. She may even have welcomed the idea of a trip to Germany, enthusiastic as she always was for new places and experiences, and pleased to practise the language she had studied with the much-admired Walter Rippmann at Queen's; the Trowell boys had studied in Germany too, and Cousin Elizabeth had by now extracted several bestsellers from her German husband's Pomeranian estates.

In the Hotel Kreuzer, Katherine signed herself in unabashedly as Käthe Beauchamp-Bowden, *Schriftstellerin* (i.e., woman writer). She had published nothing in her ten months in London, but the entry reads like a bold prediction that now at last she is about to find her direction as a writer; and, indeed, she began at once to discover raw material for stories, simply by looking round. Much as Isherwood did a generation later in Berlin, she cast a coolly satirical eye at the crassness, affectations and chauvinism of the German bourgeoisie. Bad Wörishofen, like so many German spas, owed its success to the health theories of one man, in this case a local priest, Sebastian Kneipp; in the 1890s he thought up a particular form of treatment, hydrotherapy, or the *Wasserkur*, which involved baths in the local water, hosing, walking barefoot and a vegetarian diet. Pfarrer Kneipp's ideas became immensely popular, spreading to other parts of Germany, and the village in the pine forests throve, the local peasant farmers suddenly finding themselves surrounded by hotels, casinos and bathing establishments. From Mrs Beauchamp's point of view, it must have seemed a suitable place to leave her daughter, since it was a health resort, with plenty of doctors, as well as being remote from anyone who knew anything about Katherine or her family.

Because she destroyed her own records of this period, and because there is almost no other testimony available, her experiences in Bavaria remain partly conjectural. Ida was made to destroy her letters, and Katherine burnt her notebooks. It was, nevertheless, an absolutely crucial time for her; without an understanding of what happened to her in 1909, the rest of her life simply does not make sense.

At first, everything was straightforward enough. Local records show that she moved out of the Kreuzer almost as soon as her mother left, on 12 June. She settled, instead, in the Pension Müller, which became the 'German Pension' of her first book, with its little garden boasting a lilac bush, summer-house and an arbour where guests might take coffee in their dressing-gowns, its dinner-gong summoning them to enormous meals – not everyone was a vegetarian – and mealtime conversations in which the company exchanged details of the bodily functions, its changing guests all curious about one another's symptoms, histories and social status. Katherine watched and gave nothing away, placing everyone else admirably, refusing to be placed herself, keeping her secrets.

Her room had a chestnut tree immediately outside, its green boughs against the window, a horsehair sofa too stiff to be comfortable, and a red pillow she would put on the floor if she wanted to lie there; and in this room, at some point in late June or early July, she suffered a miscarriage, possibly as a result of lifting her trunk from the top of the wardrobe. Garnet's baby, dreamed of and lamented for the rest of her life, was lost. It was too small to be registered as a still birth, and we do not know whether it was the 'son' she had always imagined.

It must have caused a stir at the Pension Müller; no husband in evidence, and now no baby either. Clearly, Katherine had conflicting feelings about the loss; she was satirical about the German matrons' enthusiasm for babies in the stories she was beginning to write, and she shared the distaste for the process of childbirth expressed by many educated British women at this time. 'I consider childbearing the most ignominious of all professions,' remarks the narrator in 'Frau Fischer'. All the same, she wrote to Ida, asking her to send out an English child for her to look after. Ida, for whom no service seemed impossible, duly found a boy of eight who had been ill with pleurisy, from a London family only too grateful to get him out of the filthy town air. His name was Charlie Walter; he was sent out to Bavaria, with a label round his neck, to this totally unknown young lady. Katherine kept him for his summer holidays, telling him to call her 'Sally': another secret name, as though she could not bear to be the same person for too long.

She did not explain the circumstances of the miscarriage to Ida then or later, but she did behave with remarkable resilience, moving herself out of the Pension Müller to rooms in the flat of a woman who ran a lending library above the post office, Fräulein Rosa Nitsch. Here she recovered her health and presumably improved Charlie's too; and she began to make new friends among the summer visitors, notably a group of Polish intellectuals, and among them in particular a good-looking and smooth-tongued young man of twenty-eight with ambitions to be a writer – or at any rate a translator – himself. His name was Floryan Sobieniowski; he came, or he said he came, from an impoverished landowning family in Terezski, a part of Poland then annexed by Russia. He had studied at the University of Cracow and acquired a good command of German, and a little English.

Floryan and Käthe Beauchamp-Bowden got on well. They were both quick, clever and attractive, both interested in literary careers; both had good voices and a passion for singing, both were travellers and adventurers, and she, at any rate, was licking some emotional wounds. He appears to have had nothing but his wits to live on and he may have observed that she had at least a small, regular supply of money, dispatched, no doubt, by Mr Kay. By the autumn, Charlie Walter had been sent back to London with another label, Katherine had moved again, this time into lodgings with the Brechenmacher family (he was a postman whose family name she borrowed for a story), and she was studying the Polish language busily with the help of a fat dictionary in a green leather binding. Floryan was now allowed to call her by her old name, Kathleen. He had interested her in Polish and Russian literature and was suggesting that they should set off eastwards together. They might go to Munich, that great centre of cultural and Bohemian life; they could go on to Russia, or perhaps turn west again to Paris, earning their livings by translating and writing. It was just the sort of proposition Katherine found attractive; and Floryan, who never had much difficulty in talking himself into people's good graces, knew how to paint a glorious picture of their future life and achievements together. In due course, she would get a divorce, and they would be married.

In a work of fiction, the part played by Floryan in Katherine's life would appear so extraordinary and melodramatic that one might shrug it off as improbable. In a biography, the problem is one of documentation; it is not possible to prove every detail of the story I propose to trace, but it does fit all the facts we know, and has an inner logic which makes sense of everything else that happened subsequently in the lives of both Katherine and Floryan.

The story is complicated, and divided into two parts – cultural and medical – which have to be followed carefully and separately, but which run in parallel through the whole course of her life. For when Floryan fell in love with her, as he undoubtedly did, and when she responded to him, as she certainly did also, when they sat smoking and talking about Polish and Russian, English and American literature, about translating and publishing and fame, laying plans for a brilliant pair of careers, when all this was being set in motion, Floryan, without evil intentions at that point, surely – for were they not both adventurers and equals in the same field? – like some demon dropped into the plot of her life, was offering her poisoned gifts.

The first of these gifts seems innocent enough. Floryan, a Russian speaker and professional translator, must be the likely candidate for introducing Katherine to the work of Chekhov, who had died only a few years earlier, in 1904, in Germany, and was still relatively unknown in western Europe; only two small volumes of his stories had been translated into English, attracting very little attention, and none of his plays. Katherine herself begins to mention Chekhov only years later: 1914 is the first journal entry, and the letters contain nothing until 1918, when Murry had begun to tell her that her stories resembled Chekhov's.

Let us suppose that Floryan showed Katherine a German translation of one of Chekhov's stories, or translated one that he thought likely to interest her, or read it aloud to her and encouraged her to make an English version; however it happened, she produced as her own work a story she called 'The Child-Who-Was-Tired', which was, in essence, Chekhov's story '*Spat' khochetsia*', a highly sensational account of child slave-labour and baby-murder. Different critics and apologists have seen this as an adaptation or a plagiarized version, but there can be no shred of doubt that Katherine's story is drawn directly or indirectly from a specific Chekhov story, and should properly be described as a free translation.* Of course, there is absolutely nothing wrong with such an exercise, provided that acknowledgement is made to the original; the fact that this became the first work of hers to be published in England (in February 1910), and that it appeared in her first collection (in 1911), each time without any acknowledgement of its source, may have seemed a light matter to her at the start; but the use to which Floryan put his

* There were at least four German editions of the story, called '*Schlafen*', in print at that date.

knowledge later made it something quite different, as we shall see.*

As for Floryan's other poisoned gift: medical evidence given by Katherine later suggests that she was infected with gonorrhoea late in 1909. It is hard to see any other candidate for this particular honour, unless we believe that she was totally promiscuous, which seems unlikely. In Floryan's favour, it must be said that it was all too common for men to believe themselves cured of the disease when they were, in fact, still contagious.

Katherine's last extant letter from Wörishofen is dated 10 November; it is a Christmas message to her younger sister in New Zealand, and speaks of the Polish dictionary purchased with her birthday money, which had presumably arrived in mid October, adding that it was her constant companion. From Ida's reminiscences we gather that Katherine made a visit to Munich at this time; and from another friend's letter, who wrote urging caution, that she was in love with a Pole and planning to marry him after her divorce,[1] and to live with him before it.

A story of Katherine's written about this time, 'The Swing of the Pendulum', may build up the picture a little further. Its heroine, Viola, is a young literary woman sharing lodgings in a large German city with a lover with the Polish name of Casimir, also a would-be writer. As the story opens, Casimir is out seeking work from editors. He and Viola are described as having fallen in love when both had been unhappy: 'They had been like two patients in the same hospital ward – each finding comfort in the sickness of the other – sweet foundation for a love affair.' Troubled by conflicting feelings about Casimir, she reflects,

I believed in him then. I thought his work had only to be recognized once, and he'd roll in wealth. I thought perhaps we might be poor for a month – but he said, if only he could have me, the stimulus ... Funny, if it wasn't so damned tragic! Exactly the contrary has happened – he hasn't had a thing published for months – neither have I – but then I didn't expect to.

In the story, the heroine finds herself almost tempted into prostitution: 'If I'd the clothes I would go to a really good hotel and find some wealthy man ... I wasn't born for poverty – I only flower among really jolly people'. She saves herself, just in time, for Casimir; though she keeps a would-be client at bay only by taking a bite out of his hand.

In real life, something made her change her mind about Floryan. In mid December, when he made a visit to Poland, they were exchanging

---

* For a full account of the arguments about the plagiarism, see pp. 208–11. See also Appendix 2.

love-letters; his from Warsaw (dated 12 December) thanks her for telling him she loves him and for painting a picture of their future together in Paris, where she promises to make the tea while they smoke, and talk together, and read. It is a long letter, written in a beautiful, legible hand, in bad German and with a few English words. He tells her what he has been doing, discusses the poetry of Walt Whitman and some Polish books he plans to read with her and praises her beauty in

deinem roten sweater (ist das gut?) und nur eine kleine Rezeda blume an der Brust – Was fur ein Garten war für mich ...

[your red sweater (is that right?) and just one small mignonette flower in your bosom – what a garden it was for me ...][2]

He goes on to speak of feeling like a person new-born in the two months since he has known her, imagines her room in the white forest calling him to come, and says they will be meeting, probably in eighteen days' time. This suggests she planned to be in Paris at the end of the year.

Instead, from Bavaria, she turned to Ida for help. Ida, failing to get permission from her father to fetch her, at least sent her the fare, met her in mid December and installed her in the newly opened Strand Palace Hotel.* From there Katherine wrote again to Floryan, now in Cracow, still apparently planning to join him in Paris, but mentioning that she was unwell (though not specifying her symptoms). Floryan's only other surviving letter to her makes one feel sorry for him. It is dated 9 January 1910. He has arrived in Paris, is at a hotel in the rue des Beaux Arts, and looking for a flat for them to share. He proposes to take a flat from 15 January, but is hampered in his search by his very poor French; and he cannot understand why he has had no letter from her for over two weeks. He is worried that she is still ill. He addresses her as his wife, and says he can do nothing without her:

Ich kann ohne Dich nicht leben ... weil ich Dich liebe – und diese Liebe – das ist jetzt mein Leben

[I cannot live without you ... because I love you – and this love is now my life][3]

These pathetic protestations fell on deaf ears. Although Katherine seemed to have recovered her health well enough to embark on new activities in England, she had turned against Floryan, and he appears to

* Ida dated her arrival in January, but Floryan had letters from the Strand Palace in December.

have heard nothing more from her; no doubt she hoped he would disappear back into central Europe.

Both sides deserve sympathy at this point, for Floryan probably had no idea as to the cause of Katherine's change of heart, which must have seemed an inexplicable caprice; while she, struggling with the horror of symptoms whose significance she can hardly have understood, was in no state to write and explain anything to him. He found himself cruelly and mysteriously jilted, alone in a foreign country; she found herself with a hideous new sexual problem, hardly less difficult to cope with than the previous year's.

In March she faced a new crisis, when she became violently ill with peritonitis. Ida becomes the chief witness here. She said she simply received a message from Katherine to say she was in a nursing-home (described by Ida as 'second-rate', which no doubt it was; Katherine would not have dreamed of submitting herself to a public ward, but she could not afford the fees of a first-rate nursing-home either). She had been operated on, and she complained to Ida that the surgeon's manner towards her was improper, and asked to be 'rescued', although she still had an open wound.

Ida took her at once in a cab to her flat in the Marylebone Road. The bumpy journey was agonizing for Katherine. Sensibly, Ida called in a nurse. Years later, writing in her journal in December 1920, Katherine mentioned a 'terrible operation' she had endured: 'I remember that when I thought of the pain of being stretched out, I used to cry. Every time, I felt it again, and winced, and it was unbearable.' In fact, she had had her left fallopian tube removed, and the reason for its removal was that it was infected with gonococci. The surgeon's 'improper' manner towards her may have been a display of disrespect on that account, but much more likely it was an attempt to question her, examine her, establish a diagnosis and try to cure her disease, procedures she would almost certainly have found objectionable.

Because gonorrhoea ceased to be the scourge it was, once sulphonamide drugs appeared on the scene in the 1930s (followed by penicillin), there is little understanding today of what it once meant. At the time Katherine contracted it, the attitude of most British doctors was that it was a disease that needed to be considered in relation only to prostitutes and the armed forces (the only other women mentioned in the standard Oxford text book on venereal disease at that date are

Indian women in Army cantonments). Ladies were simply unaware of its existence, because it did not impinge on their lives at all, in theory. Doctors in America and on the Continent, however, and some British women doctors too, were beginning to question this attitude; but they had not made much headway in 1910. In fact, the gonococcus had been isolated only a few years before Katherine's birth, in 1879, by a young German doctor (and for some years more, little notice was taken of his discovery).

The disease, traditionally regarded as something trivial, was usually so in men; but in women it was a completely different matter. In men, the immediate symptoms were always obvious and painful, so that they tended to seek immediate treatment which, if efficiently managed, could be successful (although men often regarded themselves as cured before they were, and thus, in practice, passed on the infection). In women, the first symptoms were often negligible or transitory (or both), so that they might easily ignore them. As a result, the gonococci ascended into the womb, the fallopian tubes and the ovaries, one after another. Once established in the recesses of the body, the gonococci might become dormant, but were usually impossible to eradicate. The disease was also quite unpredictable in its behaviour; symptoms might flare up and then disappear again; a woman might have regular sexual relations with a man without ever infecting him, but then, with a different lover, have a recurrence of symptoms herself, and possibly infect him also.

From the testimony of the most experienced specialists of the period, there was a pattern of healthy women becoming, apparently mysteriously, lifelong invalids, suffering from a whole range of symptoms which their family doctors could only seek to palliate, without, as a rule, understanding their source or, even if they did guess at it, being able to cure. Frequently they became infertile. If the bloodstream became infected with gonococci, as happened to some, the disease became systemic, producing a whole further range of miseries: painful and ultimately crippling arthritis in the joints; pericarditis (i.e., inflammation of the sac around the heart) and pleurisy (inflammation of the membranes surrounding the lungs). All of these things Katherine in due course suffered from.

One way in which the blood became infected with the gonococci was through surgical intervention. For this very reason, expert medical opinion at the time of Katherine's illness was vehemently opposed to surgery on women with infections of the tubes, preferring to nurse them carefully and lengthily through the acute phase of any such infection until the worst symptoms subsided. Then, and then only, they might attempt the removal of irreparably damaged organs, but it had to be explained to the patient that their removal was no guarantee at all of a cure of the original infection.

To summarize: doctors had found that a woman, once infected, was very unlikely to be cured unless she had immediate treatment (which was one of the reasons in favour of regulating and inspecting prostitutes). Ladies were most unlikely to have such immediate treatment, since they might not notice any symptoms and, even if they did, would probably be too embarrassed to go to a doctor with them. It was a classic Catch-22 situation.

Katherine's operation was exactly what specialists in gonorrhoea advised against, because of the risk of spreading the infection into the bloodstream. Evidently this is exactly what happened: soon afterwards, she began to suffer from gonorrhoeal arthritis, which affected her hip joints, feet, hands and back at various times. Then, one after another, she suffered the symptoms of systemic gonorrhoea: her periods were markedly irregular, allowing her to believe herself pregnant more than once; she became infertile; after the peritonitis, she began to suffer from heart trouble and then later repeated attacks of pleurisy. These attacks have been described as warning signs of impending tuberculosis of the lung, which no doubt they were, but they were also very possibly one of the effects of the gonorrhoea.

We have only to study her letters and look at her account in 1920, in which she said she was 'never quite well' from then on,* to see that from 1910 she was a chronic invalid; as such, her vulnerability to the tuberculosis bacillus must have been considerably increased. The picture

---

* The following is an extract from a medical report made by Dr Bouchage in 1921 and annotated by Murry. It was sent to me by the late Mrs (Mary) Middleton Murry.

'When I first saw her, Oct. 15 1920, she had been suffering from lung troubles for three years, and was at the time complaining of bad attacks of coughing, especially morning and evening (in spite of codeine taken 6 times a day for the last 2 years), of much stiffness and pain in the right hip joint and muscles round and also in the spine, of palpitations in the heart on the least provocation. (Digitalis mixture taken for six months previously.)

'Previous history. Age 32. Excellent health till 20. Married for the first time at 18. Had two years after an attack of peritonitis (very likely from gonococcal origin), white discharge for four months. Left salpinx was removed then. Since that time she has never been quite well. A short time after began to suffer from rheumatism, in various muscles of the body, hip joints and small joints in feet, and has been more or less troubled with it ever since.

'During the war, exertions and worries. In autumn 1917 actual disease began and since then has been more or less an invalid with lungs and heart and rheumatic troubles. No T.B. in family history.'

of Katherine as a classic case of tuberculosis is true enough, but over it we have to superimpose another picture, that of the classic female victim of gonorrhoea.

How much did she herself know? It has been assumed that she remained completely ignorant of her disease until enlightened by a Dr Sorapure in the winter of 1918. My own view is that she must have suspected something. She certainly took note of a 'white discharge' which she suffered from all through the summer of 1910. In 1914 Beatrice Campbell heard her drunkenly lamenting that she was a 'soiled woman'.[4] In 1915 she told her friend Koteliansky that she had a 'special disease'.[5] Both these remarks suggest that she had some idea of her condition.

It is likely, though, that she did not connect her arthritis with her gonorrhoea, or fully understand that she had been sterilized by it, until Sorapure told her. Even he, consoling as he tried to be, could only attempt various alleviating treatments for the arthritis: injections and inoculations in the affected joints, fashionable but of disputed worth; there was nothing he could do to cure the primary lesion nine years after its infliction.

Katherine recovered slowly from her operation. When she was strong enough, Ida decided to take her to the seaside to convalesce. She rented rooms over a shop in Rottingdean, on the Sussex coast between Brighton and Newhaven, and from there looked for a cottage. In Rottingdean Katherine became ill with what she called rheumatism, i.e., the arthritic pains in her joints caused by gonorrhoea. More doctors were called, more bills run up; they were forced to turn to Mr Kay, who took the trouble to come down and see the Sussex doctor, assuring him that all the bills would be settled. It seems unlikely that the doctor made a correct diagnosis, but, whether he did or not, there was little he could recommend except that Mrs Bowden should lead a quiet life, eat well, avoid alcohol and marital relations, and keep warm; and so, for a while, she did.

7

THE *NEW AGE* : 'YOU TAUGHT ME TO WRITE, YOU TAUGHT ME TO THINK'

■

We must now return from this long medical excursion to Katherine's arrival at the Strand Palace Hotel in December 1909. She had some stories in her bag; she had her £100 a year, still handed out by Mr Kay in the City; and she had Ida to provide loving attention, and lend her extra money, or 'T' as they called it in their private language. Beyond that, where was she now to turn? One of the first things she did was to send a copy of *Alice in Wonderland* round to Dolly Trowell, inscribed 'To Little Sister from Big Sister, Xmas 1909'; but this produced no response, although Dolly kept and cherished it. Then Katherine told Ida she was considering joining forces with a woman fortune-teller she had met at the Strand Palace: about as low a point in her career as could be reached. Soon a rather better idea occurred to her.

Bowden, who had not heard from her since the previous March, and who was staying with some rather formal people in Lincolnshire for the weekend, suddenly received a telegram, or rather a whole series of telegrams, brought to him by his host's butler, urging him to meet her at once, and signed, for maximum impact, 'your wife'. The butler must have enjoyed himself, and the manoeuvre was successful. Bowden knew nothing at all about what she had been doing, but, faced with her peremptory demands, he submitted again and invited her to come and live in his new flat in Gloucester Place. Fortunately for him, perhaps, the marriage remained unconsummated.

Katherine told Ida that, owing to Bowden's suspicious nature, she could come to the flat only when he was out, and only under a false name, 'Lesley Moore' (this is the origin of Ida's 'L.M.'). So things proceeded for another few weeks; Katherine had, at least, found free and comfortable board and lodging. And now Bowden, who, like his supposed rival Ida, deserves a thoroughly honourable place in any account of Katherine's life, offered her some of the best advice she ever had. She told him she had written some stories in Bavaria and offered to show them to him; uneasy as the ménage in Gloucester Place might be, he was ten years her senior, with a Cambridge education and literary connections. He thought her stories were good, and suggested she should submit them to the paper for which Saleeby and others of his circle wrote, A. R. Orage's *New Age*.

Bowden was then kind enough to take her to the offices of the *New Age*, which were in one of the little courts off Chancery Lane: a couple of small, smoky rooms up a lot of stone stairs. Katherine's appearance and personality made an immediate impression on Orage. He looked at her work and declared that he would like to publish something. The first story he picked out was 'The Child-Who-Was-Tired'. The dilemma for Katherine was acute. When he singled it out, she should obviously have said at once, 'That one is actually a version of the work of another writer – the Russian writer, Chekhov.' Yet this would inevitably spoil the moment of triumph, and perhaps cast a doubt over the authenticity of the rest of the stories. She said nothing. The moment passed, and could not be recalled.

By coincidence, she sold an entirely original story to another magazine at the same time. It was called 'Mary', and was a sentimental precursor of 'Prelude'. The setting is Karori, and it centres on 'Kass' and her two elder sisters; there is also a grandmother, a mother who undervalues Kass, and a mention of Pat, the handyman, who chops the head off a rooster. Kass nobly and secretly asks her schoolteacher to give a prize she has earned (for reciting, appropriately enough, 'I remember, I remember, the house where I was born') to her less gifted elder sister Mary. She suffers when family and visitors heap praise on Mary and then accuse Kass of jealousy. That night, Kass nearly blurts out the truth to Mary, but her better nature prevails, and she gives her sleeping sister a kiss.

'Mary' appeared in the *Idler*, a light, illustrated monthly magazine struggling to survive. No one has ever thought it worth reprinting. Curiously, its immediate neighbour in the pages of the *Idler* was 'En Famille in the Fatherland', the second part of a serial about a brisk English girl staying in a German family, featuring a pompous and greedy Herr Doktor Professor. The author was Cicely Wilmot. Neither

Mansfield nor Wilmot appeared again in the *Idler*, which ceased publication within a few months, but a whole series of German stories now appeared in the *New Age*.

To have stories in the *New Age* meant not only the distinction of appearing in a paper which had a reputation for being 'more acutely alive than any other journal' (or so Arnold Bennett was willing to testify in a plug for the paper that February), but also entry into a new world in which Orage offered encouragement, guidance and friendship. He followed up his first acceptance by printing three more of her German stories in March; and this time they were authentic Mansfield, dialogue sketches called 'Germans at Meat', 'The Baron' and 'The Luftbad', all obviously the fruit of her Wörishofen observations.

Katherine said later that she owed a great deal to Orage's editing: '. . . you taught me to write, you taught me to think, you showed me what there was to be done and what not to do'.[1] He certainly encouraged her to move away from the sentimental, the dreamy reminiscence or fantasy, and towards the succinct, the sharp observation, the puncturing aside. Pathos, childish charm, indefinable feelings and abstractions do not appear in the *New Age* stories; understatement, and an eye for absurdity, do. It is a giant step forwards from the juvenile problems of Juliet to the coolly impersonal narrator of these stories. She makes you feel she must be good company, and evidently Orage found she was, in life as well as on the page. She was as amusing as she was attractive, and whatever he may have heard of her past could not shock him, he knew all about unhappy marriages, the desire to escape from one's background, illicit unions, lesbianism even – he alleged that his wife Jean had been a lesbian – and fiercely independent women, one of whom he lived with: Beatrice Hastings.

He himself was the real thing at last, in Katherine's eyes, a metropolitan man of letters with the power to deliver what he promised her. He was thirty-seven, his clothes were worn, his boots patched; but he was a charmer when he chose to be. Even the red birthmark on the side of his face conferred a certain glamour. He rarely had any money in his pocket – 'No Wage' was his own private title for his paper – and his usual form of hospitality was tea or coffee and cigarettes in the basement of the ABC tea-rooms in Chancery Lane, where proofs could be read and the next issue planned in the warmth at minimum cost. When he did have some cash, it might be Chablis and oysters in a nearby hotel lounge, but, like the best journals, the *New Age* ran mostly on sweat and magic. His office was a mere cubicle, with cartoons on the walls and a roll-top desk; there was one secretary and 'manager', a darkly disapproving woman called Alice Marks, who tried to protect him and must have been one of the essential props to the whole enterprise. There were times when he would weep at the sheer grind of turning out so much of the copy himself, Monday after Monday, but he was patient and genial with his contributors, and nothing delighted him more than discovering new talent and helping to shape it. He and Beatrice lived in various miscellaneous flats and cottages, never acquiring any settled home or way of life: or rather, their way of life *was* the *New Age*.

Orage is the most difficult character to pin down among Katherine's many friends. He wrote nothing autobiographical, preserved an extreme reticence about his life and systematically destroyed his private papers and correspondence. His published writings are impersonal; although he felt passionately about many issues and some people, the tone is dry and detached. He had no talent as a reporter and his few attempts at fiction are feeble and dull, except in so far as personal attacks may be entertaining to those who know their object. His personality, which made a great impression on contemporaries as diverse as Bernard Shaw and T. S. Eliot, has to be summoned up from hints and fragments. He was born in 1873, lost his father early, and was brought up in wretched poverty by his widowed mother and unmarried grandmother in the village of Fenstanton, near Cambridge. His mother scraped a living by taking in washing. When he was fourteen she went to the squire, a Nonconformist named Mr Coote, to ask him to give the boy work as a labourer.

Fortunately, the boy's exceptional ability had already attracted attention in the village, and the squire paid for him to stay on at the school and have some extra coaching. Orage – some said 'Orridge' but he preferred a pronunciation closer to the French and never used his first names – was a tall, attractive boy, good at sports, quick to learn anything, with a passion for reading, drawing and acting. Like Lawrence, he became a pupil-teacher and so reached a training college. He was twenty-one when he finished his training and went to teach at a Leeds elementary school.

Soon he was wearing a red tie, haunting second-hand bookshops, joining in public debates, interested in the ideas of Madame Blavatsky, a member of a 'Plato' group, and engaged to an art student, a Scots girl whose middle-class parents were not pleased. In 1896 they were married, with the result that Coote, who also disapproved of this recklessness, refused Orage a loan to go to Oxford and work for a degree. Instead he settled to teaching – he would not move on from taking Standard I, in order to be sure to have time for his reading – and began to write for Keir Hardie's *Labour Leader* and to speak at Theosophical meetings. Mrs Orage, beautiful and intelligent, devoted to the ideals of William Morris, practised her craft as a needlewoman. Orage began to read Edward Carpenter, whose free-verse rhapsodies and association of advanced political thought and eastern mysticism appealed to him, in books such as *Towards Democracy* (1883), *Civilization, Its Cause and Cure* (1889) and *Sex, Love and Its Place in a Free Society* (1894).

Not wishing to remain a schoolmaster for ever, Orage struck up an acquaintance with Bernard Shaw and sought to extend his range of activities. With a Leeds businessman, Holbrook Jackson, who introduced him to the works of Nietzsche, he began to plan a movement for cultural reform which became in practice the Leeds Arts Club, whose object was 'to affirm the mutual dependence of art and ideas'. It was a success. Chesterton, Bernard Shaw, Carpenter and Yeats were among the speakers, similar clubs were formed in other Yorkshire towns, and its fame preceded Orage and Jackson when they went to London in 1905. There Orage first tried his hand at freelance journalism, produced two small books on Nietzsche – each a mixture of his own exposition and Nietzsche's aphorisms – and helped to form the Fabian Arts Group.

From both Carpenter and Nietzsche Orage drew ideas about the relations between men and women. He rejected the Victorian code of a subject sex; he began to question the value of marriage as an institution; and in his *Nietzsche in Outline and Aphorism* he wrote that 'few beings are at present wholly male or wholly female'. Carpenter's view of sexual union as having its own, intrinsic, mystical value, unconnected with procreation – a view Lawrence was to absorb and make central to his work – may have interested Orage equally. His own marriage was childless; it became unhappy; and he acquired a reputation, both in Leeds and in London, as a fascinator of women.[2] At a time when most men prided themselves on being undemonstrative, Orage was quickly moved to tears and gestures of physical affection towards both men and women.

The Orages parted about the time he came to London. Soon afterwards he met Beatrice Hastings. She was initially an ardent supporter of the suffragette movement, and burning with ambition to write: novels, poetry, polemic. Orage was somewhat bewitched by her, and she may be partly responsible for his arrest, the only man among seventy-five women, when a group of suffragettes attempted to rush the House of Commons in the spring of 1907.

A month later, he and Jackson issued their first number of a magazine they had persuaded Bernard Shaw to help them acquire, the *New Age*. They subtitled it 'An Independent Review of Politics, Literature and Art', and their formula, front half devoted to politics, back half to literature and the arts, was later to be taken over by the *New Statesman* and other weeklies as the standard arrangement. Things went very well from the start. The paper sold at first for a penny (by 1910 it was 3d, by 1914 6d) and most of the contributors, though not the regular critics, went unpaid; they either worked for other, paying papers, or had professions. Orage worked with the zeal of a man who has found his true *métier* and, although he had no business sense (he would not try to get advertising, for instance, to Jackson's exasperation), the circulation rose rapidly from less than 4,000 to 20,000. But during 1907 the two editors fell out and by the start of 1908 Orage was sole editor and about to embark on his most dazzling period.

The *New Age* was of the left – the young Enid Bagnold's father considered its politics 'near treason' – though rather of the utopian left than identified with any particular movement for long. Orage wanted controversy, and was more interested in stirring it up than in maintaining a consistent line. On the question of votes for women, for instance, the paper began with editorials as well as articles in favour, but as Beatrice Hastings changed her view of the matter, Orage followed her and by 1910 the paper was generally hostile to the suffragettes. On the other hand, he was responsible for appointing Arnold Bennett, who wrote a weekly column on books from 1908 until 1911, which was one of the great attractions of the paper for readers like Lawrence. Orage had a crazy and quarrelsome streak, but he was loved by his contributors and at his happiest in the editorial chair.

Among his regular contributors in 1910 was John Kennedy, an Ulsterman on the staff of the *Daily Telegraph*, who wrote on foreign affairs in the *New Age* for the fun of it. He became Katherine's adorer for a while, and is rumoured to have presented her with a fur coat, something none of the others could have afforded, neither the radical Clarence Norman, a protégé of Bernard Shaw, nor A. E. Randall, who reviewed books and theatre under different names and was sour, learned and penniless. It was Beatrice Hastings who seemed made to be Katherine's friend; like her, she was English and yet not English, for her parents were settled in South Africa, and she had spent some years there. Her father was a successful shopkeeper and, like Katherine's, gave his wandering daughter an allowance. Beatrice too had been married for a while and was separated but not divorced; she had simply lost contact with her husband. She had also borne a child who had died in infancy, and seen her younger sister die in childbirth, if her confessional writings are to be believed. She was thirty in 1910, and welcomed a younger woman colleague to whom she could give patronage – for her advice counted with Orage – and sisterly sympathy.

Beatrice had been writing regularly in the *New Age* for the past two years, using several pseudonyms. Most of her articles were feminist polemics, some couched in passionate language, especially when she discussed the sexual subjection of women to their husbands, or the treatment of imprisoned suffragettes. She wrote on the absurdity of the universities' refusal to grant degrees to women, and their rejection as members of the Chemical Society; still more striking were her humorous pieces, often written in dialogue form, in which 'free marriage' was discussed between an enthusiastic young fiancée and a worldly-wise older woman, or a ladies' tea-party conversation was used to explore the connections between sex, economics and childbearing. Beatrice, at her best, presented bold, clear and original arguments, while at her worst she became incomprehensible. She thought for herself, and her initial alignment with the militant suffragette movement and later criticism of it were very much her own affair, although Orage followed the same path, and both ended by believing that something much more fundamental than the vote would be needed to change the pattern of women's – and men's – lives.

Neither these issues, nor the various radical causes taken up in the *New Age*, seem to have interested Katherine very much; but Beatrice was undeniably a model and example to her, as an independent literary woman, and very much the dominant partner emotionally with Orage. Perhaps they were all a little in thrall to one another for a time; certainly Katherine loved being launched and noticed, part of a world dominated by proofs and next week's issue, so-and-so's article, letters to the editor, a world in which Orage and Beatrice and she sat up late, discussing one another's work and ideas. She was still officially living at Gloucester Place, but Bowden was receding rapidly into the background. Ida too, whose dreaded father had decided to emigrate to Rhodesia, leaving her free at last in a flat shared with her sister, was made aware now that Katherine had found more congenial companions.

Only then came the episode of her illness and operation, cutting across the excitement of the new friendships, but also giving her a simple exit from Gloucester Place. Orage and Beatrice, in the full flush of their enthusiasm for Katherine, wanted to be near her and came to Rottingdean to look for a summer cottage too. When they appeared, Ida moved back to London, and when they found their own place, she returned. She disliked Beatrice, predictably perhaps, but accepted Katherine's enjoyment of her company; and for Katherine, they were the best friends she had yet made, filling her life with talk and laughter that overcame the pain of her illness, encouraging her to become the person she wanted to be. A picture taken of her at Rottingdean was, she said, the first to show any character (we may disagree); and, once recovered and with no thought that her illness would recur, the summer of 1910 looked very bright to her. The kindly Bowden came to visit her once or twice, but Katherine maliciously sent him off with Ida to admire the local church, and made it clear that he was unwelcome. 'Your wife' had decided to be George Sand or George Eliot again. Meekly, he withdrew, and heard no more from her for two years.

In July, Katherine returned to London to stay with Beatrice and Orage in a mansion flat in Kensington,* and a new series of her stories, still set in Germany, began in the *New Age*. The first two were concerned with the horrors of childbirth and marriage respectively, with special emphasis on the insensitivity of men, a topic on which Beatrice may have encouraged her to express herself, although she needed no encouragement to present a view of things in which people were divided between tormentors and victims. Beatrice herself had held forth so ferociously about the indignity of women forced into perpetual child-bearing by ignorant and brutal husbands that E. Nesbit, the children's author and Fabian, had written to the *New Age* to point out that many women did, in fact, enjoy both their husbands and their children: a point that has continued to trouble vehement feminists. Had Katherine and Beatrice been able to write about contagious sexual disease, they would have been on stronger ground.

In August, Katherine asked Ida to write to Garnet for her, returning

* Abingdon Mansions, Pater Street.

the ring he had given her and telling him she was now finally separated from Bowden, and intending to use the pen name of 'Mansfield' only in future. If she expected a response, she was disappointed; there was no more contact with the Trowells, although Garnet kept her letters till he died.*

Orage and Beatrice were exerting themselves on her behalf and found her a two-room flat in Chelsea, belonging to a painter friend, Henry Bishop, who was going to Morocco for the winter; it was in Cheyne Walk, with a view over the river and decorative touches that appealed to Katherine, such as a human skull used as a candle holder. She decided to sleep in the big front-room where she could see the trees in the lamplight at night; Ida, who had now given up any pretence of studying music, helped her to install herself, and observed with admiration as she started off in several new directions at once.

First, there was a revival of her interest in performance. In the flat above, a Madame Alexandra who trained opera singers heard Katherine singing and – this is Ida's version – insisted on giving her lessons. Katherine bought a grand piano from her new teacher, but soon found she had not the stamina to practise for the hours expected of her and gave up, though she continued to play and sing for her own pleasure. The desire for impersonation appeared again when she visited a Japanese exhibition and at once began to receive guests in a kimono, with a bowl of chrysanthemums beside her. She had until now worn her hair long, parted in the middle and put up in a curly mass, but in the autumn she had it cropped into a fringe and brushed sleekly against her head, the style that was to become her hallmark long before short hair became generally fashionable. At once she took on a Japanese air of her own; she spoke of visiting Japan, and acquired a Japanese doll, Ribni. She also discovered a dressmaker and began to order a new wardrobe described by Ida as 'small coats of lovely colours and soft velvet materials and ... dresses with long fitting bodices and pleated skirts'.

When she was not planning clothes, sitting at the piano or writing, she found time to go to tennis parties, and at one of these she met a young schoolmaster called William Orton, who responded to her question 'Do you believe in Pan?' by becoming shyly attached to her.[3] He was earnest and humble, and wanted to be a writer himself; his father, like Katherine's, was a tradesman. Orton, fascinated as he was by Katherine,

---

* Garnet worked as a musician in South Africa and then settled in Ontario with his Canadian wife; he gave up music during World War II to work in the Ford factory, and died in 1947.

already had a girl-friend called Edna Smith. Undeterred by this, Katherine bestowed the name 'Lais' on Edna, 'Michael' on Orton, and divided her attentions between the two of them. According to Edna, her love-affair with Orton was effectively broken up by Katherine, 'who took rather a fancy to my lover and myself. She played with us both for a little while and then went on her way. She was a beautiful, wonderful creature and I never bore her any grudge.'[4] Generous words, and for a nineteen-year-old the adventure of being taken up by an infinitely sophisticated woman of twenty-two was, perhaps, worth the loss of her lover. The three-cornered relationship, as long as she was dominant, was always to Katherine's taste. 'What very pretty hair!' wrote Katherine of 'little Lais' to Orton, 'I expect I shall see her quite often and take her to concerts and I am sure I shall take her to the National Gallery.'[5] Meanwhile, she gave him her opal ring and discussed marriage, though it was far from certain that either of them seriously desired it, quite apart from the fact that she was already married. They set up a communal note-book, in which she practised decadent phrasemaking and provocation:

I have red and white tulips growing in the centre of the praying mat. The red ones look as though they have fed on brackish blood. But I like the white ones best. They are dying – each petal ever so faintly distorted – and yet such dainty grace. I wish you were here.[6]

When she was not being decadent, or a follower of Pan, or Japanese, she tried being Russian. Another friend gave her a toy Russian village to play with, and she began to call herself Yekaterina and Katya; Diaghilev was in Paris, and Russia-mania was reaching England. Entertainment of all kinds abounded: Thomas Beecham was conducting his first season at Covent Garden, giving Richard Strauss's *Elektra*; in October, Elizabeth von Arnim's one-time tutor, E. M. Forster, published a novel called *Howards End*, charting with perfect accuracy the rift between the world of Katherine's parents and the world she was moving into; and in November, the post-impressionist exhibition opened, organized by Roger Fry and hailed by the *New Age* and Bloomsbury alike. Katherine gazed long at the Van Goghs, and said later they taught her something about writing, 'a kind of freedom – or rather, a shaking free'.[7]

There was nothing from her in the *New Age* that winter though according to her notebook she was intent on writing and, according to Orton, produced a great deal which she then destroyed. One story ap-

Kathleen Mansfield Beauchamp, aged about nine: the third, difficult, least loved daughter, already with a rebellious and inquisitive glimmer behind the glasses

Mrs Harold Beauchamp, possessor of a weak heart and a steely will; her children were taught that self-control was the prime virtue

Sir Harold Beauchamp, the hugely successful colonial banker and businessman, who wanted his daughters to be perfect ladies, and sent them to school in London, with unexpected results

The Beauchamp clan in full splendour, photographed at Las Palmas on the way to England in 1903 (see description on p.19). *(standing, left to right)* K.M., Harold Beauchamp, Ship's Officer Crow, Uncle Dyer, Vera Beauchamp. *(sitting, left to right)* 'Chaddie' Beauchamp, Mrs Beauchamp, Leslie Beauchamp, Captain Fishwick, Jeanne Beauchamp and Belle Dyer

Queen's College, Harley Street: something between a boarding school and a college

Ida Constance Baker, Katherine's faithful 'wife' (in about 1908)

(above) Katherine in 1906, before her reluctant return to New Zealand: 'the idea of sitting and waiting for a husband is absolutely revolting'

(right) 'She enthrals me, enslaves me . . . her body absolute – is my worship': the artist Edith Kathleen Bendall, nine years older than Katherine, who fell passionately and guiltily in love with her in Wellington in 1907

Garnet Carrington Trowell, Katherine's first lover and the father of her lost child: a gentle, dreamy, bookish young musician, and, like her, transplanted from New Zealand to study in Europe

Another of Katherine's lovers, the translator Floryan Sobieniowski, who became her evil genius, here with famous friend Bernard Shaw

Floryan as Polish correspondent to *Rhythm*

George Bowden, King's College Cambridge music scholar, whom Katherine decided to marry in 1909

peared in a magazine called *Open Window*, a melancholy fairy-tale with traces of both Hans Christian Andersen and Oscar Wilde, full of wrong choices and loss of innocence and love, which no reader of the *New Age* would have recognized as her work (and it has never been collected).

The following May, her best piece of writing to date appeared in the *New Age*: 'A Birthday'. The story has a childbirth theme and a New Zealand setting, converted summarily into a 'German' one, but what makes it so remarkable is that it is almost a piece of divination into the mind of its central figure. The middle-aged Andreas Binzer, self-loving, irritable, pompous and nervous, inhabits the story in every phrase, and his dissatisfied examination of the photograph of his wife – the more he studies her smiling face, the more he sees her as a freakish stranger, not at all a suitable mother for the son he is expecting – is an entirely original and distinctive effect. It is remarkable too that she should have written about birth entirely from the perspective of father, maid, grandmother, doctor, rather than her own grim personal experience: fledgeling writers so often find their own sufferings irresistible as copy. Reading 'A Birthday', you know at once that this is the work of a real writer who has hit an inspired vein.

Yet there is a feeling of randomness about the achievement too. Katherine did not seem to be interested in building on a successful piece of work, but persistently dispersed herself in different styles and tones. In her writing, as in her life, she revelled in change, disguise, mystery and mimicry: the last she saw as the key to creation and understanding of character. It gave her freedom, but it also became a weakness; lacking stamina, she dispersed herself too widely in different effects. Considering how good 'A Birthday' is, you can't help regretting that she wasted energy on so much lesser work.

Katherine stayed at Cheyne Walk until April, when Bishop was due home and she had to find somewhere of her own. She decided to move nearer the *New Age* offices and found a flat high up over the ugly Gray's Inn Road, on the fringes of Bloomsbury and the City, in a solid, handsome red-brick block called Clovelly Mansions.* No. 69 was on the fourth floor, but when the stone steps had been scaled the views

* In 1913, Clovelly Mansions was renamed Churston Mansions,[8] and No. 69 became No. 19. The views are not quite what they were, especially at the back, but the five front windows let in lots of sun. For some years – until 1986 – the next-door building housed the *Sunday Times* newspaper; for six years the author shared K.M.'s view, with the addition of the Post Office Tower and one or two other later features.

were tremendous, over the city spires to the east, the roofs of Bloomsbury and distant Hampstead hills to the west; and the rooms were comfortable, two at the front which she called the Writing Room and the Music Room, with a bedroom, kitchen, bathroom and hall at the back. As usual, Ida helped out with the decorations: bamboo matting on the floor, brown paper and travel posters on the walls, a lot of yellow cushions, one black 'sofa' (a divan with the legs cut off), the piano from Chelsea and a few chairs. In the Writing Room, pride of place was given to a stone Buddha belonging to Ida – her family had brought it back from Burma – before which a dish of votive flowers was kept; and in the Music Room stood a bowl of water with an ornamental lizard in it, and a pawa shell from New Zealand. Katherine had a roll-top desk, like Orage's, to work at, and Ida also contributed a basket chair that had belonged to her mother; there was no table, and tea was habitually served from the floor. In the bedroom, a procession of elephants waving their trunks covered the cotton bedcover. The rent was £1 a week, and the lease was taken boldly in the name 'Katerina Mansfield'.

At this juncture Ida recalled that Katherine believed herself to be pregnant again and said she was looking forward to having a child, undeterred by the absence of a husband or, indeed, any certainty about its possible paternity. Obviously, there was a lover about, but there is no knowing who he was;* and, in fact, it is extremely unlikely that she was pregnant; but Ida, summoned away to Rhodesia in April, left some money in a bank account to help with the supposed baby. Katherine saw her off with a bunch of carnations. A letter to Orton speaks of having been sad, unreal and 'turbulent', but says she is happy in the new flat, where she lies on the floor, smoking.

By May, when the Beauchamps were due to arrive in force for the coronation of George V, Katherine was staying at Ditchling-on-Sea with Beatrice and Orage; she was in a very jolly frame of mind, and writing a series of skits on popular writers for the paper. These included Bennett, Wells and the Poet Laureate of the day, Alfred Austin, who was made to extend greetings to the 'bronzed Colonial' over for the coronation. Relations between the bronzed Beauchamps and their problem daughter proved polite without being enthusiastic or intimate. There is no mention of any parental visit to Clovelly Mansions, although the seventeen-year-old Leslie was given a key and was thoroughly impressed by his sister's

* It has been alleged by Antony Alpers that this was Francis Heinemann. He denied this categorically to the present author.

success. She took him to meet Orage, who praised her work; and when Leslie found she was usually out on the evenings when he called, she explained that she was acting as theatre critic to the paper (which was not true). Fired by this glimpse of the cultural scene, Leslie tried to persuade his father to let him go to Oxford or Cambridge rather than continuing with commercial shorthand in preparation for the business, but he had no luck. Harold Beauchamp was far from convinced that an English education had done his daughters good.

In July, Leslie was horrified to find Katherine lying in bed with a fever so high that it induced the sensation of levitation (so she told Ida later). Pleurisy or bronchitis was diagnosed; and whatever caused her illness, she was advised by a doctor to get away, since London was stiflingly hot that summer. Orton wanted her to go to Brittany with him; the Beauchamps advised her to go to Spain, without volunteering to accompany her. She chose neither of these options, but set off for Bruges alone, having suggested in a letter to Ida, who was due to return to Europe, that they should meet in Paris. Characteristically, she changed her mind and hurried on to Geneva, leaving a telegram of apology for Ida; and when Ida got back to London, Leslie Beauchamp, who was still worried about his sister's health, urged Ida to set off again for Geneva. When she got there, she found Katherine reduced to £1, although apparently confident that something, or someone, would turn up. They shared a pension room for a while and then Ida, sensing that Katherine had better things to do, left. She was, in fact, seeing some friends from Wörishofen: not Floryan, whose whereabouts at this time are unknown, but a married couple with a child. In September she was in London again.

The trip gave her some good travel notes, which she duly wrote up for publication in the *New Age*, and which show the free, cool Mansfield, who refuses to be pinned down and always runs away with a laugh, in fine form. But she was not well; nor was it in her nature to be careful with herself. Soon she was writing in the Orton notebook about a mysterious 'Man' who called at Clovelly Mansions at five o'clock, carried her off to the 'Black Bed' – presumably the divan – and proved an appreciative audience for her silver stockings bound with spiked ribbons, and yellow suede shoes fringed with white fur. 'How vicious I looked! We made love like two wild beasts,' she boasted; she also described herself performing a topless dance for his delectation.[9] Poor Orton was no match for this sort of thing.

Who was this mysterious and exotic 'Man' with whom Katherine chose to tease Orton? Antony Alpers speculated that he could have been Katherine's old German teacher from Queen's, Walter Rippmann, on the grounds that Ida Baker remembered him calling on them in Chelsea, and suspected his intentions. Ida, however, tended to suspect all Katherine's callers; besides which, she was not in England at the time of this entry in Katherine and Orton's joint journal.

A far more likely candidate is a Viennese journalist, Geza Silberer, generally known by his rather fancy pseudonym of 'Sil-Vara'. We know for certain that there was a love-affair of some kind between Katherine and Sil-Vara, because after her death, J. M. Murry wrote a long letter to Ida in which he inquired about this period and specifically asked, 'When was her love-affair with Sil Vara [*sic*]? She once gave me all his letters to her to read and then burned them.'[10]

Sil-Vara was living in London at this time, collecting material for articles on English life and characters. He was also interested in the theatre, and looking for plays to translate; his version of Synge's *Playboy of the Western World* was published in Germany in 1912. His journalism seems to have been fairly light-weight stuff. He turned out profiles of well-known writers and statesmen, and a series of sketches of London life, describing the Season, the Music Halls, the Royal Academy, Whitechapel and various *causes célèbres* of the day such as the Crippen murder case and the activities of the suffragettes; the articles were collected and later published in Munich (in 1914) under the title *Londoner Spaziergänge*. Scattered among the general pieces are more specific tales of his introduction to a cultural and Bohemian circle through a Chelsea hostess called Gwendolen, who liked to entertain theatre people, painters, poets, novelists (male and female) and writers for small magazines. Gwendolen herself is well to do and well connected, but she has a taste for the slightly bizarre and outrageous; she sounds as though she could well have been drawn from Gwen Otter, a Chelsea literary hostess who was certainly known to Katherine (she refers to her affectionately, and expresses nostalgia for her parties, in a much later letter[11]).

Sil-Vara was twelve years older than Katherine. Since Orton and Katherine were of an age, and Orton by his own confession sexually innocent, a 34-year-old Viennese journalist would have offered a considerable contrast. Sil-Vara lived on until 1938; but he does not appear to have said anything about his love-affair with Katherine. Perhaps she wounded his pride, or perhaps he was simply a discreet Viennese gentleman of the old school. It would be nice to know which of these two strong personalities dominated the other during this particular love-affair, or whether it was more a matter of posing than loving for both at this juncture of their lives.[12]

At the same time, Katherine was writing to Edna in a flurry of exclamatory phrases:

not yet do I know what it is that clamours for utterance at the gates of my heart – rather there are so many, with the richness of spoil in their hands (& the East! quite suddenly) that I still pause – deliberately – terribly – rave. I cannot afford anything in the faintest touch unworthy – Edna to write like that! Suddenly stir the wings of a giant and all-powerful desire – one wing stretched over the Future – the other over the past – and the flight of the wings is rapture – Art! Art! Do you too exult in the very word and lift your proud head ...[13]

This is pretty unfathomable nonsense by any standards, and the cry of 'Art!' is always a danger signal. Perhaps it is not surprising that the agent James B. Pinker, whose clients included Henry James, Conrad and soon D. H. Lawrence, returned the story Katherine sent him in October and appears not to have taken up her suggestion that they should meet to discuss her work.*

It looks, understandably enough, as though she were trying to find outlets for her work other than the non-paying *New Age*; and yet it was the *New Age* that now helped her to her greatest triumph so far. A friend of Orage called Charles Granville, who had already published several books derived from *New Age* articles under the imprint 'Stephen Swift', offered Katherine an advance of £15 for her German stories. The success must have been particularly sweet, since her family was still in London to witness it. She rearranged them, putting 'The Child-Who-Was-Tired' towards the end, and adding two stories Orage had not printed, 'The Swing of the Pendulum' and 'The Blaze', a poor story about a respectable woman who ensnares men only to tease them; she also removed her name where it had appeared in the text of certain stories.

In a German Pension appeared in December, nicely printed in green boards with an orange cover, and priced at 6s. The publisher described it as a 'delightful literary novelty', and talked in the blurb of Katherine's 'malicious naïveté' in describing the 'quaint Bavarian people', and also

---

* Pinker did become Katherine's agent in 1920, however; see p. 213.

of her cynicism and satiric strokes. The blurb went on,

The one or two chapters which might be called Bavarian short stories rather than sketches are written in a most uncommon – indeed thoroughly individual – vein, both in form and substance. Miss Mansfield's style is almost French in its character, and her descriptions will remind the reader of Russian masters like Turguenieff [*sic*].[14]

Today this edition is so rare as to be almost unobtainable. On publication it was acclaimed as 'impish', 'lively', 'caustic', 'amusing' and 'original': all of which it was. Considering what its author had been through during the past three years, it was also a triumphant personal achievement. If there was a small Chekhovian time bomb ticking away inside, it was not going to cause any trouble for a long while yet.

8

'MAKE ME YOUR MISTRESS'

■

Katherine now commanded the fame and dignity of a published author. Her name began to reach wider circles than those of the *New Age*. One of its contributors, a poet and novelist called Willy George,* arranged a dinner in order to introduce her to an Oxford undergraduate who was already co-editing a bilingual quarterly magazine called *Rhythm*. His name was John Middleton Murry, and he was to play a crucial, and largely unfortunate, role in her life.

Murry himself had just done an article for the *New Age*. Orage was quick to notice the contents of other papers and, seeing that *Rhythm* had reproduced some studies by a painter yet unknown in England, Picasso, had commissioned a piece on him in November. George, for his part, had sent a fairy-story of Katherine's to *Rhythm*. Murry turned down the fairy-story; if he had admired her satirical writing, he was understandably baffled by this other voice. He was to spend the next eleven years being baffled by her, and still longer trying to shape her image into something he could cope with. Meanwhile, he wrote to her, expressing an interest in seeing something else of hers; and when she sent him her story set in the New Zealand backblocks, 'The Woman at the Store', he accepted it enthusiastically and pressed George to give him an introduction. The story was, indeed, a striking piece of work, and marked another departure in an entirely new direction. It dealt obliquely with a murder, and drew on her memories of the Urewera trip. It was also her first deliberate portrayal of her native country, a

* Walter George was half French, an ex-literary editor of *Vanity Fair*, prolific author, ardent for women's emancipation, hospitable, with a finger in every pie; he had just published a best-seller about a respectable young widow driven to prostitution, *A Bed of Roses*. Though generous and ambitious, he was not a gifted writer.

vivid and almost sinister evocation of the atmosphere of the sparsely inhabited wilderness, the poverty and ignorance of the people settled there, the 'savage spirit' of the place. But there is another theme: the woman at the centre, once a pretty barmaid with 125 ways of kissing, has been broken by marriage, childbearing, solitude, and responded with violence. The story is left coolly at that, neither characters nor author passing judgement. Anyone would have been excited to publish such a story by a young writer, and it is not surprising that Murry reacted so strongly.

Katherine was nearly a year older than him, and George had told him she was immensely sophisticated, so that he set off from his parental home in Wandsworth in a slightly nervous frame of mind, although he was not quite an innocent in the London literary scene. He had, for instance, discovered Dan Rider's bookshop in St Martin's Lane, where you could hang about with the other hopefuls for a glimpse of a famous author; but he cherished the belief, so common in the literary world, that other people were in the swim while he was not. Yet to Katherine he appeared enviably brilliant, an editor at twenty-two, with the benefit of a classical education and studies at Oxford, Paris and Heidelberg.

As to what Murry was really like, the question is not much easier to answer at this stage than it is about Katherine. He was young and unformed and certainly outstandingly gifted as a scholar. At school, he had learnt to be ashamed of his family – often an integral part of English education – but he had also learned to work hard and effectively. Getting from Christ's Hospital to Oxford was a way of escaping from the ugly little London and suburban houses in which his holidays had been spent, and from the tyranny of his father, a grinding petty civil servant whose highest hope for his scholarship-winning son was that he should follow him into the civil service, albeit at a higher level. In Murry's own accounts of his young life, he appears as a bewildered and sometimes beleaguered hero, always in search of Love, Faith, Art and other assorted abstractions and often ruefully puzzled by his own bad behaviour. He hardly mentions the one obvious driving force that ran through everything he did: ambition. It was not his father's ambition, and it was going to drive him in some surprising directions, but it was the real thing.

The other immediately noticeable thing about him, testified to by many who met him in his youth, was his physical charm. He had what was called a fine head, with large hazel eyes and thickly springing dark hair. Katherine talked of his 'lovely, frightening mouth'; and some attraction drew both men and women to him like flies to honey. Older people wanted to help him, younger ones sought his friendship or fell in love with him. Murry's characteristic stance was passive, bewildered delight at receiving all this kindness and affection. People who took against him said his eyes were blank or even reptilian, but this was rarely the initial impression. He was earnest, eager to listen and learn from new friends, and prone to hero-worship. One other striking thing was his sheer capacity for work, for mastering a subject or a language, or turning out a serious review to a deadline; well-informed words poured neatly from his pen. His hours at a desk had given him a scholar's stoop, so that although he was five foot eight and a half inches tall (as he noted with characteristic meticulousness in one of his many autobiographical musings), he seemed smaller.

The story of his Oxford years, which he told in his autobiography *Between Two Worlds*, is instructive. They did not turn out at all as he or his family had expected. Instead of proceeding steadily through Modern Greats towards the civil service examination, he was thrown off course by the experience of university life itself. For most scholarship boys in 1910, Oxford was an opportunity, but not likely to be much fun. Murry overcame the disability of poverty with ease. During his first year he won his tutor's heart and was invited to a reading party in Suffolk. The experience, which turned out to be more a matter of sailing with carefree friends in the Alde estuary than reading, was so congenial that he decided he must simply sever himself from his shameful background, and this he proceeded to do. He found a farming family in Gloucestershire that took in paying guests and presented himself to them as an orphan who needed somewhere to spend his Oxford vacations. (It is the sort of adventure Katherine could well have gone in for, but which she would not have sought to explain or justify afterwards.)

In Gloucestershire Murry at once became a favourite with his hosts. He bought a horse, which they taught him to ride, and he took up fox-hunting. He embarked on a romance with the niece of the local vicar; but he also met a young Frenchman, a fellow lodger on the farm, who interested him in the idea of visiting Paris. At the speed of a picaresque hero with his eye on the next chapter, Murry abandoned Gloucestershire without farewell to the farmer, his wife or the vicar's niece, and spent his next vacation as tutor to a young golf-playing aristocrat in the Borders, in order to earn the money to go to France. In one sense this was an admirable plan: if the system of snobbery is there, better to use it rather than let it crush you. He found the pleasures of life in a stately home congenial, and grew more confident about his ability to plot his own life.

He was, in any case, growing bored with classical studies and becoming more interested in modern languages and literature. His first visit to Paris, in the winter of 1910 (Katherine was living in Chelsea at the time), finished any prospect of becoming a civil servant. He began by spending his days reading Bergson and covering the city conscientiously on foot, district by district. In the evenings he sat in a café in Montparnasse. Presently, he was seduced by a sweet-natured girl who, as soon as she had won the heart of her innocent Englishman, gave up her life of easy virtue and adopted one of strict morality, in the hope of marriage.

Her plan failed: after some severe pangs of conscience, Murry deserted her, again without explanation. It was an unkind but pardonable act of self-preservation; he was not cut out to be a Puccini hero, and Paris had other things more to his purpose on offer. An Oxford friend, Frederick Goodyear, with enough money from his father to live as he chose, arrived in Paris; he had many friends among painters and writers, and introduced Murry to groups ranging from Aleister Crowley and his black magic disciples to the more interesting entourage of Picasso and Derain. Here he made friends with 'George' Banks, a forceful and eccentric woman cartoonist who dressed like a man, revered the memory of Wilde and teased Murry for his innocence; and a genial Scottish artist, John D. Fergusson, who proclaimed himself a Fauve, and asserted that art was not a profession so much as a quality of being. It was a dangerous doctrine to give a young man on the brink of regarding himself as an artist; and at about this time Murry decided to become a poet and novelist. This was a serious mistake, for his gifts did not lie in that direction, and he wasted energy and paper for years on bad verse and flaccid novels, determinedly seeing himself as the heir to the English Romantics.

As an editor he was a more credible figure; young as he was, his earnest enthusiasm impressed people, and he had a quick responsiveness to fashions in taste. In the summer of 1911 *Rhythm* was hatched with Fergusson's enthusiastic support and money provided by the father of another artistic Oxford friend, Michael Sadler. They did not plan it as an undergraduate magazine, but as something much more ambitious that aimed to cover the French and English avant-garde in literature and art, with forays into other languages, and to sell as far afield as

Munich, New York and Glasgow. From the start Fergusson was a strong art editor; he provided fine woodcuts and drawings of his own, introduced the decorative work of his Irish-American girl-friend from Philadelphia, Anne Estelle Rice, and established a high standard in all that he commissioned. Almost all the plates and drawings look as good today as they did when they were chosen, from the Picasso in the first issue to the Derains, Ihlees, Peploes, Jessie Dismorrs, Orpens, Augustus Johns, Rothensteins and Gaudier-Brzeskas; and George Banks proved a clever cartoonist. The quality of the writing, unfortunately, rarely approached that of the artwork. The format, with its thick, wide-margined paper and large type, seems oddly inappropriate to the text but well matched to the illustrations.

In the first issue Murry appeared as the disciple of the philosophers Bergson and Croce, proclaiming his allegiance to intuition and 'the spiritual vision of the artist'. 'Art is beyond creeds,' he wrote, 'for it is the creed itself. It comes to birth in irreligion and is nurtured in amorality.' There were chunks of untranslated Croce and prose poems by a 25-year-old French writer Murry had made friends with and hailed as another Rimbaud: this was Francis Carco, *fantaisiste* poet, novelist of low-life Paris and friend of Colette; he had been one of her ex-husband Willy's ghost-writers. Later, Carco contributed *Lettres de Paris* alternately with another poet, Tristan Derème; the plan looked good, but the articles provided were not, Carco and Derème both being better poets than journalists.

English poetry was represented at first by Murry himself and by Willy George. Murry's efforts were along these lines:

> Poor fools! We part. I am not heartless, yet
> I dare not see you. You must live your life,
> I mine, forgetting ...[1]

Later, he was writing under a different influence, but no better:

> The twinkling feet of all the little stars
>   Have danced in my hair tonight:
> They made bright music at the golden bars
>   About my heart tonight.
>
> Tonight my lover came over the hills,

His feet were a bright fire;
He strode across the black slopes and the rills
With limbs that never tire.

Despite this sort of thing, *Rhythm* was noticed, by artists and journalists, at any rate; in the third issue Orage's one-time fellow editor, Holbrook Jackson, appeared with a long polemic against charm in art, and better poets – W. W. Gibson, Harold Monro, Walter de la Mare – contributed later on. Murry's judgement remained shaky, both of his own powers and of other people's.

His meeting with Katherine in December 1911 at the Georges' dinner-table, where she appeared in a grey dress and spoke with cool authority about the superiority of German to English translation from the Russian, was a momentous event in his life. She was all that he had expected, and more. What particularly struck him from the start, he wrote later, was that 'she was not, somehow, primarily a woman'.[2] He could enjoy listening to her talk without the distraction of sex. She seemed wonderfully simple and pure. Murry had gone through a bad time after his break with his Parisian girl; in a manly gesture intended to rid himself of remorse, he had persuaded an Oxford friend to take him to a brothel. The experience had been hateful in itself, and it had given him gonorrhoea; unlike Katherine, he had had his diagnosed and treated quickly, and was cured. But the experience had left him frightened. Katherine's cool independence seemed both refreshing and safe; he could fall in love with her without being required to do or decide anything.

After their first meeting, he immediately wrote to her, suggesting she should contribute reviews to *Rhythm*; he sent her a volume of Crowley's verse, and asked for more of her work. She sent him some poems of her own, saying they had been turned down by Orage because they were in free verse,[3] but nothing more for the moment. He returned to Oxford; but he had lost interest in his work there completely, although he was expected to achieve a First in the summer, after his years of scholarships and exhibitions.

Katherine was maintaining fairly distant relations with her family, who were still in London, although in January she pressed them to patronize the beauty salon in South Moulton Street where Ida was trying to earn some money by what was optimistically called 'Scientific Hair-Brushing'. Katherine was struggling with a story, and also apparently with bad health again, which she gave as her reason for returning to Geneva in February; perhaps she had found a congenial doctor there.

On her return, she went to stay with Beatrice and Orage in Sussex. It was the last friendly time the three of them spent together. Orage chose to regard her readiness to contribute to *Rhythm* as an act of treachery, a quite unreasonable attitude since, with its tiny circulation and purely aesthetic aims, it was in no way a rival to a political weekly. In any case, it was absurd to expect her to write for the *New Age* alone if she hoped to make a living from her work; but paranoia flourished in Chancery Lane, Orage and Beatrice both being hypersensitive and quarrelsome. They were also fond of Kennedy, who was suffering the pangs of rejected love for Katherine. As soon as they began to see an enemy in her, she could expect to feel their wrath, and in March they began to attack *Rhythm* in the pages of the *New Age*, singling out her poems – already familiar to Orage – for their 'flapping and wappering', and suggesting that other items were vulgar or stupid. Their criticism was not ill founded, but it was scarcely called for.

Murry, meanwhile, was seeking Katherine's editorial advice. When the Easter vacation arrived, he wrote to her from his parents' house, complaining that '*je m'étouffe* here',[4] saying that he proposed to call on her with a batch of manuscripts, and that he was thinking of trying to find a job in London. She gave him tea at Clovelly Mansions, serving it in bowls from the floor and sympathizing with his troubles. He told her how guilty he felt at letting down his college's hopes, but how impossible it had become to continue his studies. Then they both laughed, and Katherine pronounced that he should give up Oxford.

Since this was, in any case, what he wanted to hear, Murry obediently visited his tutor and told him he could not continue at Oxford. His tutor, while disapproving, acted with extraordinary kindness and gave him an introduction to J. A. Spender, editor of the *Westminster Gazette*, who promised him freelance work and advanced him £5: another example of Murry's power to charm and impress. It was obviously absurd to give up Oxford within months of his final examinations, but no doubt he appeared, as so often throughout his later life, sincerely and helplessly in the grip of some idea too great to combat. Murry's self-justifying sincerity was always absolute, and he was never at a loss for words.

He went straight to Katherine with the good news, telling her he felt he owed it to her, and then invited her to dine with him and Goodyear, who was about to take a job in advertising himself, and was full of envy and good advice for Murry. He must, for instance, leave home at all costs. When this had been generally agreed – Katherine and Goodyear took to one another – she suddenly offered Murry the Music Room in her flat, at 7s 6d a week. Somewhat dazedly, Murry accepted and was told to arrive the following Thursday; and, inquiring whether he liked eggs, she departed with a cool *auf Wiedersehen*, leaving Goodyear still more envious.

Ida was called in to help Katherine prepare the room for this new male rival. She also contributed another fiver, which was discreetly placed with the eggs and other provisions laid out for Murry's use, and departed with some sense of being excluded, not entirely dispelled by Katherine's offering of a consolatory poem, written out especially for her (it later appeared in *Rhythm*). No one mentioned love at this point. 'Mansfield' and 'Murry' – so they addressed one another at first – shook hands at night if they happened to be in at the same time, and lived separate lives.

This was in early April, a little after the Beauchamps – father, mother, Chaddie, Jeanne and Leslie, who had failed to win permission to go to Oxford or Cambridge – sailed for New Zealand again. There is no indication that Katherine felt the parting as a painful one. Since 1909 she had been calling her mother 'Jane' (another Beauchamp nickname) and neither troubled to preserve whatever letters they exchanged thereafter; nor did 'Jane' adjust her will to reinstate her difficult daughter. The two women never met again, and Katherine's later tributes to her read oddly in the light of the tenuousness of their bond. It was the all-forgiving Ida, always ready to come to her assistance however often she was slighted, responding to demands and infantile rages with absolving love and patience, who gave Katherine the real mothering she needed from then on.

Murry's attempt to introduce Katherine to his family was, predictably, a disaster. Her single visit to Nicosia Road in Wandsworth was followed by the appearance of his mother and aunt together at Clovelly Mansions, intent on removing him bodily from proximity to the dangerous married woman. Murry (feeling sick, he says) pushed them out and did not see them again until 1914.

Katherine was shedding encumbrances too; her interest in Orton and Edna now faded rapidly, but there were other complications. For a time she seems to have tried to conceal Murry's presence in the flat from some of her friends. Orage's cruelly funny account of these manoeuvres had Katherine whispering at doors, leaving false messages, sending telegrams and building up brilliantly complicated series of lies rather than let him know she had a young man installed on the premises. Another new friend, an Irish barrister with literary leanings called Gordon Campbell, introduced to her by the indefatigable Willy George, also went through the bizarre experience of spending several hours in conversation with her in one room, thinking they were alone in the flat, and then hearing Murry summoned from behind a closed door. The incident could well have come straight out of Orage's story, which he ran in the *New Age* in May: five episodes of pseudonymous private jokes and hostile portraiture in which Katherine figured as 'Moira Foisacre', a young widow with cultural pretensions and a complicated private life. Mrs Foisacre has had a brute of a husband, and currently possesses plenty of friends who are 'the debris of her wrecked past', and whom she keeps in careful compartments. Her clever writing has both a satirical and a sentimental streak, and her admirers think she has it in her to become a playwright; but, according to the severe narrator, 'promiscuity of reflection, taste, judgement, character and intelligence is her distinctive and peculiar quality'.*

Mrs Foisacre enjoys wide-ranging literary conversations (Maeterlinck, Whitman and Wells all figure) and is planning a sketch about Christian Scientists. She offers her visitors tea with the remark 'Isn't tea in the afternoon like a sonnet of Rossetti's?' Her flat is decorated with modern French drawings, she has installed a fountain in the middle of the room on the matting, and other furniture includes a piano and divans. Within this familiar-sounding setting, she is apparently concealing the presence of a young literary man.

Orage ran his 'Tales for Men Only' on other occasions also; they represent his streak of general misogyny, but this particular one is a clear and blatantly personal attack, designed to wound and also to be unanswerable. Katherine never attacked him in return, whether for fear of him or because she accepted the truth of some of his criticism; and she never lost her respect for him.†

For the present, Murry, who found her flawless, did not presume to

---

* The judgement is strikingly similar to that of Aldous Huxley in *Those Barren Leaves*, written after Katherine's death, where she is satirized as Mary Thriplow.
† Orage's view of Katherine fluctuated: after her death, he told Frieda Lawrence that she was the only woman he had ever truly loved.[5]

question or criticize, and was prepared to publish almost anything she offered him, was in the ascendant. He, after all, was also an editor and, though he talked of being 'so awfully out of it',[6] was better educated, and treated with respect by other intellectuals. The *Westminster Gazette* was giving him serious German works to review as well as a round-up, which provided him with a batch of books to sell each week. Life at Clovelly Mansions was not too uncomfortable. Poor Ida reports that at this time she was reduced to eating the oats from the face-packs at the beauty salon, where she worked for 10s a week.

Katherine now invited Murry to 'make me your mistress'. He declined, saying he felt it would spoil everything, reluctant to give up his role as the little boy in the ménage. Concealing her deeply hurt pride, Katherine continued to listen to his confidences about the past, his Parisian love-affair and the ensuing miseries. She offered no confidences in return, nor did Murry invite them. Either he lacked the nerve, or he preferred to keep her image untarnished by reality.

It did not take her long to overpower his resistance; within a very short while of her first onslaught, they began to sleep together. By his account, their relations remained very childlike; although both had had sexual experience, she was wholly reticent about hers, and his had been slight and nervous; Murry adds that he found no real sexual fulfilment until his *fourth* marriage, when he was in his late fifties, and that it came as a revelation to him. Katherine also wrote later that their love was 'child love', and this remains a sad, underlying inadequacy of their relationship, and helps to explain much of their mutual dissatisfaction later. For the moment, though, they were happy and busy, with brilliant hopes for the future. Like children, they lived mostly on the junk food of the day, meat pies and the cheapest possible restaurants; Katherine had no time or wish to cook, even though Murry tried to teach her to make stock out of cheap ham bones, throwing in a few vegetables to make a '*pot-au-feu*'.

She began to think about getting a divorce and wrote to Bowden, inviting him to visit her and discuss the matter. When he did call politely, he had the impression – or so he said later – that she was rather enjoying her role of free woman of letters, living outside the confines of convention like George Sand or George Eliot. They discussed the possibility of an American divorce, but found it would not be valid in England, and she was not prepared to be divorced as the guilty party, a process that would inevitably bring her name into the newspapers.

Nothing was resolved, but in May she and Murry took a few days' 'honeymoon' in Paris, where she had so ecstatically imagined living in the Latin Quarter in her letters to Garnet in 1908 and to Floryan in 1909 (and where she had subsequently stood up both Floryan and Ida on different occasions). This time Murry took her the rounds, and she met his Paris correspondent, Carco, who offered to give her French lessons; they had something in common, for he had been born in Tahiti (albeit of Corsican parents) and liked to affect a South Seas persona, much as she had played at being a Maori.

On their return to London, Katherine suggested, with considerable cheek in view of Granville's association with Orage, that her publisher might like to back *Rhythm*. He agreed, taking on the financial dealings with the printers, and offering Murry and Katherine £10 a month to edit. For the moment, it looked like a good arrangement. Murry had also written to Rupert Brooke in the hope of a poem, and he introduced them in turn to Edward Marsh, private secretary to Winston Churchill and a generous patron of the arts, who offered to help with the finances too.

With things apparently going so well, Murry, under some friendly pressure from his old tutor, agreed to sit his final examinations in Oxford. He took a supporting party of Katherine and Gordon Campbell, who was now a close friend, and they all stayed together outside the city at Boar's Hill while Murry underwent the ordeal, from which he emerged with a second-class degree, which was good under the circumstances. Katherine was promoted to the official position of Editorial Assistant and taken to meet Murry's current literary idol. This was Frank Harris, in his fifties and still possessed of the panache that had made him a good editor of the *Saturday Review* in the 1890s; his latest success was a life of Shakespeare, and he had a reputation for opposing Victorian prudery, which naturally attracted the young. Katherine wrote him an outrageous, flattering letter, saying he was her 'hero and master – always' and enthusing about how he has made

'this art business' far more serious than ever before to me – and I thought it meant almost everything in the past years – but now I seem to realize for the first time what it may mean – and knowing you, and hearing you – I must needs go humbly. Ever since I have loved Tiger we have spoken of you.[7]

'Tiger' was of course Murry; or rather, he and Katherine had been given the joint nickname of the 'two Tigers' by another new friend,

Gilbert Cannan, who had begun to write for *Rhythm*. In private the tigers began to call one another Tig and Wig.

Wig's flattery of Harris was encouraged to the hilt by Tig, who was himself preparing a eulogy of their hero for *Rhythm*. Murry described one of Harris's novels as the greatest in the language, his short stories as the greatest, himself 'a prince among men, a prince of talkers and critics' compared with whom 'Coleridge and Goethe have had but a half-vision'.

Just as this tribute appeared on the bookstalls in the July issue, Murry's enthusiasm received a check. Harris had recommended Stendhal to his young disciple; when he began to read Stendhal he found that Harris's story 'An English Saint' was, in fact, plagiarized boldly from Stendhal. 'I kept my discovery to myself,' wrote Murry, 'but my attitude to Harris was changed in a moment. I did not trust him any more.'[8] Murry felt so strongly about the matter that, when Harris invited him cordially to become a director of the new fiction magazine he was setting up with comfortable financial backing, *Hearth and Home*, Murry refused. In his view, plagiarism was an unforgivable sin.

Murry adds that, in addition to keeping the discovery to himself, it prevented him from contributing to *Hearth and Home*. He does not say whether he discussed the matter with Katherine, although it would seem surprising not to, given the closeness of their association, both personal and professional, since by now she had her name on the masthead of *Rhythm*. In the event, one of her stories did appear in the November issue of *Hearth and Home*. How had Murry accounted to her for his change of heart? If he did tell her about the plagiarism, how did she react? These are interesting questions, but they have no answers.

She may have worried about the matter more than she cared to disclose to Murry, not least because her old friend Floryan had now tracked her down; he appeared in London bearing enough luggage to suggest that he intended to settle. Whatever her private feelings about this were, she persuaded Murry that he could make a contribution to *Rhythm*, and his name duly appeared as 'Polish correspondent'. A full-page drawing of the new correspondent was prepared for the September issue. Murry accepted this incursion as obligingly as he usually fell in with what she proposed; in August, Sadler's name (and his father's backing) disappeared, and a prose poem of Orton's was in. Outwardly, at any rate, Katherine adopted an attitude of kindly mockery towards Floryan.

He was not the only Pole to complicate their lives in 1911. Murry was introduced to a young French artist of outstanding promise, Henri Gaudier, at this time. Gaudier was primarily interested in sculpture, though he was also offering drawings to *Rhythm*. Part of his education had been in England, but his main reason for residence currently was to avoid military service. He was twenty-one and living with a Polish woman twice his age, Sophie Brzeska. Their relationship may or may not have been platonic, since Gaudier gave different accounts to different people, and, in any case, asserted that lying is indispensable to an artist. However things stood, the couple, half starved for both food and friends, were enchanted to discover a similarly artistic and unconventional pair who were good company and also promised to be a source of patronage.

At first the friendship flourished. Gaudier started work on a head of Murry. He and Katherine enjoyed singing together, and carried on enthusiastic conversations in which they planned to go and live on a Pacific island. But when Sophie was introduced, Katherine's enthusiasm lessened. Sophie was undoubtedly a neurotic as well as an unfortunate woman, her life a long catalogue of woes and ill treatment by her family, lovers and employers. She had travelled the world from one miserable experience to another, and all this she began to confide to Katherine at length, including a period of intense lesbian attachments during a stay in New York. This was the wrong subject to raise with Katherine just then; she shuddered and retreated into Beauchamp gentility. An invitation to tea to meet her other Polish friend, presumably Floryan, was withdrawn by telegram, and Murry was told to invite Gaudier on his own. Later he too was grilled by Katherine as to whether he was a homosexual – to which the answer was probably in part yes – and she was responsible for breaking his friendship with Murry. This Murry minded very much; it was also sad for *Rhythm*, since Gaudier's drawings of birds and human heads are among the most attractive things in its pages.

The other new friend who appeared about this time, offering himself as ally, contributor and helper, was Gilbert Cannan, fair-haired, handsome, pipe-smoking, dog at heel, the very model of the successful young Georgian man of letters. At twenty-eight he had already published several novels, and was translating Romain Rolland's ten-volume *roman-fleuve, Jean Christophe*, as it appeared; several of his plays, mostly dealing with social problems such as alcoholism, had been produced in the West

End, and he had even been satirized by Bernard Shaw in *Fanny's First Play*. To Murry and Katherine, he represented the peak of achievement. Lecturing and reviewing in national papers came easily to him; he was a member of the Savage Club, and he lived in respectable Kensington. The publisher Martin Secker was his close friend, and when his novel *Round the Corner*, which dealt with the problems of adolescent sex, was published in 1912, it was banned by many circulating libraries and enthusiastically praised by Wells, Compton Mackenzie and Hugh Walpole; it also led to invitations from Lady Ottoline Morrell, and the beginning of an intimate friendship with her.

Despite all these promising signs, Cannan's life was not altogether easy. After being cited by J. M. Barrie in his divorce, Cannan felt obliged to marry Mary Barrie, who was seventeen years older than him. The case had been widely reported and, although many people expressed sympathy for Mary, there was a good deal of awkwardness. This made an obvious bond with Katherine and Murry, who seem to have gone around accusing Bowden of being obstructive in the matter of her divorce. In fact, Mary and Katherine did not altogether admire one another: Mary thought Katherine insincere, and Katherine envied Mary her comfortable life. In one of her nicely equivocal statements, she wrote to her mother, 'Mary Cannan is a charming woman; I wish that you had met her. I feel sure that you and she would get on beautifully.'[9] But there were no doubts about Gilbert: he was impressive, likeable and had connections that were going to be very useful to *Rhythm*.*

Also in the course of this busy summer, Gordon Campbell brought his Dublin fiancée, Beatrice Elvery, a painter who had trained at the Slade, to London to approve the house he had found in Selwood Terrace, off the Fulham Road. He took her to Clovelly Mansions to meet Katherine and Murry. Beatrice remembers how they were dressed in matching navy fishermen's jerseys, how they all sat on the floor to talk and how the conversation

was about people going to bed with each other and other things that I had never heard mentioned in public before. I felt Katherine was trying to shock

* Although largely forgotten today – Cannan became schizophrenic and spent his life from the age of forty in a mental hospital – in 1912 he did appear to be one of the most promising young English writers, singled out for praise by Henry James, among others. He was also a pivotal figure in the intellectual community, not only introducing Murry and Katherine to Secker, but establishing a 'poor man's Garsington' in the Chilterns, with the same people visiting him and the Morrells, and Ottoline and Gilbert calling on one another. Cannan introduced both Mark Gertler and Lawrence to her.

me and frighten me away. She was hard and bright and hostile.[10]

Despite this bad beginning, the two couples became good friends. Gordon and Beatrice went over to Ireland to be married. The Cannans were also tired of living in London, and Katherine and Murry began to dream of a cottage in the country. Almost immediately they found a small house in the village of Runcton, set in the salt-marsh land between Chichester and Selsey, with a walled garden and trees. It charmed Katherine, who saw it as their wedding house and imagined having a child there. 'At present I don't care any more for cities,' she announced to her cousin Sylvia.[11] They were so sure of their feelings for the place that they took a three-year lease, furnished it entirely on hire-purchase from Maples, had headed letter-paper printed, and engaged a manservant. Since it was a considerable journey from London, they did not give up the Gray's Inn Road flat; but they appeared to be launching into a settled domestic life in the country, with a useful *pied-à-terre* when they needed to be working in town. All this was so far from what they could actually afford that it is hard not to think they were encouraging one another into realms of high fantasy. Things went badly from the start.

A few welcome visitors came. Goodyear, who arrived at the same time as Edward Marsh and Rupert Brooke, charmed everyone with his talk and his singing when they went out walking on the marshes. Ida's visit was not such a success. She and Murry decided they had nothing in common except Katherine, which was not really a basis for friendship between them. Ida noticed that the manservant was not keeping the place clean, and soon everyone noticed that he was a drunkard; he was also a thief. This was one problem. Another was the arrival of Henri Gaudier, who was hoping to bring Sophie to stay, and who 'overheard' Katherine saying rude things about her: how she felt their life in the country would be spoiled by a visit from her, how she pitied her but did not like her and wanted to shrink away from her, and so on.

Gaudier's version is that he had walked half the way from London to Runcton because he could not afford the whole fare, arrived exhausted, heard Katherine talking at a window while she was hanging curtains and was so outraged that he departed again without speaking to them. Possibly Katherine was less innocent than she seems; at all events, the Gaudier-Brzeskas did not arrive to spoil life at the Runcton cottage, and he became a sworn enemy to Katherine and Murry, in his rage even shattering the head he had been sculpting.

The next visitor must have been even less welcome. The paper's Polish correspondent, unwilling, it seemed, to return to Poland, arrived on the doorstep with two trunks full of books and papers and no other visible means of support. Katherine did nothing to turn him away, but the place was poisoned. From this potentially disastrous situation they were rescued by a different disaster. The publishing house of 'Stephen Swift' collapsed and Granville fled abroad, having increased the print order for *Rhythm* and leaving a debt of £150 (he was later arrested in Tangier and charged with fraud and bigamy).

Katherine and Murry hurried to London to try to sort things out, leaving Floryan in sole possession of Runcton for the moment. The printers were proposing to sue for their money, convinced that Murry could easily raise it; a solicitor engaged to help them come to an arrangement managed only to run up another large bill for his unavailing services. Katherine then engaged to pay her allowance directly to the printers. She and Murry were intent on saving *Rhythm*. This meant finding another publisher, which they did without too much difficulty: Martin Secker, keen to build up a list of new writers, proved very willing. Meanwhile, Edward Marsh advanced them money with his usual generosity, and said he would pay the salary of an editorial assistant, who was to be Wilfred Gibson (his poems appeared regularly from then on). Other influential figures, including Wells, promised to help with money or contributions; no one in the literary world likes to see a small magazine shipwrecked.

Something was to be salvaged then, but the dream life by the salt marsh was not. Katherine had hoped briefly that she was pregnant, but now found this was only part of the dream. Maples was invited to repossess itself of all the new furniture. Even the Gray's Inn Road flat had to be given up. The two tigers moved stoically into one room in Chancery Lane, with only a camp bed, two chairs and a packing case. At least there was no room for Floryan. Returning to Runcton for a final clear-out, they gave him some money and devoutly hoped he would disappear. They had enjoyed little more than a month in the country.

The first Secker *Rhythm* contained some items of personal significance to its editors. One, Harold Monro's 'Overheard on a Salt Marsh', was a sad reminder of the marshes at Runcton; it was also one of the best poems to appear in the magazine, and was later much anthologized, and memorized by innumerable schoolchildren. From Gilbert Cannan came a plea for divorce reform that sat rather oddly among the literary contributions; and at the end appeared a review of a novel which had been out for some months, *The Trespasser*, by D. H. Lawrence. The review was almost certainly the work of Goodyear, and it failed utterly to take note of the striking originality and brilliance of Lawrence's gift in this book, which describes an adulterous love-affair ending in suicide; the story was substantially a true one, told to Lawrence by a woman colleague and, with her consent, turned into fiction. The condescending tone adopted by *Rhythm*'s reviewer, who attacked Lawrence for being insufficiently objective and for his morbid psychology, is altogether beside the point and would seem a bad portent for relations between Lawrence and the magazine; but, in fact, Lawrence wrote to his friend and adviser Edward Garnett from Lake Garda inquiring 'if *Rhythm* would take any of my sketches or stories'.[12]

Lawrence, then twenty-eight years old, was a miner's son from the Midlands, a slight, arrestingly bold-faced young man with vulnerable lungs; there was tuberculosis in his family. He had been a pupil-teacher, a clerk and a scholarship winner, prodigiously quick to learn and prodigiously well read in the English and French classics. From the time of his studies at Nottingham University, he had rejected the chapel faith of his forebears, expressing the view that there should be more 'thou shalt' and less 'thou shalt not' in moral teaching. In 1908 he had found a teaching post in Croydon, and was already determined to become a professional writer; Hueffer and the *English Review* had given him his first encouragement, and Edward Garnett became his editor for his early novels. His background was totally different from Katherine's but he shared with her a rebelliousness, a bold curiosity, a belief in his own powers and an intense delight in the natural world. He had told his first sweetheart, Jessie Chambers, that he needed to be happy in order to write, and that 'I think a man puts everything he is into a book'.[13]

Lawrence had finished his third, and greatest, novel (described in a letter as 'my novel *Sons and Lovers* – autobiography') and was awaiting its publication in the new year, together with a volume of poems. The previous spring he had eloped with Frieda Weekley, taking her from her husband and three children, first visiting her family in Germany and then wandering south, alternating between ecstatic happiness and quarrels over her misery at the separation from the children. To Lawrence, life on the Continent was a revelation, and he hoped to be able to go on earning his living as a writer, and not be forced back into teaching.

In January Katherine wrote to him in Italy, sending him a copy of *Rhythm* and asking him to contribute; and he agreed.

A literary supplement was planned, in which Murry was to write on Baudelaire, and Cannan on Chekhov, who was just beginning to be noticed in England, following a performance of *The Cherry Orchard* which had baffled most of the audience but entranced a select few. Someone had to be found to review the first volume of *Georgian Poetry*, anthologized by *Rhythm*'s patron Edward Marsh. John Drinkwater declined (probably because he was in it) but Lawrence (who was also in it) agreed, and sent a rhapsodic 'review' that must have puzzled the editors if they were expecting a sober assessment of the merits of Masefield, W. H. Davies, Walter de la Mare, Rupert Brooke, John Drinkwater and W. W. Gibson:

> Life is like an orange tree, always in leaf and bud, in blossom and fruit … What are the Georgian poets, nearly all, but just bursting into a thick blaze of being? … We believe in the love that is happy ever after, progressive as life itself … If I take my whole, passionate, spiritual and physical love to the woman who in return loves me, that is how I serve God. And my hymn and my game of joy is my work. All of which I read in the Anthology of Georgian Poetry.[14]

Some of the Georgian poets must have been startled to hear themselves characterized in these terms; but the article does give a very clear impression of Lawrence's state of mind at the time. He was never to be so happy again as during these months of newfound love with Frieda and confidence in his work, backed by Garnett's judgement. Lawrence next promised Katherine a story for nothing; he told another correspondent that *Rhythm* was 'a daft paper, but the folk seem rather nice'.[15]

Nice as they might be, the editors were in increasing trouble. Although there were contributions from Katherine in almost every issue, often under pseudonyms, they consisted, for the most part, of weak and sickly poems, pointless stories about little girls and the rather forced humour exemplified by the theatre review written in dialogue between the 'two tigers', all so far below the standard she could reach, and had reached in the *New Age*, that Murry must be arraigned either for critical obtuseness or for being too besotted with her to use his judgement. The former is the more likely diagnosis, since he printed equally abysmal prose poems, stories and critical essays by other contributors: Richard Curle's halting account of how he loved Conrad but could not really explain why, Arthur Crossthwaite's leaden stories and, worst of all, Murry's own contributions. They are so awful that they make you wonder how any backing was found for *Rhythm* under such an editor. They range from his long, confessional poems to stories of staggering ineptitude. In one, a little boy (Dicky – the name he said he and Katherine intended to give the baby which failed to materialize) plays house with the little girl next door, who falls ill and dies, leaving him tragically alone. The most noteworthy thing about it is perhaps the fact that Dicky has a small blue lamp in his toy house, which is a particular point of attraction: the distant forerunner, presumably, of the famous little lamp in Katherine's later story 'The Doll's House'.

Still the paper staggered on. In December, Katherine and Murry moved into a combined flat and office at 57 Chancery Lane, and spent long hours trudging round London canvassing for advertising, a chore Katherine carried out with more success than Murry, being both bolder and more persistent. Between canvassing and trying to write, they were also dodging their enemies. Orage was just along the street, sneering at them, and Gaudier was sending increasingly menacing letters, accusing Murry of being a liar and a thief who got his drawings for *Rhythm* on false pretences, and failed to pay for them. Then Floryan arrived on their doorstep again, expecting to be put up in Chancery Lane. At this point Katherine announced that her heart was giving her trouble, and Murry agreed that she must be got away.

Fortunately, Anne Rice had written from Paris, inviting them to a Christmas party. The Cannans and the Campbells, back from Ireland, were all keen to make the trip; somehow the money was scraped together and they went off in a party. Beatrice Campbell remembers Katherine being very cheerful in Paris (her heart presumably working normally again):

I remember her gaiety, the way she would flounce into a restaurant and sweep her wide black hat from her bobbed head and hang it among the men's hats on the rack. I remember a group of men at a table running their tongues round their lips saying 'Oh là là' and her little muted laugh, delighted with herself ... At night we went from café to café; there always seemed to be some terrific psychological drama going on, and we had to keep avoiding someone or other.[16]

Anne Rice has also left a record of a self-conscious and self-dramatizing Katherine who appeared at the Closerie des Lilas on different nights in clothes so different they seemed almost disguises, now a hat covered in cherries, another time a cloak and a white fez, or a turban, with bright, red-lipsticked mouth: a bold and confident Katherine; a Katherine who reminds one of her own heroine in 'The Swing of the Pendulum', telling herself, 'I wasn't born for poverty – I only flower among really jolly people, and people who never are worried.'

9

'ALL I REMEMBER IS SUNSHINE AND GAIETY'

■

Back in England, she was, all the same, embarking on a comfortless, disorganized and restless year, a year in which their projects failed and she and Murry were unproductive, ill and often unhappy. Katherine, though still contributing, appears to have given up editorial work for *Rhythm*, her last letter on its business being an apology to Edward Garnett, who had objected to Lawrence giving them a story for nothing. She wrote to Garnett in February, saying, 'I explained to Mr Lawrence that we dont pay';[1] and they sensibly held the story so that its appearance should coincide with the publication of *Sons and Lovers* in May.*

Lawrence was still in Gargnano on Lake Garda, working on a new novel called *The Sisters*, and reluctant to leave Italy, although Frieda was desperate to return to see her children. Should *Sons and Lovers* fail, Lawrence would have to return to teaching; although they were quite prepared to live on next to nothing, they still had to eat. The same problem beset Katherine and Murry in London. Even without paying the contributors, *Rhythm* continued to lose steadily; her allowance was going to the printers against their debt, and he had to slave at reviews for the *Westminster*.

Penniless as they were, it was agreed that her health required she should leave London; and when the Cannans, who were moving to Cholesbury in the Chilterns, about thirty miles west of London, suggested they should rent a small house near them, they agreed. The Cannans' was a converted windmill, 'Mill House', into which Gilbert

---

* The story, which Lawrence had written in Croydon several years earlier, was called 'The Soiled Rose', and described the visit of a young, successful man to his old sweetheart, a farmer's daughter, now engaged to a passionate gamekeeper. Lawrence reworked it after its magazine appearance and renamed it 'The Shades of Spring'.

piled his huge collection of books and Mary put all her passion for interior decoration. The Murrys' was a small semi-detached brick villa on the Common; called 'The Gables', it had a ground-floor bathroom that stuck out at the back, an outdoor lavatory and an inadequate supply of hot water. The plan was that Katherine should live in the fresh air there, with Murry coming down for weekends. The Campbells generously agreed to share the rent, with the idea that they should share the place in summer. In practice, Beatrice Campbell went there exactly once and pronounced her visit 'not a success'. She and Katherine managed to block the drains with congealed mutton fat while trying to wash up, and the landlord objected forcefully, in person, to Gordon and Murry's attempt to build a stone causeway across the garden to the lavatory shed, to protect Katherine's feet from the damp. Cholesbury was high up, and notoriously cold and windy.

The Cannans did their best to keep Katherine amused, taking her out into the country to see friends and teaching her to play poker as an evening amusement at Mill House. When Ida came to stay, she disapproved of the atmosphere, but surprised herself and everyone else by winning large sums at poker. She needed cheering up, because she had been forced to move into a single rented room when her sister decided to join their father in Rhodesia; and she was still living on her beauty-parlour pittance.

Cholesbury was no more immune to Floryan than anywhere else, and he soon turned up in quest of some of his possessions, which had been left with Katherine. Ida was deputed to hand them over from Katherine's box in Chancery Lane; and then something Floryan did caused Murry to post off a letter to Katherine 'which you must keep. It only is definite proof of what a liar & Scoundrel Floryan is, and how he'll get us into trouble everywhere.'[2]

Murry was under a different siege when Gaudier, accompanied by George Banks, invaded his office in May, insisting that he had promised to pay them for the work they had done for *Rhythm*, which he denied stoutly, and probably truthfully. More reasonably, they demanded the return of their originals, one of which was Banks's cartoon of Katherine. Gaudier then slapped Murry, reducing him to tears – for he still revered him as a genius – and left. Murry sat down immediately to write to Katherine, asking her to get Gilbert to 'crush' Banks, 'or I shall kill her'.[3] She was highly indignant on his behalf ('Do not answer the door after office hours'[4]) and promised to get Cannan to do his stuff. She also returned Banks's drawing without further ado.

In a last desperate attempt to keep afloat, *Rhythm* had now acquired a new name, the *Blue Review*; it was, in fact, in the first *Blue Review* that Lawrence's story appeared. Perhaps he heard rumblings of the Gaudier quarrel, because he asked a friend if he intended to give any drawings to 'that scoundrel, the *Blue Review*? "Scoundrel" is half affectionate, of course,' he added.[5]

All their difficulties had not made Katherine and Murry any more practical; Katherine heard that Bowden was about to serve divorce papers on them, and suddenly decided to look for a farm; but Bowden departed for America with no divorce settled, and the prospect of living on a farm disappeared as the *Blue Review*'s debts piled up.

Katherine's cousin Sydney Waterlow, in an attempt to be helpful, asked Murry to tea with Leonard and Virginia Woolf, who had been married for a few months and were planning to earn their living by their pens. To them, Murry appeared 'a moon calf looking youth'; he reported to Katherine, 'I don't think much of them. They belong to a perfectly impotent Cambridge set.'[6] Still, Leonard did send him a story, and he wrote back praising it, although it was by then too late for the dying *Blue Review*. Its third and last issue contained a story of Katherine's set in a women's Turkish bath in Geneva – a bitter attack on supposedly respectable married women, suggesting that in secret they envy the women they profess to despise, more in her *New Age* style – and a fine review of Thomas Mann's *Death in Venice* (in its original German) by Lawrence.

He and Frieda called at the Chancery Lane office with it almost as soon as they arrived in London in June, and were struck by the sight of Katherine, who happened to be in town, sitting on the floor by a bowl of goldfish, and showing her legs. Both couples had moved very fast through life lately, both had largely cut themselves off from their pasts, and both needed friends and the encouragement of feeling their loyal support. Lawrence was especially shaken that Garnett had expressed reservations about his new novel. There was an immediate attraction and sympathy between the two couples. 'Love and running from husbands is desperate ticklish work,' wrote Lawrence to Constance Garnett, describing Katherine and Murry to her.[7] All four were equally involved from the start. Lawrence saw a critic and influential editor (or so he thought); Murry saw a heroic and productive writer; Katherine saw a tragically deprived mother who had lost her children for love; and Frieda appreciated

Katherine's humour and her physical beauty, which complemented her own. Both men admired both women, Katherine witty and dark and exquisite, Frieda like a big, bold lioness with her mane of fair hair. 'All I remember is sunshine and gaiety,' wrote Murry of their first meeting, only one vivid picture remains, of ourselves sitting in opposite pairs on the two sides of an omnibus as we went off to lunch somewhere in Soho. Lawrence was slim and even boyish; he wore a large straw hat that suited him well. Mrs Lawrence, a big Panama hat over her flaxen hair. Straw hats, and sunshine, and gaiety.[8]

Friendship sprang up and flourished at once. Frieda confided to Katherine her misery at being separated from her son and daughters; their father, Professor Ernest Weekley, refused to allow her to see them. Katherine at once offered to intervene as best she could, by delivering messages to them as they walked home from school. It was a kind action, and one can also see that it must have appealed to her taste for odd aspects of human behaviour, and that she enjoyed taking on middle-class morality in this dramatic fashion.

From the start, Lawrence called Murry and Katherine 'the Murrys', just as he referred to Frieda as 'Mrs Lawrence', although she was not yet divorced from Weekley. Frieda and Katherine were both more deeply defiant of convention than Lawrence and Murry, and in both women the same streak of sexual anarchy that had first attracted the men later disconcerted them. But for the moment it was all serene. The Lawrences took a holiday flat at Broadstairs on the Kentish coast and urged the Murrys to come down for a weekend of talk, swimming and seaside pleasures.

Before they could go, the *Blue Review*'s debts had grown too large for Murry, Secker or any of the backers, and it came to an end. Katherine had been growing restless and resentful of her domestic role at The Gables, and abandoned Cholesbury without regret. She moved with Murry into a flat in Chaucer Mansions, Queen's Club Gardens in West Kensington. Ida took her furniture out of storage to lend them, Murry commandeered the sitting-room as his study, and Katherine was left with the kitchen/living-room in which to do her work. From here they went to Broadstairs for the last weekend in July, with Gordon Campbell accompanying them, as Beatrice had gone to Ireland for the birth of her first baby.

In the evening, when the sands were deserted, the whole party went swimming, naked in the half light, and then feasted on beefsteak and tomatoes. Gordon was captivated by the Lawrences, and invited them to stay whenever they wished at Selwood Terrace. Lawrence gave them a copy of *Sons and Lovers* to read on the train back to London. Both Murry and Katherine saw at once that this was a great and powerful novel. The impression on Katherine was so strong that, within days, on 2 August, she wrote out a complete 35-chapter plan for an auto-biographical novel of her own, and began work on it.[9]

Both the plan, which runs to eight pages and in which every chapter is sketched out, and the two fragmentary chapters she wrote later in the year are of considerable interest, not only because they stand for the novel Katherine Mansfield never wrote, but also for the way in which they present the heroine, obviously based on herself, although she is given the name 'Maata' from her old friend, and another character, equally obviously drawn from Ida, who is given the name 'Rhoda Bendall'. Maata appears in a harshly unsympathetic light as a young woman of great physical beauty, with ambitions to become a singer; she manipulates her various friends and admirers, using the devotion she inspires for her own ends. She justifies her taste for luxury with a defiant, 'I need these things. They help me, I can't sing if I'm draggled and poor.' She also suffers from violent swings of mood, sometimes loving and cheerful with her friends, sometimes withdrawing into periods of black depression for days at a time: a trait clearly drawn from Katherine's own nature.

Rhoda, who is given the opening chapter and who plays a major part in the story, is presented as pathologically self-sacrificing and masochistic in her devotion to Maata. Before a picture of Maata, Rhoda places a shell filled with incense dust, and addresses the photograph as though it were a shrine. Grotesquely humble and subservient, she falls in with every whim of Maata's, dreams of the touch of her lips, spends all her money on buying her flowers, paying for her lessons and even a fur coat for her, expecting nothing in return but the pleasure of being allowed to continue serving her idol. All this romantic – indeed neurotic – excess is presented without a trace of humour. Katherine seems to be attempting a wholly serious presentation of obsessive love. Whether Ida would have accepted this version of herself as containing much truth, we simply do not know. She was at pains in her old age to dismiss the notion that she had been masochistic.

The plot is melodramatic in parts, though not always more so than the episodes in Katherine's life to which it seems to refer. Her heroine does not become pregnant, but she does enter into a loveless and unconsummated marriage with a well-to-do aesthete she hardly knows, and deserts him. There are no Beauchamps at all in the story, the dominant family being that of the 'Closes', clearly modelled on the Trowells, who talk jolly Edwardian slang and have lots of music, but are also discouragingly common compared with the exquisite Maata. Her relations with them appear to be very similar to Katherine's with the Trowells, although she makes Maata's lover, Philip Close, commit suicide.

Only the first two very short chapters were actually drafted, the first entirely devoted to Rhoda, the second describing Maata arriving at a London railway station after two years' absence, met by Philip Close with his little sister, and also by Rhoda: Maata has sent telegrams to them both, and they are in competition for her company. She goes off with Rhoda in a hansom to the room she has found for her, promising to spend the evening at the Closes' – and that is all.

This is no lost masterpiece, but it is a considerable curiosity. It is unlike anything else that has survived of Katherine's work. Throughout the synopsis Maata is shown as powerful and dominant in her relations with the other characters; even when she suffers, she does not behave like a victim, but more like a Nietzschean figure who makes her own fate, without regard for morality or kindness. She also justifies her behaviour by referring to the needs of her art, in line with the view of the divine rights of artists expressed in the editorials of *Rhythm* which she and Murry had concocted in 1912.

There can be little doubt that it was her reading of *Sons and Lovers* that inspired her to plan a *Bildungsroman* of her own, in which a central autobiographical character is shown undergoing formative experiences through various friendships and love-affairs, some morbid and destructive (although there is no Oedipal conflict). One or two touches suggest that Lawrence had put his fingerprint on her imagination: Maata's skin 'flames like yellow roses' when she undresses, and when Rhoda leans out of her bedroom window in the morning, '"A-ah," she breathed, in a surge of ecstasy. "I am baptized. I am baptized into a new day," which certainly does not sound like anything else in Mansfield.

Why did she not work on it? Perhaps she soon realized that her gifts did not lie in the direction of a long book. As a writer, she always lacked stamina. Perhaps the setting of London's Bohemia, with its pleasures and perils, proved too shallow; when she did come to write well about her past, she went back to her origins, as Lawrence had done. Nothing suggests that *Maata* was going to be a very good book, but it might have been an intriguing one. A short first chapter was written within two weeks of the plan; in November another chapter, and then nothing more. During the same period she turned out an excellent New Zealand story 'Old Tar', and spoke of doing more.* They too failed to appear. Something was awry, and getting worse, and part of the trouble was her growing dissatisfaction with Murry.

The Lawrences left England early in August, going first to Bavaria, and urging their new friends to join them later in Italy. Instead, Murry took Katherine over to Ireland to stay with the Campbells at Howth for a beach holiday. She was restless and ill tempered as they all pottered about, fishing, bathing, sailing and flying kites on the cliff top, while Murry and Gordon pursued knotty points in metaphysics together. Murry noticed that Katherine disliked him spending his time in this way with his men friends. He thought she was mistrustful of what he called his 'intellectual mysticism'; a simpler diagnosis would be jealousy when she felt her dominance threatened. As so often in this situation, she set up an alternative focus of attention. She invited Ida to take a holiday in Ireland too. It was one of her calculatedly bizarre gestures, for the hospitable Campbells, who would gladly have found a bed for Ida, were told that she 'preferred' to stay away from the rest of the party, in rooms alone. Katherine would meet Ida on the rocks at the end of the beach for private conversations, contriving to give Beatrice, at any rate, the impression that she was telling Ida how much she disliked being in Howth.

Back in London, uneasy himself and aware of Katherine's dissatisfactions, Murry wrote to Lawrence – who was happily installed in a small pink house in the bay of Spezia – seeking advice both as to his relations with Katherine and his own future. Murry would not consider going to Italy, but he did want to try living somewhere abroad; yet he was perpetually anxious about money, whereas Lawrence had the divine capacity of living for the moment and trusting a few pounds would turn up before he and Frieda starved. Then too Lawrence had published three novels, as well as poems and stories, and his work was in demand, whereas Murry had nothing to show for the past few years but his degree, some experience of running a magazine that failed, and a mass

---

* 'Old Tar' was printed in the *Westminster Gazette* in October 1913, but has been reprinted only once, by Ian Gordon in his *Undiscovered Country*.

of hack book reviewing which he was beginning to loathe. True, Martin Secker had now commissioned a book on Dostoevsky from him, and he also had the chance of a teaching job in a small German university; but what tempted him most was the idea of living in Paris, where he felt fairly confident that he could earn something in the literary line. In his letter to Lawrence, he explained that Katherine needed 'little luxuries' and that he felt worn out trying to earn enough for them. Lawrence replied to Murry in a long and wonderful tirade (of which this is only a small part):

she doesn't want you to sacrifice yourself to her, you fool. Be more natural, and positive, and stick to your own guts. You spread them out on a tray for her to throw to the cats. If you want things to come right – if you are ill, and exhausted, then take her money to the last penny, and let her do her own house-work. Then she'll know you love her. You can't blame her if she's not satisfied with you ... A woman unsatisfied must have luxuries. But a woman who loves a man would sleep on a board ... Get up, lad, and be a man for yourself. It's the man who dares to take, who is independent, not he who gives. I think Oxford did you harm ...[10]

Lawrence obviously enjoyed giving advice from his position of impregnable authority as the elected consort of an older, experienced woman; and he may have underestimated how difficult Katherine could be. At different times during the autumn she was unwell; or she was pursuing work as a film extra, but finding the experience too grim to carry on with; or, according to Ida, experimenting with hashish; or taking refuge in Ida's room in order to be alone; or indulging in what the Campbells called 'Dostoevsky nights', when they sat up late drinking and there were displays of emotion. It was on one such occasion that Katherine burst into tears and declared she was a 'soiled woman'. Murry, for all his talk of the artistic temperament, could never cope with her wild bouts. There is something of the small boy whining in his appeal to Lawrence; but Lawrence understood Katherine better than he did, and his advice was probably good, even if Murry was incapable of taking it.

As for where they were going to live, he and Katherine now agreed on Paris. Murry visited the editor of *The Times Literary Supplement*, Bruce Richmond, who promised him he could review French books, and they persuaded themselves they could live much more cheaply in France than in England. In December they borrowed some money from Katherine's sister Vera, who happened to be in London, and commandeered all Ida's furniture, which was sent over to Paris; and after a few days in the Hôtel de l'Univers they moved into a flat in the rue de Tournon, which runs from the Luxembourg Gardens to the pont des Arts. Katherine wrote to her sister Chaddie to boast that she and Murry were now talking French together, and anticipating much happiness:

The weather is icy, but Paris looks beautiful. Everything is white & every morning the sun shines & shines all day until it finally disappears in a pink sky. The fountains are just a bubble in their basins of ice – And now the little green Xmas booths are lining the streets – I am going to enjoy life in Paris I know.[11]

And Katherine did love Paris; but Murry took fright almost immediately. He hated going to the office of *The Times* to request a reference for the estate agents letting the flat. He found that Carco, who was assiduous in his attentions, and other French journalists he was introduced to, were convinced that he could place their work in *The Times Literary Supplement*, which they insisted on seeing as some sort of official organ, for which Murry was virtually an ambassador. They offered him articles which he did not know how to turn down. Meanwhile, his own first piece (on Stendhal) was rejected by Richmond, and the six critical articles on 'the present state of English letters' which he toiled at for the *Westminster Gazette* met the same fate. Very soon he was panic-stricken at the gap between his income and their expenditure. A glimpse of Proust in a café one evening, 'a tall slim man in black with a sickly yellow face', a sight of Charles Péguy tying up a parcel of books in his own shop – these were thrilling, but not enough to overcome Murry's despair. In England, bankruptcy proceedings were threatening; even the patient Edward Marsh wrote to ask what was happening about the debt to the printers of *Rhythm* and the *Blue Review*.

Friends in London came to the rescue. At the beginning of February, Spender offered Murry the job of art critic at £5 a week, and Gordon Campbell offered to put him up while he came to London to consider it. Once he was in London, Gordon advised him well about the impending bankruptcy; Murry went to the official receiver, explained how things were, and found officialdom sympathetic.

There was obviously no point in going back to Paris, although Katherine wrote that the weather was deliciously springlike and was clearly not eager to leave at first. Goodyear turned up to visit her in February, and Carco was about; and it may have been at this time that she began to read Colette, whose novels about the conflict between love and independence in women's lives, *La Vagabonde* and *L'Entrave*, appeared in 1910 and 1913, and were certainly known to her (in November 1914 she reread *L'Entrave* and wrote, 'I don't care a fig for anyone I know except her' [i.e., Colette]).[12] Colette's success on stage, her bisexuality and her acquaintance with the *demi-monde* were all likely to have interested her, and her vision may have played its part in Katherine's falling in love with France itself, although none of this was shared with Murry. While he took against France, she was drawn all her life to the beauty of French skies, townscapes and countryside, the 'warm sensational life' – a phrase she applied to Carco later, when she fancied herself in love with him. He disappointed her, but the idea of France remained powerfully enticing, and she wrote loving descriptions of it until the end of her life, her sense of pleasure as intense as Colette's, if more precarious.

But now it was time to beat a retreat. Murry came back and Carco helped him to sell Ida's furniture (the only buyers he could find were brothel-owners). Katherine gave Carco a few souvenirs, 'an egg-timer which *charmed* him and some odd little pieces like that',[13] which Ida must have heard with mixed feelings. They returned to England with little more than their books. Even Katherine's overcoat was stolen by the *femme de ménage* as a parting gesture and, to add to the doom-laden atmosphere, the concierge died as they moved out.

The next four months were the bleakest Katherine and Murry had yet spent together. They had to borrow from Gordon Campbell to pay for a borrowed, furnished flat in Chelsea, while Katherine looked for cheap rooms (10s a week was what they thought they could manage); and Murry prepared himself for his new job as art critic for the *Westminster Gazette*. Ida was due to leave for Rhodesia again, this time on a more permanent basis, at the end of March, and on the same day Murry had his bankruptcy hearing. Katherine worried about money and went for long walks with Ida, revisiting the streets around Queen's nostalgically. She found her friend oppressive, but knew she would miss her and noted in her journal her awareness of the extraordinary quality of Ida's devotion and her own lack of response; except that, when Ida dressed her for an evening out, she felt 'hung with wreaths'.[14] Then she began to dream of New Zealand, and there were other twitches of memory. At a concert with Beatrice Campbell she fancied the violinist looked like Garnet; the crocuses in Battersea Park made her think of Bavaria in autumn. She worried about her writing becoming 'pretty-pretty', with some reason, for the only story that survives from this period is one of her most vapid, 'Something Childish But Very Natural'. Both she and Murry were trying to produce work that would bring in money: he a novel, she a play, which she tore up.

In April she found some rooms in Edith Grove, Fulham, which seemed just possible, in spite of a squalid communal staircase; they furnished them with a table and two chairs, and a mattress on the floor, and settled down miserably. Then Murry had an attack of pleurisy, and as soon as he recovered she collapsed in turn, with a galloping heart on top of the pleurisy. A decent doctor, seeing how things were, looked after them for nothing; and another friend got Murry the offer of a job in the Imperial Library in St Petersburg. While they thought this one over – and it is tempting to speculate on what might have happened had they set off for Russia just then – the Lawrences arrived back from Italy to be married. They went to stay with the Campbells. The Murrys were impatient to see them again. It was the end of June 1914.

10

1914: 'OTHER PEOPLE, OTHER THINGS'

■

The return of Lawrence and Frieda in June 1914 delighted Katherine and Murry, and for the next two years Lawrence was a dominant figure in their lives. They were to spend a great deal of their time together, swapping friends, planning magazines, setting up club rooms and communal living arrangements, talking, quarrelling, scolding and complaining, both to each other's faces and behind one another's backs. It was during these years that Katherine probably told Frieda and Lawrence things about her New Zealand girlhood she did not tell Murry and that, as we have seen, Lawrence used in *The Rainbow*; and that she also unconsciously became, in part, a model for a character in *Women in Love*. Although their affection was deeply riven by malice, misunderstanding and bad behaviour, in essence it survived, and was reasserted before their deaths.

For the moment Murry, at any rate, felt the contrast between their respective fortunes painfully. Frieda was now free to marry Lawrence, whereas Katherine had no divorce in prospect, as Bowden had gone to America with nothing resolved between them. Lawrence had been offered an advance of £300 by Methuen for his next novel, while Murry was struggling hopelessly with his first, *Still Life* (the title is apt enough) and had become almost entirely dependent on Katherine's allowance, which her father had providentially raised to £120 a year. Beauchamp always disliked Murry and regarded him as a scrounger, in contrast with his other sons-in-law, all of whom earned good salaries and supported their wives properly, as men were expected to do. Katherine was writing nothing and had been trying to find work as an actress, but there too had failed. In one of Murry's reminiscences of the period, he writes of 'the enchanted and irrecoverable paradise of before the war',[1] but elsewhere records how, when the Lawrences came to supper in their wretched lodgings in Edith Grove, Katherine burst out with complaints against their squalor. After their guests had gone, she and Murry sat up half the night quarrelling about this 'betrayal'.[2]

The next day they agreed they would look for something better and found a flat they liked the look of, still in Chelsea; but here again disaster struck. The rooms were infested with bugs, and they were obliged to wage secret war with paraffin and sulphur, too mortified to tell anyone about their problem. (Lawrence and Frieda would undoubtedly have laughed and come to their aid in an entirely practical way.) Katherine gallantly tried to make a joke of it in private, by suggesting that they should imagine they were Russians, who would presumably take bugs more easily in their stride. Later, Murry was to say Lawrence accused him of being a blood-sucking bug; poor, respectable Murry, it was a more hurtful gibe than Lawrence knew.

The two women were especially close at this time. With Ida away in Africa, Katherine had no other woman friend to confide in. The gloss had gone from her life with Murry, now that he was no longer an editor but simply a struggling, ill-paid art critic, and his loss of confidence in himself was not good for either of them. Frieda too was in an agonized state about her children. She thought of bringing her mother over from Germany to support her claim that she should at least be allowed to see them. As it was, when one day she approached them in the street, their aunt shrieked, 'Run, children, run,' and they obeyed with frightened faces; and when Frieda tried to address her ex-husband on the subject, he told her she was worse than a prostitute. However one may judge Frieda, this was less than Christian behaviour, and Katherine was very naturally full of sympathy.

Also on Frieda's behalf, perhaps, she took a somewhat guarded view of Lawrence's other women friends. When they were all invited to Hampstead for a picnic with two, Catherine Jackson (later Carswell) and Ivy Low, and Katherine saw them running enthusiastically down the hill towards Lawrence, skirts flapping and calling out greetings, she turned tail and fled back to the underground station, muttering, 'I can't stand that,' with Murry in tow, protesting ineffectually.[3] It was a pity, because they were both highly interesting and able women, but the whole Low connection aroused Katherine's tendency to mock. Ivy's aunt Edith was married to David Eder, who had turned from his *New Age* theorizing to another field, setting up as one of the first British psychoanalysts. *Sons and Lovers* being so clearly a study of the Oedipus complex, Eder was interested in Lawrence; and, although he never accepted Freud's doctrines, the two men became friends and there was much earnest talk of sex. The Katherine who had shocked Beatrice Campbell by talking brazenly about who went to bed with whom had now grown more reticent; or perhaps the whole subject seemed less amusing after two years with Murry, and she became caustic at the expense of the Freudians.

Her flippancy did not prevent Lawrence and Frieda from inviting her with Murry to their wedding on the morning of 13 July at Kensington Registry Office in Marloes Road. Lawrence had first wanted Edward Marsh and an old teaching colleague as witnesses, but they were unavailable; so he fell back on his host, Campbell, and Murry. The men put on formal three-piece suits, Frieda enveloped herself in flowing silks, Katherine wore a sombre suit and another of her black hats, and all of them piled into a cab early on Monday morning. On the way, they suddenly realized that Lawrence had not yet bought a wedding-ring, and they had to stop while he hurried into a goldsmith's for one. This was the moment when Frieda took off her old, ill-omened ring and gave it to Katherine. She wore it in preference to any other for the rest of her life.

'I don't feel a changed man, but I suppose I am one,' wrote Lawrence,[4] and made preparations to visit his sister in Derbyshire, leaving Frieda to pursue the question of the children. Lawrence had mixed feelings about being lionized in London. Murry was exasperated by Frieda's sublime indifference to her husband's appearance at social gatherings (he had to wear a dress suit to H. G. Wells's, and it did not flatter him); she took the view that he was simply a great man; but Murry felt an almost proprietorial concern for Lawrence's dignity. On another evening, the Lawrences took Murry and Katherine to a dinner in Soho organized by David Garnett to bring his Bloomsbury friends into the same orbit: a gesture of friendliness with many repercussions.

The Lawrences planned to return to the continent in October. Meanwhile, he went north with some men friends for a walking-tour, and Murry and Katherine tried to organize a holiday of their own. Hearing of a cheap schoolmistress's cottage at St Merryn, near Padstow in Cornwall, they decided to go at the end of August. Then, on the fourth, taking them all by surprise, war was declared.

Lawrence was sick at heart, not only because of his German wife and in-laws, but also because his escape abroad was now cut off. He came hurrying to London. Murry and Katherine were stunned and did not know what to feel.

We drifted about London, bought newspapers, read them in tea shops; in the evening we swirled with the crowds from one embassy to another, were caught in strange momentary eddies of mass emotion, and flung aside, bewildered. We were neither for the war, nor against it. To be for or against a thing, it must belong to one's world; and this was not in ours.[5]

Both were moved by the sight of the departing regiments as they stood in the hot, dusty night outside Green Park, and the next day, inspired by an old friend, he rushed off to Putney to enlist in a cycle battalion. He began to have doubts on the bus back to Chelsea, and when he got home and told Katherine she would have to go to Cornwall alone, she refused. Murry decided he must have a holiday after all and, having failed to interest the Army in this idea, went to his own doctor, who kindly wrote him a note saying 'Query TB.' This set him free again at once and, feeling better, he called on his parents for the first time since the brawl at Clovelly Mansions. He and his father quarrelled over the question of German guilt, but at least they had their private armistice.

A week after the start of the war, Lawrence, back in Selwood Terrace, invited Katherine and Murry to the Café Royal to meet a new friend, Koteliansky. Kot, as he became to all his friends – his full name was Samuel Solomonovich Koteliansky – was a Ukrainian Jewish law student who had come to England from Kiev with a scholarship in 1911 and remained, partly for political reasons, partly for sheer love of England, earning his living precariously as a translator. He was hampered by a very poor command of English, but helped in due course by many admiring collaborators (including Katherine). A serious and passionate man, generous to chosen friends, he took strongly to Lawrence, who reciprocated fully; in his invitation, he referred rather grandly to Murry and Katherine as 'two little friends'.[6] Perhaps this was insufficient inducement, for the introduction was postponed.

The Murrys set off for Cornwall, while the Lawrences moved to a cheap cottage found for them by the Cannans, ever eager for neighbours, at Chesham in Buckinghamshire. It was called 'The Triangle', and stood a few miles from Mill House. 'I can't say we're happy, because we're not, Frieda and I,' wrote Lawrence to Marsh.[7] The war portended many difficulties for them, personal and financial. An entry in Katherine's sparse journal shows she was no happier, mistrustful of Murry and wishing she had another lover, one who would 'nurse me, love me, hold me, comfort me'.[8] Murry's memoirs insist, however, that all was well once they left town for Cornwall. They lived cheaply on cream, blackberry jam and eggs, and decided to look for a more permanent cottage, turning south to Fowey and the Truro River with no luck; then they travelled across to Kent and searched further for somewhere in Rye or Romney Marsh. As the sun shone and the war gathered momentum (Frieda was furiously denying tales of German atrocities) they enjoyed, according to Murry, one of the brief periods of contentment together that were always associated with good weather and isolation from rivals or treacherous confidantes.

Katherine found time to write a patriotic letter to a friend of her mother's in Wellington, describing the piteous scenes as Belgian refugees arrived: orphaned children carrying dolls or kittens, an 'old lady of 93, who had walked miles to escape the soldiers'.[9] It made a good piece, and was printed in the *Wellington Evening Post* in November. Katherine then tried to get herself a job, 'not far from the fighting line' she told her father,[10] and said she was going to be a reporter for a newspaper syndicate. Meanwhile, her brother Leslie had volunteered and was preparing to come to Europe to fight; Vera's husband joined a Canadian regiment and Chaddie's was a regular Army officer. No wonder the Beauchamps were scornful of Murry, and no wonder Katherine felt obliged to tell them later how hard he had tried to enlist.[11]

There were no cottages to be found in Kent. Lawrence now suggested they should come and stay with them, and try to find a place nearby. So, about the time of Katherine's twenty-sixth birthday, they returned to their previous year's haunts and installed themselves in the Triangle. They noticed that Lawrence had lost his bloom of the summer; he looked thin and unwell, and had begun to grow a beard. Murry set off daily on a bicycle to look for a second cottage, leaving Katherine to talk. 'She trusted me. I was older and she told me much of her life,' said Frieda.[12] When Murry found 'Rose Tree Cottage', three miles or so across the fields, going for 5s a week, Lawrence insisted on helping to prepare it, and expressed great scorn of Murry's languid way with a paint brush, hissing, 'Get it *done*!' and finishing the job for him at double speed.[13]

When the Murrys moved out, the two couples continued to dine together twice a week, the men sharing the cooking. Frieda found Katherine 'gay and gallant and wonderful'[14] and was struck by her hard-working habits, which were in considerable contrast to her own. Katherine was always up at seven to get her housework done by ten, she said; but gallant as she may have been, she resented having to do it. When her father sent her five sovereigns extra for Christmas – produced by the avuncular Mr Kay with a little flourish – she immediately took on a woman to do the cleaning and reported that she much preferred to sit snug in her little sitting-room and hear someone else scrubbing. All this came in a gushingly affectionate letter to her mother, who had been ill. Katherine was trying to re-establish good relations after a long period of silence. She could not resist mentioning that Frieda was the daughter of a baron, but she did not venture any explanatory remarks about Lawrence's origins or work.

Some time in November the meeting between Katherine and Kot took place, though not at all in the way Lawrence had planned it. One of the rolling quarrels about Frieda's misery over the loss of her children had arisen; Kot, who was staying at the Triangle, took Lawrence's part, and Frieda fled to Rose Tree Cottage in tears. From there, Katherine, no doubt playing her role in the drama with some zest, set off in the dark in her wellington boots and with her skirts tucked up – the duck pond went right across the lane in rainy weather – to inform him that Frieda did not intend to return. Lawrence shouted, 'Damn the woman, tell her I never want to see her again',[15] at which Katherine simply disappeared into the night. It was a good scene, and Kot was instantly bewitched by her.

As he got to know her over the next few weeks, he made this quite plain: he was happy to perform services for her and pressed presents upon her with a generosity that contrasted strikingly with Murry's stinginess. She was naturally charmed to have an adorer; and was quite prepared to flirt with him. Her intentions were never serious, but he became one of the people to whom she could safely complain about Murry. At various times in her life she put various friends in this role – Ida, Lawrence, Kot, Virginia Woolf – regardless of their sex, involving them in a private game in which she denigrated Murry while at the same time professing love to him. Only to her family she always praised him. Even if it was a way of working out a fundamental conflict for a strong-willed person who resented dependence on a lover, it proved baffling to her friends. Many of Kot's friends also disapproved of his love for Katherine, feeling she exploited him. He simply said, 'she could do things that I disliked intensely, exaggerate and tell untruths, yet the way she did it was so admirable, unique, that I did not trouble at all about what she spoke it was just lovely'.[16] Although he had more than one falling out with her during her lifetime, he would not hear anything against her after her death.

Kot was invited for Christmas, which the three country-dwelling couples had determined to make as festive as possible, in spite of the war (and the lack of Frieda's children); Lawrence promised to make punch 'up in the attics, with a Primus Stove',[17] which he did to devastating effect. Gordon Campbell was invited also, since Beatrice was away in Ireland again, and a protégé of the Cannans, Mark Gertler. He was two years out of the Slade and already regarded as an artist of high promise, a lively and attractive young man with the exotic background of an East End Jewish family from central Europe and 'the face of a Lippo Lippi cherub' according to Edward Marsh, who was hoping to produce a volume of Georgian drawings to match his *Georgian Poetry*.[18] Parties were planned at the Lawrences' on the twenty-third and the Cannans' on Christmas Day. According to Gertler's account (sent to Lytton Strachey),

These were really fun. On both occasions we all got drunk! The second party, I got so drunk that I made violent love to Katherine Mansfield! She returned it, also being drunk. I ended the evening by weeping bitterly at having kissed another man's woman and everybody trying to console me.[19]

The episode took place during a game of charades suggested by Kot. Later Gertler told his adored friend from the Slade, Carrington, that nobody knew whether to take it as a joke or a scandal, and the Lawrences were excited and intrigued. Gertler decided that he liked Katherine, and wanted to know her better. Her journal is discreetly silent about it; the charade had cast Murry as an abandoned lover and Gertler as his rival, and Katherine had refused to be 'reunited' with Murry at the end, as planned. In truth, she had already been writing genuine farewells to him in her journal: 'Darling, it has been lovely. We shall never forget – no never. Goodbye! When once I have left you I will be more remote than you could imagine.'[20] On New Year's Eve, which she spent soberly, alone with Murry, she went into the frosty garden with the thought of just walking away for ever; and Ida's 'ghost ... ran through my heart, her hair flying, very pale, with dark startled eyes'.[21]

The next day she went to London and visited Kot in his office, the smoke-filled Russian Law Bureau in High Holborn, with its horsehair furniture and pictures, one of Christ with children, one of kittens with a basket of pansies, which pleased her by its ugliness.

All through January she and Lawrence were both restless, finding the wintry discomforts of cottage life in the Chilterns more than their spirits or their health could stand. He and Frieda quarrelled on, Murry increasingly taking Lawrence's part and becoming hostile to Frieda; and Lawrence dreamed of setting up an island community with a group of chosen spirits. At this time Katherine found even his talk about sex congenial: 'Lawrence was nice, very nice, sitting with a piece of string in his hand, on true sex.'[22] She consented to let Murry make love with her several times, but was in a state of fevered passion for the idea of Francis Carco, with whom she was exchanging love-letters, photographs and locks of hair.

She and Murry were officially planning a party for the end of January – both Kot and Gertler, who had become good friends, were looking forward to it – but at the same time she had it in mind to take a flat in London, or even go to France. She wrote a long story, 'Brave Love', about a heartless and fascinating woman kept by a rich man, who breaks the heart of an innocent Russian sailor, possibly modelled on Gertler. Murry was noncommittal about it, understandably, for it is both artificial and melodramatic, one of her real failures, which he never collected.

She spent a few days in London with Anne Rice, now married to an art critic, Raymond Drey, from *Rhythm* days; and when the Lawrences announced they were moving to Sussex, where Viola Meynell had offered them a cottage at Pulborough, the charms of Rose Tree Cottage diminished still further. The Murrys cancelled their party and spent the last night of the Lawrences' residence at the Triangle with them: 'very untidy – newspapers and faded mistletoe' commented houseproud Katherine, adding, 'I hardly slept at all, but it was nice'.[23] Then she went to London again, visited another agent (Curtis Brown: nothing came of it) and allowed Kot to escort her to several music halls and give her chocolates, cigarettes and clothes.

On her return, she again told Murry she wanted to live apart from him in future. He was unresponsive, busy with a different emotional crisis over a fancied slight from Campbell. A few days later, a letter from Carco pressed her to come to France as soon as possible. Again she hurried to London where, at Mr Kay's, she unexpectedly came face to face with her brother Leslie. He took her to lunch to hear her news, which turned out to be two unblushingly delivered lies: one, that she was still as much in love with Murry as ever; two, that he was about to accompany her to France to do some reporting. Leslie passed this misinformation on innocently to the family; then, fulfilling his old ambition to attend an English university, went to begin his training to be an officer at Balliol, while his sister set off alone for Paris.

Murry was left so disconsolate that he fell ill and fled to Pulborough immediately, to be looked after tenderly by Lawrence. Murry's dislike of Frieda was now well established; Katherine, on the other hand, sat down to write to her as soon as she reached her destination in France.

She had to hoodwink the French Army officials to get into the war zone to visit her would-be lover. Today it seems an act of grotesque foolhardiness, but it was just the sort of adventure she thrived on. She had gone so far as to ask Beatrice Campbell to lend her some maternity clothes so that she could pose as a pregnant wife, but Beatrice had managed to dissuade her, and she fell back on the old tale of a sick relative. The weather was unseasonably warm and, despite the chilling sight of wounded soldiers, she was thrilled to be in France again, 'such wonderful country – all rivers and woods and large birds that look blue in the sunlight'.[24] Gray, where she was bound, was on the Saône, just east of Dijon; women were not allowed in this area, but Carco was as amused by the adventure as she was, and had taken a room for her in a village house, to which he conducted her, pretending to be a stranger. She describes their encounter charmingly and quite dispassionately in her journal:

In the most natural manner we slowly undressed by the stove. F. slung into bed. 'Is it cold?' I said. 'Ah, no, not at all cold. *Viens, ma bébé*. Don't be frightened. The waves are quite small.' With his laughing face, his pretty hair, one hand with a bangle over the sheets, he looked like a girl.

The sword, the big ugly sword, but not between us, lying in a chair. The act of love seemed somehow quite incidental, we talked so much. It was so warm and delicious, lying curled in each other's arms, by the light of the tiny lamp ... only the clock and the fire to be heard. A whole life passed in thought. Other people, other things. But we lay like two old people coughing faintly under the eiderdown and laughing at each other.[25]

Neither she nor Carco could even try to sustain the idea that they were passionate lovers. He had doubtless never expected anything more than a passing, friendly episode; he offered her the use of his flat in Paris afterwards and probably thought he had been of service to her, since she enjoyed adventures. But she felt obliged to work up a pique against him. Perhaps it was a way of squaring her guilt feelings; she and Murry, after all, took 'Love' seriously.

In 'An Indiscreet Journey', the story she drew from the adventure, Carco hardly exists as a person; but in the much later '*Je ne parle pas français*', which is usually supposed to contain a portrait of him as Duquette (indeed, Katherine suggested he was partly drawn from Carco), he is depicted as sexually passive, a gigolo, but not predatory. He is also possibly bisexual, a fantasist and a writer. Perhaps in truth Katherine felt too complicit with him, too like him, for comfort; and since she could not dominate him as she liked to do, she preferred to give up the affair. She then made him into an emblem of what she did not like about France, what she called its 'corruption' to Murry. But she kept her love of its 'warm, sensational life' intact.

A week later she was back in the cold of Rose Tree Cottage. Murry, summoned by one of her telegrams, met her in London and accompanied her. He observed that she had had her hair cut very short, and seemed 'aggressive and ill'.[26] For two weeks or more she suffered from rheumatism so severe that she could hardly move, she told Kot, who sent her whisky and cigarettes. She sent him her story 'The Little Governess', in which she explores the vulnerability and terror of a young girl who falls into the hands of an apparently benevolent old gentleman. Its settings – a trans-European train, a hotel, Munich – were known territory for her, and she managed to combine a direct narrative simplicity with the frightening aspect of a fairy-tale about innocence, pride and wickedness. Not only is it a very successful story, it is also of a genre in which Katherine excelled.

Kot was enthusiastic about the story, but he failed to place it for her. Anxious about her health, he pressed her and she wrote, 'Yes, I have a special disease. Pray your Ancestors for my heart.'[27] As far as we know, no doctor ever suggested to Katherine that she had heart disease, but she did have a special unnameable disease. What was she trying to tell Kot? The mystery increases when she told him a few weeks later (29 March), writing from Paris, that 'the illness that I had in England and longed to be cured of – is quite gone for ever – I believe it was my "heart" after all'.[28] Since she continued to suffer from agonizing rheumatism, she may have had other symptoms in mind, which cleared up in Paris, or possibly she just regretted the impulse to confide to Kot something so intimate that she would hardly acknowledge it even to herself.

Before returning to Paris, she was well enough to go to Pulborough to see the Lawrences, with Kot in attendance. Murry was at a very low ebb. Lawrence had finished *The Rainbow* at last and even Campbell had nearly completed a novel, while he struggled on with *Still Life*. Katherine sent him a breezy, loving letter with drawings, and then went straight on to Paris, to stay in Carco's empty flat on the quai aux Fleurs, high up over the Seine, with Notre Dame and its gardens at the back.

Lawrence was preoccupied with new friends: Lady Ottoline Morrell, E. M. Forster, Bertrand Russell. Murry found himself a two-room flat in Elgin Crescent, Notting Hill, and spent his time miserably, looking for linoleum and curtains. In his desperation he wrote to Orage, soliciting some work; the snub he got made him wince. Kot and Gertler called, but it was obvious they came to see Katherine, and went away disappointed. The only person who seemed pleased to see Murry was Floryan Sobieniowski, whom he ran into in the street, and who also asked for news of Katherine, and boasted of being very 'bussy': secretary to the Polish committee, translator of Synge, and with many projects under way, though his English seemed no better. Murry could not resist a friendly response, to Katherine's annoyance.

She was also spending time with an old enemy, Beatrice Hastings, who had left Orage and settled in Paris, where she held court among writers and painters: Max Jacob was her friend, Picasso and Modigliani both reputedly her lovers. Katherine regaled Murry, who had never met Beatrice, with accounts of her drunkenness and her fashionable Bohemian parties in Montmartre, where she described herself dancing with 'a very lovely young woman – married and *curious* – blonde – passionate'.[29]

She was deeply divided between her enjoyment of the pleasures of living in Paris alone and her sense that Murry was, after all, a safe lover, a refuge, not to be thrown away lightly for the sake of any unreliable French person. For his part, he sent her a letter at the end of March in which he spelt out the attitude he had determined to take in order to square his romantic view of love with the actual situation they were in. He began by referring to Beatrice Hastings, saying she and Katherine had some points in common: 'I mean the Cabaret bit ... that used to terrify me and almost killed me dead' (perhaps he meant her performances at the Cave of the Golden Calf). But, he went on, Katherine was 'the eternal woman', envied by other 'inadequate women' who put up right and wrong against you, whose greatness is that there is no right and wrong save what you feel to be you, or not-you ... Well with so much against you, it's a hard row to hoe, to be really *you*. (You is a type – the wonderful type from Aspasia to B.B. – [Beatrice Hastings] – Colette Vagabonde and you above all moderns). Naturally the tendency is to be extravagant and outrageous, retaliating against the hostility that puts up right & wrong against you. You by the sheer fact of your genius – genius is with you only being wonderfully what you are – have got through that without hurting yourself, and are very near to getting absolutely rid of your wickedness (that's only a figure of speech). Because of that, you'll stick to me; not so much because you love me, which you do, but because you know that you are more the real you, the good you, with me.[30]

Murry cannot be blamed for his ignorance of Katherine's actual experience ('you ... have got through without hurting yourself'), although it must have taken exceptional obtuseness to be as unaware of it as he was. His encouragement to her to think that she was somehow a genius simply by 'being wonderfully what you are' is culpably stupid, as is his nervous suggestion that she was both above right and wrong and yet at the same time wicked; but evidently the last suggestion, that only he could provide the right conditions for the 'real' and 'good' Katherine to flourish, did find a measure of response in her.

Her letters grew more affectionate; descriptions of walks along the banks of the Seine and meals taken alone replace the Montmartre parties, and in this benign state she began work on a new story, which she planned as a novel. It was called 'The Aloe', and was the germ of 'Prelude'. She also, for good measure, wrote flirtatiously to Kot; you can feel her determination to keep this new admirer on the leash as she coyly describes the pretty violet corset she has bought herself, fantasizes about a house far away in which 'we' might sit on the balcony in the evenings, smoking and drinking tea, tells him he is 'one of my people', and signs herself 'Kissienka', a name reserved for him: poor Kot, with his head too big for his body and his heart sometimes bigger than his good sense.

At the end of March she was again in London, but she hated Murry's rooms in Elgin Crescent, and April passed in dissatisfaction. She returned to France for the third time in as many months and reinstalled herself in Carco's sunny flat; by day she enjoyed the blossoming trees and warm weather, and worked hard on her book: '*Ça marche, ça va, ça se dessine*; it's good'.[31] By night she dreamed: of Rupert Brooke, news of whose death had just reached England, striking a chill into them all, and of Murry, improbably 'dressed in khaki – very handsome and happy'.[32]

Lawrence told Kot he found her letters from Paris 'jarring as the sound of a saw'.[33] He was going through trials of his own, being pursued to pay the costs of Frieda's divorce, unable to extract the full amount of his advance from Methuen, and in a state of quarrelsome crisis with David Garnett and his Cambridge and Bloomsbury friends. Lawrence had suddenly become aware of their tendency towards homosexuality, and reacted with mixed disgust and fascination; he found the idea loathsome, but he could not leave it alone. Murry, meanwhile, was moving into the position of favourite disciple. His dislike of Frieda had grown to such proportions that he wrote to Katherine in mid May, saying he planned to take Lawrence away for a summer holiday in which he would 'see if I can urge him to the point of leaving her'.[34] 'I have an idea that he might be happy were he away with me for a bit, because he would know that I was loving him,' he continued, to which Katherine responded very sharply with a short note: 'Fancy GIVING YOURSELF UP to LOVING someone for a fortnight.'[35] She began and ended with references to her rheumatism – 'I am ill and alone *voilà tout*' – and a day or two later she was back in London again.

Murry was prevailed on to leave Elgin Crescent, and in June they moved to a small stucco house in Acacia Road, St John's Wood; Katherine was delighted to have a garden and an attic-study of her own (Murry was always inclined to think she could work in the living-room). The Campbells moved into a nearby house, and in August the Lawrences arrived in the Vale of Health, in Hampstead, and there were plans to hatch a new magazine, to be called *Signature*. Lawrence was counting on the publication of *The Rainbow* in September to bring him a pot of gold, as he put it, and his faith in Murry's powers led him to tell Ottoline that his disciple would in due course surpass him.

Leslie Beauchamp, now at Aldershot, came to Acacia Road in August and September; Katherine and he sat talking over memories of Wellington together, and she was inspired to write a short, nostalgic sketch called 'The Wind Blows', which appeared in *Signature*'s first issue (on 4 October). Her much sharper, longer story, based on her escapade with Carco, remained unpublished; perhaps she and Murry judged it simply too indiscreet about her and about the war. News came of another death in France, that of Henri Gaudier-Brzeska. He was twenty-four.

All through September Lawrence was busy and excited about *Signature*, which was to contain Murry's essays on 'personal freedom, what it means to feel free in my own soul', Katherine's sketches, and Lawrence's ideas on 'impersonal freedom, the freedom of me in relation to all the world'.[36] He tried to persuade Bertrand Russell and Cannan to contribute also, and to sell by subscription; it was to be printed in the East End, and the contributors were to have a club room in Bloomsbury for regular meetings and discussions.

As it turned out, only three issues appeared, two in October and one in November, and the club hardly got going. At the end of September Lawrence brought Katherine and Murry a prepublication copy of *The Rainbow*, lovingly inscribed to them both. How they responded is not on record, but on 5 October Lawrence called again with the first review the book had received, from Robert Lynd in the *Daily News*, and sat watching them as they read it. Lynd said the book was 'windy, tedious, boring and nauseating', a waste of its author's powers, and specifically drew attention to the lesbian episode by likening the book to Diderot's *La Religieuse* (with which it certainly has nothing else in common). After this, other reviewers went in to the kill: Clement Shorter also picked out the lesbian theme and the chapter 'Shame', and another critic said the book betrayed the young men at the front. The publishers did nothing to defend their author from police intervention. There was a prosecution, and the book was ordered to be destroyed. It was a shameful episode from which Lawrence never really recovered.

We have only Murry's testimony that Katherine 'hated' parts of *The Rainbow*, especially its 'glorification of the secret, intimate talk between women, the sexual understanding of the female confraternity, which Katherine could not abide'.[37] It is easy to see that Murry might have wanted her to feel this, but, in fact, she appears to have said nothing to Lawrence; and to have remained on good terms with him. Then, suddenly, literary questions were eclipsed for her. News came that Leslie, who had recently crossed the Channel, had been blown up while giving grenade instruction, on 7 October.

She reacted in bursts of bitter grief, alternating, naturally enough, with fits of frenetic gaiety. She continued to see friends and go out, and we know, for instance, that she attended a party given by Gertler's friend Brett in her Hampstead studio, where she took Lytton Strachey's fancy, attracted a dinner invitation from Mary Hutchinson* and met and admired Carrington.[38] Sometimes she was hostile to Murry, but then suddenly she carried him off abroad in the middle of November. They were to go to the south of France; Murry acquired a new certificate of exemption from Army service on grounds of health, and the house was passed on to a friend of Kot's.

Like many travellers, they expected the Mediterranean coast to be perpetually warm and sunny, and were taken aback by the cold. Marseilles gave Murry food poisoning, and he hated their first hotel in Cassis, although Katherine wrote to Kot that she liked the place and was happy. Murry wrote too and she instructed Kot to 'ignore the conjugal "we"', saying it had no meaning for her.[39] They moved on to Bandol, and by then 'my little John Bull Murry' had had enough.[40] He said he wanted to buy a printing press, and returned to the metropolitan literary life where he thrived best, and where he soon received an invitation to Garsington for Christmas. It had been engineered by Lawrence.

Katherine, for all her boasting to Kot of her single pride, was within a week again reduced to a state of shattered dependence on Murry. He had left believing her to be comfortably installed in the Hôtel Beau Rivage, and happy, and then, as if by malign magic, the coolly independent Mansfield disappeared. Letters suddenly became a lifeline for her, an umbilical cord through which reassurance – that she was loved and needed, that Murry was planning their future together, that he missed her – had to be pumped steadily. For her, letter-writing was never a problem. She could produce sheets every day, minutely observant, sometimes funny, sometimes lyrical, but then also reproachful, agonized, alternating declarations of perfect love with flashes of disappointment, jealousy and rage. His replies were irregular, less frequent, less detailed and shorter. Proudly as he published most of hers after her death, he must have shrunk from them at times when they first reached him, sometimes several in a day, inexorably reminding him of her loneliness, her ill health, her needs. He reacted with guilty confusion to this punishment. When he promised to come and join her, she would tell

* St John Hutchinson, a barrister, and his wife, Mary, were friends of the Campbells and also of the Bloomsbury group. Mrs Hutchinson was generally known to be the mistress of Clive Bell. They had a house in Hammersmith and a holiday farm in Sussex, and were exceedingly hospitable.

him not to, yet she could not help painting pictures of the ideal happiness they might enjoy together if only he were at her side.

All this, soon to become the standard pattern of their life, was now just beginning. Katherine was, of course, already chronically ill long before tuberculosis was established, and it is possible that, if her health had been good, she might have been able to make the break with Murry that half of her being desired. But with the fever, sore throat, 'dysentery' and above all rheumatism she went down with as soon as he left, so that she was confined to bed, her imagination turned to Murry at once. When she did not hear from him as fast as she expected to, she fired off a passionate letter of despair to Lawrence, who then attacked Murry in person, telling him he should not have left her alone, and suggesting that her illness was entirely due to his bad behaviour in 'always whining & never making a decision'.[41] Unfair as this may have been, Lawrence also took the trouble to send her a loving letter in which he did not mention his own troubles, but returned to the idea that they might form a community together. He and Frieda were going to borrow a small house in St Merryn, where Katherine and Murry had spent their 1914 holiday; they were there by the end of December, and wrote to Katherine kindly again early in January. Murry, meanwhile, had rushed to the Foreign Office to get his passport endorsed again, so that he could return to France. First, however, he spent Christmas at Garsington, installed in a cottage, going for walks with Lytton Strachey and Clive Bell, and rather pleased with the impression he was making:

they seem to be rather deferential to what I say ... I've come to the conclusion that the reason for it all is that they have a suspicion that between you and me there is actually happening that incredible thing called a *grande passion* ... And I imagine that something of the glamour of it hangs about me nowadays.[42]

For Murry, everything in life had to be turned into literature; even his feeling for Katherine was an occasion for self-congratulation because it interested (supposedly) the members of a new, distinguished group of people to whom he had been introduced. Clearly, he had no inkling that he was saying something that makes one quiver with embarrassment on his behalf.

Katherine forgot about her rage and loneliness as her health improved. She wrote to Kot, saying how happy she was, and sent Murry conflicting telegrams, but also a description of the 'perfect villa' she had found for them just outside Bandol:

It stands alone in a small garden with terraces. It faces the 'midi' & gets the sun all day long. It has a stone verandah & little round table where we can sit & eat or work ... It is very private and stands high on the top of a hill. It is called the Villa Pauline.[43]

She saw their perfect life together in her mind's eye, and on the last day of the year, having received his telegram to say he was coming, she ordered food, wine and wood for the stove.

All the windows are open – all the doors – the linen is airing. I went to the flower market and stood among the buyers and bought wholesale you know, at the auction in a state of lively terrified joy 3 dozen rose buds and 6 bunches of violets.[44]

He arrived on the first day of January. The spring flowers had begun to appear and the sea was showing its required Mediterranean blue in the sunshine. While the war waged to the north and thousands of young men followed Katherine's brother to the grave, she and Murry settled down to the most peaceful months of their life together.

They were in many ways happy, he writing his Dostoevsky book on one side of the table, she for the first six weeks worrying about whether the impulse to write had died in her. Late in January she wrote in her journal that she wanted to try poetry and some sort of elegy for her brother, and thought she might keep 'a kind of minute notebook, to be published some day'.[45] By the middle of February she had done nothing, but then she took out what she had written in Paris the previous spring, 'The Aloe', and saw that it could be made into what she wanted to do; she started work, the weather grew cold and windy, and they sat by the fire, writing together all day. Their health was in equilibrium and, during this brief, confident period, Katherine noted her intention 'to make enough money to be able to give [Ida] some. In fact, I want to provide for her.'[46] She knew she was doing good work and, full of the sense of her own powers finding fulfilment, she wished to make provision for her 'wife', even while she enjoyed the company of her 'husband'.

The nature of their happiness together is caught in a phrase she used to him when, on a two-day visit to Marseilles to see her widowed sister Chaddie in March, she sent him loving letters. (It is worth noting that, for Katherine, letters were an end in themselves: she never hesitated to write them even when she would be seeing the recipient before they could possibly arrive.) Dwelling fondly on their good times at the Villa

Pauline, she said, 'I feel we are about 15 today – just children. You and I don't live like grown up people, you know.'[47] She went on to console him that the Army 'wont catch you', as he feared it would, after Verdun. No doubt Chaddie was given a different version.

They had been exchanging letters with the Lawrences, telling them how happy they were and receiving his warm pleasure in their happiness; *'Cari miei ragazzi'* (My dear children), he addressed them. Only he lamented his own ill health, which made him miserable through the cold winter. Why did they not make plans to live together in the spring, he again asked. Katherine wrote to Ottoline (whom she had barely met, but who had lent Murry £5 for his journey south), telling her they planned to spend the summer with the Lawrences in a farmhouse near the sea, and later she wrote to Frieda saying how glad she was they would all be together. To Murry's friend Goodyear she wrote enthusiastically about England too, complaining now about the poverty of French cooking and the discomfort of French houses. Consistency was not her chief characteristic: no wonder Murry was often confused. But there is no doubt that she was in favour of the plan with the Lawrences. He wrote twice, insisting that he had no wish to bind them to any house-sharing arrangement, and Katherine then sent a telegram of her own to say she was definitely coming. She also wrote independently to him and he, anxious not to mislead her about the charms of Cornwall, said in his next letter to them both, 'Do let the winter be gone, before Katherine comes to England.'[48] He knew from the winter of 1914 that she feared the cold winds and the damp as he did, and he was tender towards her. When he found two cottages standing together, he hoped they would come to the bigger one with a high room which he christened 'Katherine's tower'.

So, at the beginning of April, warm from the Mediterranean spring, her happy, boyish lover at her side, her grief for her brother put behind her, the manuscript of 'The Aloe' in her bag, Katherine left France for Cornwall where, only eighteen months earlier, she and Murry had tried in vain to find a cottage in which to settle, and where now their dearest friends had found one for them. Frieda wrote to Katherine,

I am so looking forward to your coming and to show you this place ... I am so anxious now to *live* without any more soul harrassing [*sic*], we are *friends* and we wont bother anymore about the *deep* things, they are all right, just let's live like the lilies in the field.[49]

This was charming; but Frieda also felt obliged to warn them that Lawrence had had a really bad time ('Some of the wonder of the world has gone for him'), and for Katherine too the omens were not entirely good. In Marseilles, she had again suffered from a fever: 'I shivered and my blood buzzed as though bees swarmed in my heart'.[50] Her sickness, unnamed but chronic, was as closely woven into the fabric of her life as any friend or lover.

11

CORNWALL 1916: 'A WHOLE SPRING FULL OF BLUE-BELLS'

■

The north coast of Cornwall near Zennor is a bleak, barren and wind-swept place. In full sunshine the sea turns deep blue and green and peacock-coloured, and the coves with surrounding rocks and cliffs make perfect bathing places, isolated and romantic, with the tide crashing in and pouring out again to leave smoothly washed sand. But it is a treacherous sea – many ships are wrecked along that coast – and treacherous weather, turning black and terrifying in a moment. Snow was falling in March 1916, and into April the coast was shrouded in mist for days at a time. Still, Lawrence busied himself setting up his little community.

The group of cottages he had found was called 'Higher Tregerthen' and stood about five miles north of St Ives; they belonged to a Captain John Short, who was prepared to let them cheaply. The Lawrences took a one-up, one-down stone structure at £5 a year for themselves, and sent sketches and descriptions of the more substantial building standing at right angles to theirs, which Short had previously converted for another writer, to Katherine and Murry. Its rent was £16 a year, and 'Mrs Murry' was to be the tenant. It was made up of three cottages in a row, with three doors opening into kitchen, dining-room and study at ground-floor level; above were bedrooms, the room over the study being known as the tower room, with big windows and panelled walls. This was to be Katherine's domain, set as far as possible from the kitchen, and accessible only through the downstairs study. It seemed a good place in which to work. 'There is a little grassy terrace outside, and at the back, the moor tumbles down, great enormous boulders and gorse.'[1]

Lawrence's delight in planning for Katherine shines out of his letters, even if there was an element of self-interest involved. His suggestion that a maid hired by them in common would prepare meals, which would be held in Katherine's house, would make things just about possible for him and Frieda in their cottage. Neither place had running water or inside sanitation, but he carefully arranged to have a privy moved so as not to offend Katherine, the ladylike member of the group (Frieda was indifferent to such things). He also insisted on damp-sealing and new white and colour washes, to please her. His descriptions of the site show how enthusiastic he became:

It is a most beautiful place: a tiny granite village nestling under high, shaggy moor-hills, and a big sweep of lovely sea beyond, such a lovely sea, lovelier even than the Mediterranean. It is 5 miles from St Ives, and 7 miles from Penzance. To Penzance one goes over the moors, high, then down into Mounts Bay, looking at St Michaels Mount, like a dark little jewel. It is all gorse now, flickering with flower; and then it will be heather; and then, hundreds of fox gloves. It is the best place I have been in, I think.[2]

Katherine shared his love of flowers, and her first letters after she arrived speak of the primroses, bluebells and violets growing by the creek that ran near their house and down to the sea; and later she gave this description of the atmosphere of the place to Virginia Woolf:

Perhaps the house itself is very imperfect in many ways but there is a — something — which makes one long for it. Immediately you get there — you are free, free as air. You hang up your hat on a nail & the house is furnished — It is a place where you sit on the stairs & watch the lovely light inhabiting the room below. After nightfall the house has three voices — If you are in the tower and someone comes from the far cottage — he comes from far away — You go by the edge of the fields to Katie Berryman's for bread. You walk home along the rim of the Atlantic with the big fresh loaf — & when you arrive the house is like a ship. I mustn't talk about it — It bewitched me —[3]

To Brett, at the end of her life, she also recalled, 'I had a whole spring full of blue-bells one year with Lawrence. I shall never forget it. And it was warm, not very sunny, the shadows raced over the silky grass and the cuckoos sang.'[4] Frieda remembered walks on sunny days to Zennor, and a calm time when they all went out in a boat and sang together, 'Row, row, row your boat'.

Despite such sweet memories, Murry says Katherine fell into gloom as soon as they reached Cornwall on 7 April and found they had to spend ten days at the Tinner's Arms in Zennor, waiting for their cottage to be quite ready; and within a month she was writing letters that indicate how cross she felt at the situation she now found herself in.

She described days in which Murry and Lawrence disappeared into the mist with their rucksacks on their backs, while she lay alone beside a fire in her tower, like Mariana, smoking and listening to the sound of her maid at work in the kitchen. She had stopped writing. Her health was not improved by the Cornish damp. She also attributed some of her unhappiness to the bleak, stony landscape, but there was a more personal reason underlying this. Instead of being absorbed in writing and love games, with Murry entirely in thrall to her, she began to fear that she might become the odd one out in the foursome.

Lawrence struck her as changed, his moods alternating between a rather suspect 'feminine' gentleness in which he sewed and painted little pictures, and bouts of rage in which he beat the table and abused everybody indiscriminately, out of control and sometimes almost mad. 'After one of these attacks he's ill with fever, haggard and broken,' she wrote to Beatrice Campbell.[5] Although he himself had warned her, 'I myself am always on the brink of another collapse',[6] she either did not understand how precarious his health had become, or did not wish to. Only later, when tuberculosis attacked her as well, did she recognize the same propensity to rage in herself.

Of Frieda too she now had not a friendly word to say. She complained even of her domesticity, irritated by her habit of washing clothes with a good deal of gusto in huge tubs of water. No doubt it was a necessary process, but nothing Frieda did was right. She was a 'huge German pudding' – Katherine always jeered at fat – and had absorbed, like an ogress, the real, dear Lawrence they had known into herself. Katherine particularly objected to Frieda's talk of sex symbols; in exasperation, the younger woman suggested that the Lawrences' cottage be renamed 'The Phallus', which Frieda good humouredly 'thought a very good idea'.[7] Frieda admired Katherine for her fastidiousness, saying later,

If I had to describe her in one word I would choose the word exquisite. She was exquisite in her person: soft shiny brown hair and delicately grained skin, not tall and not small and not thin nor stout, just right. When we went bathing I thought her as pretty as a statuette.[8]

Evidently the wild young Katherine, once so intent on sexual gratification, had now subdued herself. She believed that her relationship with Murry was all the better for being a form of child-love, and his temperament went along easily with this. The two tigers had turned out to be kittens. Katherine told Beatrice that Lawrence and Frieda 'are both too rough for me to enjoy playing with'.[9]

After a few weeks she decided that she could not put up with the Lawrences at all in their current state. Her descriptions of their behaviour are uncharitable but brilliant pieces of reporting. Never has the choreography of a full-blown marital row, with every detail and bit of timing perfectly observed, been so well set out. It is as good, or better, than anything in her stories, and shows what she could do with her gloves off and no straining for effect:

Let me tell you what happened on Friday. I went across to them for tea. Frieda said Shelleys Ode to a Skylark was false. Lawrence said: 'You are showing off; you don't know anything about it.' Then she began. '*Now* I have had enough. Out of my house – you little God Almighty you. Ive had enough of you. Are you going to keep your mouth shut or aren't you.' Said Lawrence: 'I'll give you a dab on the cheek to quiet you, you dirty hussy.' Etc. Etc. So I left the house. At dinner time Frieda appeared. 'I have finally done with him. It is all over for ever.' She then went out of the kitchen & began to walk round and round the house in the dark. Suddenly Lawrence appeared and made a kind of horrible blind rush at her and they began to scream and scuffle. He beat her – he beat her to death – her head and face and breast and pulled out her hair. All the while she screamed for Murry to help her. Finally they dashed into the kitchen and round and round the table. I shall never forget how L. looked. He was so white – almost green and he just hit – thumped the big soft woman. Then he fell into one chair and she into another. No one said a word. A silence fell except for Frieda's sobs and sniffs. In a way I felt almost glad that the tension between them was over for ever – and that they had made an end of the 'intimacy'. L. sat staring at the floor, biting his nails. Frieda sobbed. Suddenly, after a long time – about quarter of an hour – L. looked up and asked Murry a question about French literature. Murry replied. Little by little, the three drew up to the table. Then F. poured herself out some coffee. Then she and L. glided into talk, began to discuss some 'very rich but very good macaroni cheese.' And next day, whipped himself, and far more thoroughly than he had ever beaten Frieda, he was running about taking her up her breakfast to her bed and trimming her a hat.[10]

This has the ring of exact truth; what a war reporter Katherine might have made, if only she could have found a newspaper to send her to the front. But truth seemed less in evidence when she got on to the subject of Murry. To Beatrice she painted him as a comic character, forever losing his horn-rims as he jumps over stiles. To Ottoline Morrell she wrote, 'Murry and I are so happy together – it's like a miracle,' but a few days earlier she had told Kot that she was planning to come to London in June and that her dissatisfactions were by no means all with the Lawrences: 'I am very much alone here ... It may all be over next month; in fact it will be. I don't belong to anyone here. In fact I have no being, but I am making preparations for changing everything.'[11] She was silent on the subject of Lawrence's ideas of *Blutbrüderschaft*, which were originally meant to include her ('Let it be agreed forever. I am *Blutbrüder*: a *Blutbrüderschaft* between us all. Tell K. not to be so queasy.'[12]). Now, perhaps because of Katherine's earlier queasiness, the question was discussed with Murry alone, and he says he shrank back, fearing a 'pre-Christian blood-rite' of some kind on the moors. All this could have made rich material for the satirist in Katherine. The fact that she made no comment – in writing at any rate – but simply grew gloomy and resentful, suggests that, however timid Murry was (thus disappointing Lawrence), he was not resistant enough to Lawrence's spell to keep in her good graces either. For her, Murry was good only when entirely subject to her.

She was, in some ways, the least innocent of the party. The two men could wander the moorland, intensely discussing the meaning of male friendship, and Murry could be drawn in and out of sentimental hero-worship; but Lawrence, for all his painful interest in the subject, and the confession of his physical attraction to certain men (made in the suppressed Prologue to *Women in Love*), did not practise homosexual acts, and Murry had an extreme aversion to them also; according to his friend and biographer, Frank Lea, he had been the object of an indecent assault as a schoolboy, which had left him frightened. Katherine, though, knew a good deal about bisexuality and its discontents. She said nothing; but Murry felt her anger and withdrawal.

Once again she began considering her escape routes. Although she had scarcely met Ottoline – a large Bedford Square party hardly counted – she was now into a gushingly flattering correspondence with her. It was a well-chosen moment for establishing her own private relations with the benefactress of Garsington, because Frieda and Ottoline were at the same time quarrelling furiously by post. Ottoline confided in Murry and Katherine: Murry himself was privately begging for money from Ottoline, and he repaid the £10 she sent him with a treacherously disparaging letter to her about Lawrence and Frieda, dated 12 April, even before he moved into Higher Tregerthen.[13] Lawrence alone behaved with any dignity in this mêlée with Ottoline – for the moment, at any rate.

By late May Katherine was insisting that Murry should look for another cottage on the south coast of Cornwall, which he obediently set about. The two couples withdrew from one another, Lawrence baffled, hurt and at times angry. It was at this stage that he accused Murry of being a 'blood-sucking bug'; but, as he wrote to Campbell, 'Why should I not bellow, if I am of the bellowing sort?'[14] Frieda took the whole thing lightly, as usual; she had known worse. They all accepted the excuse that Katherine needed a warmer climate. Yet, as soon as she was installed in 'Sunnyside Cottage' at Mylor, she wrote to Kot, 'Life is so hateful now that I am quite numb.'[15]

She prepared her assault on Garsington, characteristically inviting herself:

May I come and stay with you on the 13th July for a few days? I have to go to London on the 8th and I should so love to come to you. Only I don't know whether you will have me – for I'll be alone – Murry can't be with me. I feel as though I have so much to tell you and talk over. Even though we have barely met – its strange – With my love to you always[16]

Intimacy was thus established with a mixture of wheedling and lying, for it does not appear that Murry was consulted as to whether he could be with her or not. It seems too that she made something like an assignation with Mark Gertler at Garsington; Kot was in the secret of this, and received Gertler's complaint when he arrived at the Morrell's only to find that Katherine had stood him up and returned earlier than planned to Cornwall – and Murry – again.* Lawrence, meanwhile, had been writing to Kot about Katherine:

I think – well, she and Jack [Murry] are not very happy – they make some sort of contract whereby each of them is free. She also talks of going to Denmark! But don't mention to her that I have told you anything. She has so many reserves – But really I think she and Jack have worn out anything that was between them – I like her better than him. He was rather horrid when he was here ... [Katherine] needs to be quiet, to learn to live alone, and without external stimulant.[17]

---

* This letter is given with the date 20 June in Gertler's letters, but such a date makes no sense, because Katherine invited herself on 27 June, and it is clear that this was to be a first visit. If Gertler's letter is, in fact, 20 July, it fits with the other facts and letters.[18]

A few days later, Lawrence wrote again, telling Kot,

> When you see Katherine, tell her to write to us and send us all the news: we are thinking of her, up in London. – You are quite right about her wanderings – she wants to run away from herself – but also from Murry, which complicates matters ... I do wish she could learn to be still, and alone.[19]

This is the voice of a friend, full of real interest and affection. Once Katherine had left her tower, Lawrence took it over as his study, and it was from here that he wrote his letters and continued work on his new novel, in which, of course, she figures.

Women in Love was written between April and the autumn: thus it was begun while Katherine and Lawrence were in daily contact, and finished when they were on more distant, though still friendly, terms. By common consent, not only is Hermione drawn (in part) from Ottoline, Birkin from Lawrence himself, Ursula from Frieda, but also Gerald Crich and Gudrun from Murry and Katherine. Murry denied any resemblance to himself and Katherine, detested the book and read it, in part, as an attack on his kind of love. It is true that Crich has little in common with Murry beyond a few remarks that have a ring of him, and a refusal of *Blutbrüderschaft*: he is the worldly son of an industrial magnate, frequenter of Bohemian circles and models, with a brutal attitude to his workforce.

With Gudrun, it is another matter. There is no doubt that, in many respects, she is clearly based on Katherine and, except at the very end of the novel, the portrait is a warm and affectionate one: perhaps this is what Murry disliked. Gudrun is exceptionally pretty and attractive, with dark, sometimes 'dilated' eyes and well chosen, boldly individual clothes. She is very much admired wherever she goes; she is gifted artistically, charming, spirited, a good talker, a bit of a feminist, a bit of a cynic. Gudrun, like Katherine, is 'a restless bird ... a bird of paradise', always liable to drop her art if anything else catches her attention, always planning to go off abroad to Russia or Munich or Rome, lacking stamina and often on the defensive. When Lawrence describes Gudrun envying the freedom of men, we can hear Katherine's voice: ' "The freedom, the liberty, the mobility!" cried Gudrun, strangely flushed and brilliant. "You're a man, you want to do a thing, you do it. You haven't the *thousand* obstacles a woman has." '[20] And later, objecting that she can't simply take her clothes off to go swimming, 'Isn't it *ridiculous*, doesn't it simply prevent our living!' When she swims, and sings and dances with her sister, we can see Katherine and Frieda in their cheerful moments; when she steps into a small boat and says lightly, 'It's lovely – like sitting in a leaf', that is Katherine's trick of miniaturization exactly.

Her self-mockery is here too, when Gudrun says on the one hand that she could not bear to be married and 'put into a house', and then almost immediately confesses that she has a vision of

a rosy room, with herself in a beautiful gown, and a handsome man in evening dress who held her in his arms in the firelight, and kissed her. This picture she entitled 'Home'. It would have done for the Royal Academy.[21]

Novelists rarely draw exact portraits, and it is a finicky, and finally impossible, business 'proving' that a character is inspired by a real acquaintance. Nevertheless, it is not only the similarity between certain episodes in the book to known facts involving Katherine and Lawrence (among them a trip on the Thames resembling one made in the summer of 1914, and the much-cited Café Pompadour incident) which suggests that something of the essential Katherine has found her way into Gudrun. There was undoubtedly a real intimacy between them, and Lawrence remained preoccupied with her over a period of years; as late as March 1919 he wrote to her, 'you I am sure of – I was ever since Cornwall, save for Jack'.[22]

This is Gudrun, lying awake at night, as Katherine so often described herself doing,

conscious of everything, her childhood, her girlhood, all the forgotten incidents, all the unrealized influences and all the happenings she had not understood, pertaining to herself, to her family, to her friends, her lovers, her acquaintances, everybody. It was as if she drew a glittering rope of knowledge out of the sea of darkness, drew and drew and drew it out of the fathomless depths of the past, and still it did not come to an end, there was no end to it, she must haul and haul at the rope of glittering consciousness . . .[23]

Another time, while her lover is sleeping and she is tormented with wakefulness, she reflects, 'there are perfect moments', a highly characteristic Mansfield notion:

Wake up, Gerald, wake up, convince me of the perfect moments. Oh, convince me, I need it.

He opened his eyes, and looked at her. She greeted him with a mocking, enigmatic smile in which was a poignant gaiety. Over his face went the reflection of the smile, he smiled too, purely unconsciously.

That filled her with extraordinary delight, to see the smile cross his face, reflected from her face. She remembered that was how a baby smiled. It filled her with extraordinary radiant delight.*[24]

By the end of the book, Lawrence is stressing Gudrun's instability and cynicism, and her lover's disappointment; although Crich wants to invade her privacy, which she resists, he also confesses that there is something disappointing about being with her. At first it seems 'a great experience, something final – and then – you're shrivelled as if struck by electricity.'[25] As for Gudrun,

> Did she want 'goodness'? Who but a fool would accept this of Gudrun? This was but the street view of her wants. Cross the threshold, and you found her completely, completely cynical about the social world and its advantages. Once inside the house of her soul, and there was a pungent atmosphere of corrosion, an inflamed darkness of sensation, and a vivid, subtle critical consciousness, that saw the world distorted, horrific.[26]

It was Murry, of course, who wished to claim Katherine for 'goodness', and who was terrified of the cynical, critical Katherine perceived by Orage, Lytton Strachey, Leonard Woolf and other attentive observers. Lawrence's account of her is acute in a way that Murry's could never be.

Lawrence and Frieda spent one more weekend with Murry and Katherine, at Mylor in August, in which a semblance of harmony was maintained. After this Murry kept his distance, despite several attempts at restoring intimacy by Lawrence. Katherine and he exchanged letters from time to time – he wrote consolingly to her, for instance, for the anniversary of her brother's death – and she took several opportunities to defend him. The most famous is the incident in the Café Royal at the end of August. Sitting with Kot and Gertler, Katherine overheard two Indian undergraduates reading out Lawrence's newly published poems, *Amores*, and laughing; she thought they were being disrespectful and, in her characteristically dramatic way, asked them for the book politely and, when they handed it to her, simply walked straight out of the place with it. It was a striking scene, and when Kot reported it to Lawrence, he wrote it at once into his novel. Katherine also defended him later to Ottoline, sensibly telling her that the best response to his attacks and obsessions was to laugh at him. The friendship between

---

* This striking account of someone smiling in reflex imitation also occurs in Katherine's story 'At the Bay', when Linda Burnell answers her baby son's smile in the same way.

Lawrence and Katherine, in short, though not exactly flourishing at this time, was by no means at an end.

And what about Katherine and Murry? 'Life feels wonderful and different for at last I am free again,' she wrote to Kot as she prepared to take a train for London and then Garsington in July.[27] It was a delusion. She was moving into a new and larger circle, but it was not one that would release her from Murry. Whenever she grew nervous, she took refuge with him, and although over the next eighteen months they played an elaborate game of hide-and-seek with one another, at the end of that time Katherine was more dependent than ever on her old loves, Murry and Ida, who was now on her way back to England from Rhodesia.

For a while it looked as though Murry might be as ready to break free as Katherine. Significantly, he preserved none of his own letters to her between August 1916 and 1918; his memoirs are also studiously vague about their relations during this period. There is, however, a letter from him to Ottoline (dated 31 August 1916)[28] which says, 'I have a queer suspicion that I must be in love with you', and it is not the only such declaration he made. Murry appeared to be overtaking Lawrence in terms of success that autumn, with two books published (his novel and his study of Dostoevsky), and the comfort and protection of Garsington were important to him. There he met John Sheppard, who got him a place as a translator at the War Office, saving him from military service once again, and securing him a very decent salary. There too he must be the obvious candidate when one asks who warned Ottoline that she was the 'villainess' in Lawrence's new novel: she heard this in late November, when Murry was staying there without Katherine. Thus alerted, Ottoline insisted on seeing the manuscript of *Women in Love* and was so enraged by the character of Hermione that she told Lawrence she would sue if he tried to publish, and never forgave him. Lawrence was now reduced to extreme penury, his two major novels – the work of three to four years – without a publisher; though it's true that Ottoline was not the only stumbling block: no publisher was prepared to take on *Women in Love* then.

Murry continued his wooing of Ottoline, and by the next summer he had his younger brother installed on the estate, working the farm with the conscientious objectors sheltered by the Morrells; and Ottoline offered Murry and Katherine the bailiff's cottage that Lawrence had hoped to have. Even when Murry overstepped the mark and, having asked Ottoline one evening if he might 'come into' her heart and been invited for a moonlit walk, hurried back to London the next day to confess to Katherine that Ottoline seemed to be in love with him, he was forgiven by both ladies. But Ottoline never relented towards Lawrence.

Katherine too was a success at Garsington from her first visit, despite the fiasco of her failed rendez-vous with Gertler. According to Brett, who was there with her, she visited her in her room and proposed a pact of eternal friendship. Brett was pretty well enslaved. She gave a good painter's description of her friend:

small, her sleek dark hair brushed close to her head, her fringe sleeked down over her white forehead ... her movements are restricted; controlled, small, reserved gestures. The dark eyes glance about much like a bird's, the pale face is a quiet mask, full of hidden laughter, wit, gaiety. But she is cautious, a bit suspicious, on her guard.[29]

Katherine extended sisterly intimacies to Carrington, who was intrigued, to Mlle Baillot, Julian Morrell's Swiss governess (later the wife of Julian Huxley), who found her charming and attentive, and to Ottoline herself. Katherine was invited frequently thereafter, although Ottoline's capitulation was only partial; she liked to be loved and admired as much as anyone else, but she came to suspect Katherine of disingenuousness and envy. It is true that Garsington contained all the luxury she had known briefly at home in 1907 and 1908; though she had deliberately rejected this, she never ceased to yearn for it in one part of her being. Katherine felt superior to her sisters with their comfortable, easy lives, but she also felt envious rage; and Ottoline, made into an honorary sister, was appreciated and resented simultaneously.

The flattery and 'charm' of Katherine's letters to Ottoline are among her grosser effects; nevertheless, Ottoline *was* charmed. It was not simply that she was gullible; she also perceived something of her own rebellious spirit in Katherine, and found it sympathetic. Katherine's sketch 'In Confidence' reads almost like a transcript of her hostess talking:

Perhaps you and I are going to be great friends – what do you feel? Sometimes I think you like me – sometimes I am not so sure. Strange little secret person! Do you think that anything you could tell me about your life and your experience could shock me? You would not, my dear. I burn to know and sympathize and understand. I feel so strangely that we two are very alike in a way. At any rate, we will have courage ... Perhaps we even want the same things.[30]

Katherine heard and hated the note of patronage, but there is something both touching and perceptive about the Ottoline who tells her bold younger friend, 'perhaps we even want the same things'.

Garsington was described as being more like Crotchet Castle or Gryll Grange, the imaginary mansions in which Thomas Love Peacock assembled his characters for reckless conversation and intrigue, than like any place in the real world. Ottoline had, in fact, succeeded in her early ambition to surround herself with entertaining people; she had made her escape from the Cavendish-Bentincks triumphantly (although she kept on good terms with them and one of her brothers bought paintings by her friends) and established herself in the role of patroness, benefactress and muse. For five years she had inspired love in Bertrand Russell, who told her that she had not only given him the experience of passion, but actually made his mind work better. She had insisted on her freedom to conduct the affair, while at the same time refusing to abandon her marriage. It had not been easy, but it had worked, though for Ottoline the intellectual companionship had always been more important than the sexual part of the relationship. Russell grew gradually more and more restive as a result, and was beginning to look for other women; but this did not prevent him from being a constant visitor at Garsington.

The house, within bicycling distance of Oxford, was a stone Jacobean manor, and the garden was laid out with lawns, flowers in profusion, walks and ponds in which both fish and guests might swim. There were also peacocks and, according to one of the sharp-tongued guests,

Ottoline herself was not unlike one of her own peacocks, drifting about the house and terraces in strange, brightly coloured shawls and other floating garments, her unskilfully dyed red hair, her head tilted to the sky at the same angle as the birds' and her odd nasal voice and neighing laugh always seeming as if they might at any moment rise into one of those shattering calls of the peacocks.[31]

Combining her own flamboyant taste with a respect for the taste of her artistic friends, Ottoline had decorated the house with brilliantly coloured paint and fabrics. It was big enough to hold half a dozen guests at a time comfortably, with cottages for any extra (once Katherine was put into the governess's attic room: another world, she noted); and just as she mixed her colours, so she mixed her friends from the aristocracy and world of politics with other groups; the progressives and pacifists, poets, artists and writers, some famous and distinguished, others unknown and even needy.

Russell evidently put Katherine into his private mental collection of emancipated young women with good minds who might become sexually available. That summer he first met his future wife, Dora Black, a fellow of Girton College, Cambridge, and an enthusiastic devotee of free love; he also embarked on an affair with the actress Constance Malleson, without severing his links with Ottoline. Soon he was in pursuit of Katherine too. Lytton Strachey also noted that she was 'very amusing and sufficiently mysterious', or so he told Virginia Woolf, passing on Katherine's praises of her novel *The Voyage Out*, which Ottoline had lent her.

'Katherine Mansfield has dogged my steps for three years,' wrote Virginia.

I'm always on the point of meeting her, or of reading her stories, and I have never managed to do either ... Do arrange a meeting -- We go to Cornwall in September, and if I see anyone answering to your account on a rock or in the sea I shall accost her ...[32]

Only in September Katherine was no longer in Cornwall, because Brett had invited her first to stay in her studio flat in Earls Court and then to move in, with Murry, to a house she and her fellow artist Carrington were renting from Maynard Keynes, at 3 Gower Street in Bloomsbury. Brett christened this menagerie 'The Ark', and soon Russell and Lytton were constant visitors and Brett was lamenting that everyone came to see Katherine. When Ida arrived from Rhodesia after her two years' absence, she was soon made to feel *de trop*. For the time being she withdrew prudently to stay with other friends and find herself a job in an aeroplane factory in Chiswick, alongside several aristocratic ladies who had turned to war work.

Katherine was very occupied, if not with work, at least with her own popularity. Invitations came from Mary Hutchinson, from the Woolfs in Richmond (a first dinner that passed without comment on either side), from Lytton to tea-parties, from Ottoline for a weekend, from Russell to various private meetings. 'I should love to come to tea with you on Wednesday but I have an engagement which I must keep. I shall not be free before six. Supposing I were to come to your flat then?' she suggested boldly,[33] and in her next note she told him,

I have just re-read your letter and now my head aches with a kind of sweet excitement ... on Tuesday night I am going to ask you a great many questions.

I want to know more about your life – ever so many things ... There is time enough, perhaps, but I feel devilishly impatient at this moment ... I shall not read your letter again – It 'troubles' me too greatly – but thank you – Thank you for it.[34]

It is unlikely that this flirtation went unnoticed or unreported. Katherine disliked intensely being talked about and became very wary of Bloomsbury gossip, rightly fearing the malice of Lytton and Clive Bell. Of course, her own conversation was not notable for discretion or tenderness; Russell wrote later that 'her talk was marvellous, much better than her writing, especially when she was telling of things she was going to write, but when she spoke about people she was envious, dark and full of alarming penetration'.[35] Carrington also preferred Katherine's talk to her written word; she described her later as 'an extraordinary woman, witty and courageous, very much of an adventuress and with the language of a fish-wife in Wapping'.[36]

Christmas 1916 was Murry's second and Katherine's first at Garsington. All the inmates of the Ark were invited, plus Russell, Lytton and the young Aldous Huxley; Clive Bell was already in residence, officially working on the farm as a conscientious objector. Katherine took presents for everyone, including a blue enamel pot for Mlle Baillot, but Murry arrived without any. He made up for it by leaving ingratiating, not to say amorous, notes of apology on the pillows of Brett and his hostess. Christmas passed in parlour games and the performance of a mock-Russian playlet devised by Katherine, for which Lytton donned a false red beard; it was considered hilarious at the time, although the fragment that has survived makes one feel the performances must have enlivened the text considerably.

The Christmas party took the train back to London together. Katherine described in her thank-you letter to Ottoline how Russell took sheaves of documents connected with his work for conscientious objectors out of his green attaché case and spread them over her lap. She sounded cheerful, but she had already begun to withdraw from his pursuit; she had also decided to leave the Ark and find a flat of her own, independent of everyone, including Murry. Thus it is unlikely that her rejection of Russell was due to her love for Murry; rather it was a part of a general (and final) disenchantment with sexual entanglements, which had caused her so much damage.

Russell was not an easy man to control, as many of his wives and mistresses could testify; Murry's sexual timidity and ineptness, his biddable nature, made him a much safer bet for Katherine. In January she wrote to him, while she was phasing Russell out, 'My one over-whelming feeling is that we must both be free to write this year – and that even our life together must mark time for that.'[37] It was an affec-tionate letter, but absolutely insistent that she must have a place of her own in which to work, and ruthless in its evocation of their past housing difficulties:

Do you remember as vividly as I do ALL those houses ALL those flats ALL those rooms we have taken and withdrawn from ... For the time they have broken me and I must live from week to week and not feel bound ... Time is passing, and we cannot afford to waste another year.[38]

She had also been made to feel, by estate agents and by the refusal of St John Hutchinson to give her a reference for a flat lease, the humili-ations of her equivocal marital status. Respectability could extort its dues in London as well as in Wellington. At some time in 1917 it appears that Murry told his parents he and Katherine were married,[39] a lie which meant that, when they did marry, they had to conceal the fact from them.

For the moment, first she and then he moved to separate 'studios' in Chelsea, hers at 141A Old Church Street (the first studio flat she found was 'snatched' from her by a 'perfidious Pole', according to a letter she sent to Ottoline; one can't help speculating that it may have been Floryan[40]). It was a romantic place, squeezed in between two houses, with a huge, high north light at one end, glass doors at the other opening on to trees, a curtained-off bedroom and a gallery, where Katherine soon installed Ida, who sometimes surprised visitors by unexpectedly making signs of life from behind the curtain, or above.

Katherine was now embarked on several false starts. For a while she acted as a film extra, found it gruelling and gave up; as the winter went by, she had a cough, and her right hand was out of action, presumably with rheumatic pain. Then she planned a full-length play called *A Ship in the Harbour*; no trace of it survives, although she had reached the third act in April. Her old incubus Floryan leaves his trace in another way about this time, for there are fragments of translation from the Polish playwright Wyspiański in her hand and his; but she told no one about this. In the spring she began to write for another old associate, Orage, giving him a series of dialogue sketches, none of which approaches the standard of her 1911 and 1912 pieces in the *New Age*; they were crudely worked and do not suggest she would have made a dramatist, however acute her ear for speech. It is to be hoped that Ottoline did not see the *New Age*, for she was sending Katherine flowers and pressing invitations to stay, and receiving effusive 'literary' letters in return, just when the dialogue in which she figures as an affected and absurd hostess appeared.

The one good piece of work produced in 1917 was her reworking of 'The Aloe'. It came about through her developing friendship with Virginia Woolf. The approach of these two unstable, delicate and extraordinary women to one another was hesitant. Virginia's history since we last looked at it in 1908 had been quite as nightmarish as Katherine's, and she had advanced on her chosen path as a writer far less steadily than might have been predicted then.

In Bloomsbury circles she was for a long time somewhat overshadowed by her exuberant sister Vanessa, who, with her husband Clive Bell, provided the strongest focus for Virginia's emotions. She turned down proposals of marriage from (among others) Lytton Strachey in 1909 and Sydney Waterlow in 1910. She worked hard for the women's suffrage movement in that year, but also suffered a mental collapse severe enough to necessitate nursing-home treatment.

Recovered, she found and leased Asheham House, tucked into the downs behind the Sussex coast, for herself; but she still lived mostly in London, sometimes travelling with the Bells and keeping in their circle. When she did agree to marry, it was still within the confines of the group; Leonard Woolf had been at Cambridge with her brothers and Lytton and Sydney. Leonard's interests were political and literary, and his intention was to pursue them while devoting himself to keeping the balance of her precarious mental health; he resigned from the Colonial Office to marry. All this while, her first novel remained unfinished.

She and Leonard were married in August 1912. There are many indications that she felt herself sexually unfitted to be a wife, much as she loved her husband, and her mental health remained disturbed. The novel, however, was at last completed in March 1913. Later in the year, she attempted suicide and was again in a nursing-home for two months, and under the care of nurses and Leonard for many more. In 1914 she seemed to be better, but it was decreed by the doctors that she must not have any children: confirming, perhaps, her vision of herself as defective in womanliness.

In March 1915 *The Voyage Out* was finally published by the firm of her half-brother, Gerald Duckworth. (Readers familiar with her history will not need to be told that she later accused him in private memoirs of sexually abusing her as a small child.) Immediately after publication she had a severe relapse of madness – hallucinations, raving abuse of her attendants and Leonard, refusal to eat – and only in 1916 did she begin to live something approaching a normal life, dividing her time between a house in Richmond and Asheham, taking up her pen again as a reviewer and starting on another novel, always carefully and tenderly watched by Leonard for signs of strain.

In 1917 he suggested that they should set up a small printing and publishing business of their own in Richmond; his hope was to give Virginia an interest and occupation less emotionally draining than writing. She agreed, and it was called the Hogarth Press. Clearly, they were unlikely to attract established writers, and were on the lookout for those with their reputations still to be made. Katherine's name came forward as one of these.

At first, Virginia found Katherine 'cheap and hard' in her manner, 'unpleasant but forcible and utterly unscrupulous'.[41] Despite this ferocious judgement, she called on her in Old Church Street and asked for a story. Then, at the end of June, she invited Katherine to dinner *tête-à-tête*, and listened while she told stories of her past. Virginia was impressed by these adventures in the real world, but did not repeat them to her sister, merely saying, 'She seems to have gone every sort of hog since she was 17, which is interesting; I also think she has a much better idea of writing than most. She's an odd character.'[42] Katherine, for her part, told Ottoline,

I do like her tremendously ... I felt then for the first time the strange, trembling, glinting quality of her mind – and quite for the first time she seemed to me to be one of those Dostoevsky women whose 'innocence' has been hurt.[43]

It was a finely perceptive account.

Meanwhile, the story was submitted, accepted and renamed 'Prelude'. 'Prelude to what?' asked Lawrence irritably when he heard of it, although he and Katherine were exchanging thoroughly friendly letters again, and she boldly praised him to Ottoline too. The Woolfs were enthusiastic about the story, but before Katherine could visit them again both women were ill, she with rheumatism so bad that the doctor hinted, amid many thumps and bangs as he examined her, she should be wintering in the sunshine. She told Virginia she felt too ill and depressed to copy-type 'Prelude'.

When she was better, she went, without Murry, for a long weekend at Asheham. Lytton Strachey was a fellow guest, and Edward Garnett came for the day. Virginia and Katherine walked on the downs, observing thistledown, butterflies and many aeroplanes overhead. The war was entering its third year. The harvest was in full swing, and the sun shone; Katherine stayed on until Wednesday, and wrote an ecstatic thank-you letter in which she praised Virginia's latest story, declared that the two of them had very similar aims as writers, and defended herself against Bloomsbury gossip. Leonard liked Katherine, admired her work and approved the friendship.

The auguries again seemed good. 'Prelude' was among her finest stories, and her longest yet. It is a description of a family moving into a new house in the country, written in a series of short sections without explanatory or linking passages; the reader is simply plunged directly into one fresh scene, one character's thoughts, after another. It is obvious that the inspiration is taken from the Beauchamp family and Katherine's childhood, but there is nothing confessional or indulgent about the story, in which the mother's detachment from the children is clear in a few lines, the children's chief excitement is to see a duck beheaded for dinner, and the women of the family are full of dissatisfactions and dreams of escape. Both in its setting – which is unstated, and disquietingly English-seeming without being English – and its handling of mood and character, it is boldly original. The lack of stamina which prevented her from producing a novel encouraged other virtues: speed, economy, clarity. They became her hallmark, admired and imitated by later writers.

In October Katherine dined at Richmond and was given a few pages of proofs and high praise from the Woolfs. When Brett asked her about the story's form, she answered, 'As far as I know its more or less my own invention ... I don't feel anything but intensely a longing to serve my subject as well as I can'.[44] She was in a state of high excitement. Then fell the blows.

The first was that Murry became ill. He had lost weight and had pleurisy. He was also depressed, and the doctor said he must stop work and rest in the country. Katherine, fired with maternal concern, wrote at once to Ottoline, asking her to have him to stay. The next day she received a telegram which read: 'OF COURSE DELIGHTED HAVE

OTTOLINE'.[45] Katherine wouldn't go, but she saw him off and urged his hostess, and Brett, who was often there, to look after him. Murry was soon on the mend. Katherine went for a weekend at the beginning of December, and caught a chill.

By the middle of December she was very ill, her bones aching till she felt 'a crawling thing without the power of doing anything except cursing my fate',[46] her temperature soaring, Ida irritating her with cups of hot milk, the doctor on the way. 'Dry pleurisy,' said the doctor ('an old complaint of mine!'). He bound up her chest and told her she must stay in bed and not even be driven in a warm car either to Garsington or to Aunt Belle, who appeared with Chaddie to succour her.

To Anne Drey she confessed that she had been told she must never winter in England again or 'I may become consumptive'.[47] The next day she wrote to Murry at Garsington, where he was staying for Christmas again, that she had a 'SPOT' in her right lung; that she must go to the south of France; that she could not work; and that she wished they could be married before she went. She also wrote, and underlined: *'Burn my letters'*.[48]

Murry returned to London now, and he and Ida helped her to prepare to leave for Bandol. Ida asked for a month's leave from her factory in order to accompany her, but at the last minute the Foreign Office refused her permission to go. Katherine made light of everything. 'I am not an invalid really,' she told Ottoline,[49] and she and Murry went for a last visit to Garsington. After this he returned to his flat in Redcliffe Road and his job at the War Office, and she spent three days with her sister Chaddie. Then she left for France. The tuberculosis that had seemed to threaten Murry had alighted instead on her.

Tuberculosis is an infectious disease. The question naturally arises as to whom Katherine caught it from. There is one glaringly obvious candidate. In the first winter of the war, and again in the spring of 1916, she lived in close proximity with the Lawrences, sometimes staying overnight at their cottage, and eating many meals in common. Lawrence was tubercular, although he did not acknowledge it. Frieda and Murry were both robust enough to be resistant, or may have had childhood infections which immunized them effectively against the disease; but Katherine, already chronically ill, was vulnerable. This may have been the real *Blutbrüderschaft*, more sinister than Lawrence had ever intended.

12

1918: 'A GREAT BLACK BIRD'

■

Katherine set off alone, armed with little more than a doctor's certificate to allow her to travel across warring France. She had five years of life left, in which the old symptoms of her gonorrhoea would continue to torture her, while the new symptoms of tuberculosis would gradually destroy her. The comments of her friends and her own observations chart the steady weight loss, the rings slipping on her fingers, the face once plump growing drawn and haggard, the breath shorter, the temper blacker, the freedom even to move across a room slowly taken from her. At the same time, almost as though it were fattening on her sickness, her fame grew and began to blossom. Often she was too ill and low-spirited to work, but then there would be a burst of literally feverish writing, producing some perfectly judged and achieved stories. The quality remained uneven, and she was never satisfied with what she did, but she produced enough for two more collections in her lifetime, many fragments, many reviews and her poignantly allusive journal. Her letters to Murry fill up a larger volume than any of these; unfortunately, they only rarely show her at her best, and are sometimes of more clinical than literary interest, cruelly and repetitively revealing the pathological basis of her moods.

The ninety-eight letters Katherine wrote to Murry over the next three months, however, form the most vividly self-revealing of all the sequences she addressed to him; they add up to more than 50,000 words, a far bigger slab of prose than any of her stories. The two blows of first his illness and then her own had revived her feeling for him strongly, and suddenly she found herself dependent on him as never before, as she faced the shock and stress of her condition. In effect, these letters chart the transformation of a young woman expecting three months' convalescence in the sun in preparation for her wedding into someone who has felt and acknowledged the mark of approaching death. Just before she left, on the dark January Sunday afternoon, she and Murry made love; when she arrived back in April, a stone lighter, he was at first too appalled and frightened to embrace her: 'When I met her at the station, she was barely recognizable. She looked as though she had been for months in some fearful prison.'[1]

Kathrine always loved an outward journey, and her letters begin in a flurry of pleasure: the stormy Channel, the snug berth, snow on the ground at Le Havre and, for all the wartime delays and unheated trains, marvellous French food to arouse greed (seven sorts of cheese, she reported delightedly) and a blue-and-yellow brocaded room at the Hôtel Terminus by St Lazare, prudently booked in advance (this was as well, for Paris was full). But as she travelled south the next day, while her impressions remained sharply etched, the pleasure drained out. In its place came first disappointment and then fear. She had forgotten how cold it could be in the Midi in winter; only the sunny days at Bandol were fixed in her memory now. The hotel there was under new management, and even old acquaintances mysteriously failed to recognize her at first: '*Vous êtes beaucoup changée ... Vous n'avez plus votre air de p'tite gosse.*'[2] The journey had exhausted her: 'I feel like a fly who has been dropped into the milk jug and fished out again, but it's still too milky and drowned to start cleaning up.'[3] Then pain settled on her: 'My left lung aches and aches ... It is like an appalling *burn*. Sometimes, if I lift my arm over my head it seems to give it relief. What is it?'[4] Two weeks later, she wrote: 'There is a great black bird flying over me, and I am so frightened he'll settle – so terrified. I don't know exactly what kind he is.'[5]

It took only two weeks more for her to find out exactly what kind of bird it was. Jumping from her bed in the morning to look out of the window, she coughed into her handkerchief and found it red. It was her first haemorrhage. 'When I saw the bright arterial blood I nearly had a fit'; but her letter, frenetically bright too, was all reassurance for Murry:

Look here! I can't leave this place till April. It's no earthly go. I can't and mustn't – see. Can't risk a draught or a chill, and mustn't walk. I've got a bit of a temperature and I'm not so fat as when I came – and, Bogey, this is *not* serious, does not keep me in bed, is absolutely easily curable, but I have been spitting a bit of blood. See? Of course, I'll tell you. But if you worry – unless you laugh like Rib does – I can't tell you: you mustn't type it on the typewriter or anything like that, my precious, my own – and after all, Lawrence used to: so did, I think, Belle Trinder.*[6]

Pulmonary tuberculosis works in this fashion: it is an infection, produced when a tubercle bacillus gets into the lungs. In lucky cases, the body's natural resistance is strong enough to clamp down on the bacillus and lock it up in surrounding tissue, rendering it harmless; but when this fails to happen – in a person with low resistance – the bacillus proceeds to form large, cheesy masses in the lung, which break down the respiratory tissues and produce cavities. As the process continues, it eats into the bronchial passages; the tubercle bacillus can then be coughed or breathed out, and the sufferer becomes a source of infection to other people in turn. The disease advances further, eroding blood vessels. It is this which produces the haemorrhages.

Once advanced so far, tuberculosis was usually expected to be fatal in Katherine's day. Today, of course, it is chemically curable; but even then cures were sometimes achieved. They depended on encouraging the body's natural resistance. The body itself had to seal off the tubercle bacillus even at this late stage, leaving the patient with severely scarred but still working lungs. The only way to promote this self-healing process was by rest, a good diet and nursing care. For this it was not necessary to go abroad. Indeed, the first decade of this century saw the establishment of many sanatoria in the British Isles, and a determined policy of public education aimed at prevention, diagnosis and early treatment of the illness. From 1912 on there was a National Tuberculosis Scheme, and notification of the disease was compulsory throughout Britain. Much stress was laid on its infectious nature, which had been established only with the discovery of the bacillus in 1882, and on the importance of thorough disinfection of rooms in which consumptive people had been living, and objects handled by them. Special clinics and hospitals (and in some countries schools) were set up to combat infection by isolating the sick from the community, since it was believed you could catch tuberculosis even by inhabiting a room previously lived in by a patient, through dry bacilli in the dust.

Wintering by the Mediterranean was the old palliative for the disease – dry and warm air being considered beneficial – but modern treatment

---

* Murry, who had been reading the letters of Keats for the first time, may have recalled his remark at the same juncture: 'I know the colour of that blood; it is arterial blood. I cannot be deceived in that colour. That drop of blood is my death warrant.' Rib was Katherine's Japanese doll.

did not depend on travelling south. Instead it involved a strict regime of rest, fresh air, good food and nursing care, almost the exact opposite of what Katherine achieved by her journey. Had she been advised to adopt a sanatorium regime in the British Isles from the winter of 1917, it is just possible that she might have allowed her body to cure itself of tuberculosis, although in all likelihood she was already too debilitated; but it does seem that she might have been better advised under the circumstances, and when later she had better advice, she chose to ignore it.

At this moment, Murry commands sympathy. As he explained later – and the truth of his account is clear from her letters – she wanted him to join in a pretence that she did not have the illness. By ignoring it, by accepting only such doctors' advice as she chose, they could somehow make it go away. After all, she may have thought, how much good had doctors done her existing chronic illness? Katherine's courage was never in doubt, but here it verges on insanity, we may think now. Yet at no time did either Murry or Ida have the strength of will to overcome her determination not to accept the fact of tuberculosis, with all that it meant. The idea of a sanatorium, which would entail separation, loss of freedom and enforced idleness, struck her as being like 'a second lunatic asylum', she told Ida.[7] (Lawrence, of course, rejected the idea too, and died of his tuberculosis slowly, but Gertler, who had several spells in British sanatoria, appears to have recovered.)

For the rest of her life, Katherine maintained two entirely disparate sets of beliefs in her head: one that she was incurably ill and indeed dying, the other that she would recover, have children, live in the country with Murry and be perfectly happy working and gardening in a rural paradise. It is not unusual for sick people to react in this way, but Katherine's insistence that Murry should join in the fantasy of recovery made things increasingly difficult for him. Had he been older or wiser, or a completely different sort of man, he might have been strong enough to play the game in a different way. His way was not an appealing one. Sad as it is to read their plans for an impossible future, it is worse to eavesdrop on their mutual flattery, which becomes part of the fantasy. She tells him he is a 'Great Poet', he declares that they are both geniuses. Both like to see themselves as innocent children in a corrupt world; at the same time they are the true heirs to the great tradition of English literature. Murry decides they have extra-sensory powers too, since they are so often thinking about the same topic at the same time; and he urges her to preserve his letters – 'I think they may be important to us one day'[8] – in contrast to her '*Burn my letters*' of December. Poor Katherine: one especially cruel dream was that she was pregnant. In fact, her periods had stopped for the simple, sinister reason of her illness and weight loss. She noticed grey hair appearing at her temples. She was twenty-nine.

Spurred by anxiety, Ida had again sought leave from her factory, and she had sat and wept remorselessly in front of the authorities until they relented, bent the regulations and gave her the travel permit she needed. Although Katherine had been wishing for her company, by the time she arrived at the Hôtel Beau Rivage in mid February she precipitated an attack of violent hatred and resentment. 'What *have* you come for?' asked Katherine at her iciest. Off went letters to Murry, accusing Ida not merely of stupidity and insensitivity but of ghoulishly battening on her illness, of wanting her death, of being a cannibal and – as though it were part of the same constellation of hideous vices – of being greedy. 'I hate fat people,' explained Katherine, forgetting (or perhaps remembering) how her mother had chided her for being a fat little girl. Now she herself was being urged to eat, to rest, to build up her weight; and she said she appreciated the French food, but mostly she smoked cigarettes and drank cup after cup of black coffee. No wonder she suffered nights of insomnia. In her better moments, she saw that her rage against Ida was pathological, and more than once she likened it to Lawrence's rages against Frieda.

Ida was not the only object of hatred. She and Murry vied in abusing 'H.L.' (Her Ladyship, i.e., Ottoline) to one another. At the same time, Murry was seeing her, and on good enough terms to elicit a comment from Virginia ('she's got Murry back again');[9] and Katherine was sending her affectionate letters. It was not a pretty piece of behaviour in either of them. Katherine also took the French nation as a whole into contempt for the time being, her fellow guests for their coarse digestive habits, the soldiers posted along the coast for behaving like soldiers, the doctor she visited for his sexual flattery and insinuating remarks about venereal disease. She told Murry that she found 'corruption' everywhere, and wished to cry out against it in her writing; but the corruption was more within than without.

She described the story called '*Je ne parle pas français*', which she wrote and sent to him in February, as 'a cry against corruption'. Leaving aside her own physical and mental state, this remark bears little relation to the work as it appears to an unprejudiced reader. She also said the story was 'a tribute to Love'; in fact, it is about a voyeuristic but fairly harmless gigolo and an act of treachery committed by a character easily recognizable as Murry himself. Either Katherine thought she could get away with anything she said to Murry, or the gap between the artist and the tale was wider than usual: 'Never trust the artist, trust the tale,' said Lawrence wisely.

She sent Murry the story in two instalments, and he lavished praise on the first, which set up the character of the narrator, Raoul Duquette. He is a young café-haunting Parisian writer, loosely modelled – or so she volunteered – on two of Murry's rivals in the past, Carco and Gertler. Duquette is small, vain, commonplace and pleasing enough to women to earn his living as a gigolo; Katherine was at pains to establish his style and to make him an entertaining figure. Some of her dramatic devices are crude – Duquette's 'clever' remarks followed by self-deprecating corrections become tedious – but on the whole the story is effective in establishing his character and milieu of small cafés, and the seedy Parisian sexual underworld.

The second half of the story, which must have nonplussed Murry, introduced Duquette's English friend Dick Harmon, who arrives in Paris with an English girl-friend. Harmon contrives to be both wet and treacherous, abandoning the girl (who is known as 'Mouse', a name Murry sometimes used for Katherine) after having brought her to Paris and compromised her, since she has told her family and friends she is getting married. Harmon leaves a cowardly letter in the hotel where they are installed, giving his mother as his explanation for his departure: this, as Murry cannot fail to have been aware, recalls his own lies to his Parisian girl in 1911, which he had confessed to Katherine. However much he winced and swallowed, dignity dictated his response:

I wasn't prepared for the tragic turn of '*Je ne parle pas*', and it upset me – I'm an awful child. But it's lovely, lovely. I must read it right through again to taste fully the growth of the quality of that ending out of that beginning. The lift is amazing. And how the devil you get that sharp outline for Mouse I don't know.[10]

Katherine inquired anxiously if he were disappointed; and though it is hard to speak of comedy at this moment in her life, there was something irresistibly grotesque about their exchange. Mouse was certainly calculated to appeal to Murry (helpless, tiny, exquisite, etc.) and he insisted on regarding her as in some sense the 'secret' Katherine whom only he knew – the 'good' Katherine. A moment's thought tells us that this shy victim, entirely at the mercy of two equivocal men, was as far from Katherine herself – the Katherine who travelled boldly alone, who went into cafés in her wide-brimmed hat, with a thorough appreciation of the admiration she evoked from groups of unknown men – as it is possible to imagine. Yet equally, the plight of Mouse, 'abandoned' abroad by the man she depends on, can be read as a signal of Katherine's view of her current situation, as a reproach to Murry. Twist it as he might, Murry could not come well out of '*Je ne parle pas français*': and the true Katherine was to be identified with Duquette rather than Mouse, for it was Katherine who liked to sit alone in cafés, speculating about Madame and the waiters and the characters of the passers-by, savouring the time of day and the dramas of the clients; Katherine who was making a career as a writer, and Katherine who had a secret and disreputable past. But that was not something she would say, or Murry would allow himself to think.[11]

If '*Je ne parle pas français*' was a deeply subversive signal about her own complex nature and very mixed feelings about Murry, her letters continued to express entire faith in his love and literary judgement. She sent him next a purely sentimental story of children, 'Sun and Moon', and then 'Bliss', another study of a treacherous man, this time set among smart young London aesthetes. It is an uncertainly aimed piece of writing, starting as a reworking of a sketch that appeared in the *New Age* in 1912 ('Mr and Mrs Devoted') and culminating in the wife's discovery of her husband's infidelity with a friend for whom she too has a special feeling, not quite erotic but certainly passionate. The satire is too broad to be funny, and the finale fails to be poignant, but there is something powerful at work in the harsh picture of the young heroine and her feeling for her possessions: house, garden, carefully arranged dinner, boyish husband, baby whom she fights the nurse over. The almost hallucinatory intensity of some of the passages strikes with great force, if not always pleasantly.

She sent 'Bliss' straight off to Murry again for his comments, and this time he did offer some tactfully worded criticism of details, which she accepted. She told him at this time that she did not expect to make money from her serious work, only from light stories and ones about children (a prophecy which did not come to pass). Increasingly now, she discussed her reading with him, in the tone of a writer who reads to learn. Murry sent her his review copies of modern French novelists (from *The Times Literary Supplement*, where he now wrote regularly), but she asked him particularly for Dickens. 'I do not read him *idly*,' she said.[12] *Our Mutual Friend*, in which she particularly relished the Veneerings, *Edwin Drood*, *Nicholas Nickleby* and *Master Humphrey's Clock* were all read in Bandol, as well as some Mrs Gaskell, and English sixteenth-century poets.

There was plenty of time for reading: mornings and evenings had to be spent in bed. As the spring flowers bloomed, she was tempted out for short walks, but mostly she was content with the bouquets brought to her room by an attentive young Corsican maid. Ida earned nothing but scorn and hatred, as a living reminder of her past, and emblem of her present dependence and separation from Murry. Katherine was now determinedly looking forward to being married and setting her disordered past behind her, coming into the fold where both her family and his would give their healing love and approval. She sent presents and messages to his mother, and her own now became 'Mummy' again. She and Murry exchanged love-talk as embarrassing to eavesdrop on as all such talk is (though Murry did not mind publishing it); but her need to believe in the validity of their love grew with her anxiety about her own condition.

Although it had been on doctor's advice she had sought a warmer climate, even on her journey south she had begun to hear contrary opinions about its possible benefits. Two women in the train recounted with gruesome relish the speedy deterioration of a young friend of theirs who had travelled to the coast with nothing worse than bronchitis, and died within weeks of a haemorrhage brought on by the fatal climate. The Protestant graveyards of the coast too gave grim testimony to the many young patients from the north who had succumbed there. Even before her own haemorrhage Katherine had begun to think of returning to London sooner than originally planned; one reason she gave was her anxiety about the risks Murry was suffering from air raids. But travel was severely restricted because of the war, the French wishing to discourage frivolous holiday visits, and in principle she was not allowed back until she had been on the coast for three months.

Impatient with all this, instead of sitting it out, concentrating on putting on weight and enjoying the improving weather, she threw herself and Ida into a series of manoeuvres designed to get permission to return to England early. They included fake telegrams from Murry about a sick mother, exhausting visits to the authorities in Marseilles, and a determined assault on a susceptible doctor by Katherine, dressed to the nines, made up and scented with the perfume she had bought for her wedding. The doctor, duly impressed, gave her a travel chit, and the two women left Bandol for Paris; but Ida's suitcase was lost on the way, and when they arrived in the capital on 22 March they found that the city was under bombardment and no one was allowed to leave.

They went to the Hôtel Select in the place de la Sorbonne, taking rooms at the very top. Apart from the obvious folly of a lung-damaged person having six flights of stairs to deal with, they were in some danger from the German shells, which were hitting Paris every eighteen minutes or so. Katherine was frantic with dismay at being stuck out of England and treated Murry to outpourings that sound more like screams than letters at times, so great is her rage and self-pity. 'This is not Paris: this is Hell,' she told him.[13] It was necessary to report to the police every day, and there were also daily visits to be made to Thomas Cook in case there was any mail; but Murry's letters were not getting through, the authorities seemed to Katherine to take perverse delight in telling her she would be delayed for a long time yet, and her money was running out. In her more coherent moments, she described the wailing sirens, the sight of houses ripped open, the sheltering in ice-cold cellars, which were crammed with bodies and thick with cigarette smoke. These were so horrible that after a while she decided not to bother to go down. She raged against Ida, when Ida was not running errands for her, and spent the nights playing Racing Demon in her room.

The two women celebrated Easter together by going to work in a canteen under the Gare du Nord, partly to pass the time safely underground, partly to earn some money; but it was too exhausting for Katherine, and after two days she gave up. She told Murry she was tired and frightened; he was equally wretched, having been given a week's leave which he had expected to spend with her, but now instead finding himself alone in London, knowing she was under bombardment, ill and miserable in Paris, and there was little he could do. He did, however, think of asking Sydney Waterlow (at the Foreign Office) to help and eventually, after Katherine had contrived to borrow money from someone she disliked – either Beatrice Hastings or Carco – Sydney's influence was brought to bear and they were allowed to leave for England.

Once on the way, Katherine suddenly softened to Ida, and they played Patience happily together on the boat. 'Try and forget that sad and sick Katie whose back ached in her brain or whose brain ached in her back,' she wrote apologetically a few days later, when Ida had returned to her munitions factory.[14]

Her reunion with Murry, dwelt on in every letter for the past month, was not as she had dreamt. He was all too obviously aghast at the physical change in her and, she suspected, frightened of becoming infected with tuberculosis himself. The fear was not unreasonable, since the disease was known to be infectious; but his way of showing it hardly squared with the romantic image of their perfect love insisted on so often in his letters. Instead of taking her in his arms, he turned fearfully aside and put a handkerchief to his lips.

She went with him to his flat in Redcliffe Road to await the final stage of her divorce. After some false starts, it came through at last on 2 May (the same day that her old admirer Russell was sent to prison for attacking Government policy). Katherine summoned Brett to be a witness with a hectically cheerful letter.

It will be Great Fun, Larks and Jollifications. I am wearing, of course, a Simple Robe of White Crêpe de Chine and Pearl Butterfly presented by *our dear Queen*. Murry, naturally, top hat and carnation buttonhole.
Blessings on thee – I hope thou wilt be Godmother to my First Half Dozen –
Katherine.
P.S. We have decided (owing to the great war) to have a string band without brasses.[15]

Ida, apparently, was not invited to the wedding, or if she was, she did not choose to attend. Brett came up from Garsington, Fergusson was the other witness, and on 3 May Katherine and Murry were at last married, at lunchtime, at the Kensington Registry Office in Marloes Road where the Lawrences had become man and wife four years earlier. Katherine continued to wear the ring Frieda had given her then, but the two couples were out of touch, the Lawrences now in Derbyshire, struggling against poverty, ill health and bitterness, for they had been banished from Cornwall for 'military' reasons.

By Murry's own testimony, he felt nothing but anguish at his own wedding, and unhappiness during the following weeks when Katherine tried to 'keep house' for him in his rooms, which were, he said, gloomy and sunless, quite unsuited for one in her condition, and my one preoccupation was to get her away from them. She was ... almost suspicious of my eagerness to find a different place for her. I was 'trying to get rid of her'.[16]

To the world she put on a brave front. Lunching with Virginia at Richmond a few days after the wedding, she began by pretending that her marriage was purely one of convenience. 'After a good deal of worrying by me,' wrote Virginia to Ottoline,

she confessed that she was immensely happy married to Murry, though for some reason she makes out that marriage is of no more importance than engaging a charwoman. Part of her fascination lies in the obligation she is under to say absurd things.[17]

Virginia also noted, with anxious eyes, how ill she seemed; and she declared to several people her warm feelings for this friend who seemed suddenly as vulnerable as herself, and her confidence in Katherine's stature as a writer.

13

'HE OUGHT NOT TO HAVE MARRIED'

■

Just before her wedding, Katherine wrote to Ida to say that her Chelsea doctor had told her she definitely had consumption; but he appreciated, or so she claimed, that a sanatorium would kill her faster than it could cure her. He suggested a cure at home, on the condition that home should be at least on the heights of London, Hampstead or Highgate, and with this in mind she and Murry went to look for a suitable place. They came upon a narrow, semi-detached house of grey brick, high up over East Heath Road.

Like most of her homes, 2 Portland Villas existed from the start in two distinct versions in Katherine's mind. In one, it was an ugly monster, nicknamed 'The Elephant' (because of its colour, perhaps – there is no other apparent reason) and disliked because it threatened to absorb the money she and Murry were trying to set aside for their dream house in the country. In the other, it was the charming house it actually appears today, elegant, tall and airy, with pretty windows under lintels shaped like pointed eyebrows, its rooms opening off a staircase into which the light and sunshine enter freely all day long. The south-facing garden at the back possessed a vine, and from the front windows there were views over the heath and the whole of London spread out below.

While they hesitated over taking it, Katherine went down with pleurisy again. Her old friend Anne was in Cornwall with her husband for the summer, and she suggested Katherine should join them at Looe, a small resort west of Plymouth where she had found a perfect hotel on the sea, while Murry sorted out the question of where they were to live. Giving way to Murry's urgings, Katherine agreed to go, and Anne promised to devote herself to being a cheerful companion. Once more Katherine set off south, acknowledging that her presence seemed to torture her husband more than her absence.

Anne made a fuss of her, and arranged for the staff of the Headland Hotel to provide extra food for the invalid. 'I am always astonished, amazed, that people should be kind. It makes me want to weep,' she wrote to Murry.[1] Within a week, though, driven by her demons, she was raging. The hotel was too genteel; the guests changed into formal evening clothes for dinner, and raised their eyebrows at the spectacle of Katherine smoking between coughing bouts. She needed a sitting-room, not just a bedroom. She hoped Anne would find her other rooms, but then too, 'I can't really talk to Anne at all';[2] she was insensitive, tasteless, simply too healthy – '*trop forte* pour moi' – and she had a husband dancing attendance. The implied reproach is always there.

Another few days, and both Anne and the hotel had become acceptable again. Katherine was appalled by her own violent swings of mood, but she could not control them; nor could she stop herself bombarding Murry with letters that have, at times, the force of a physical assault. His responses were those of a marionette, dancing helplessly as she pulled the strings this way and that, now reassuring him, now complaining, now angry; now wanting him to take Portland Villas, now set against it. And if they did take it, how would they run it? Ida, so often reviled to Murry, must now be accepted by him as an essential part of their lives, and invited to come and be 'housekeeper'.

Katherine did not scruple to put pressure on Ida 'for the sake of all that has been';[3] she was already her secret confidante when she lost weight, when she needed money, or iron pills; and, once it was settled that they would take Portland Villas, she was persuaded to leave her job, which she enjoyed, and take on the uncongenial task of trying to run a house in which her fellow residents had decidedly equivocal feelings about her. She had misgivings, and they were justified. Katherine's instructions for the decorations of the house provided a very plain estimate of her view of the relative status and needs of the three of them: her two rooms were to be painted white; for Murry's bedroom she suggested 'a delicate flowery paper'; and for Ida's north-facing room at the top of the house, green paint, or if that was too cold, yellow.

All the while, in Cornwall, her 'spinal rheumatism' was so bad that at times she thought it might paralyse her with its 'devilish, devilish' pain. The doctors who visited her were kindly but wholly ineffectual. She got more comfort from the homely ministrations of the old Cornish woman who did her room and brought her breakfast tray. One morning, seeing Katherine was suffering, Mrs Honey offered to recite to her the poetry she had learnt as a child long ago, forty-odd verses of 'The Death of Moses'. Katherine listened, and, moved by this simple goodness, likened the old woman to a character from a Wordsworth poem. Mrs Honey also urged her to have children; it was sad advice, for in June she lost the hope she might be pregnant. The child that would not come was mourned obliquely in the increasingly frequent talk of dolls.*

Anne took Katherine for expeditions along the glittering summer coast, and painted her, a bold portrait in a brick-red frock, black eyes and fringe, lipstick mouth, a sense of strain in the pose of the head on the thin neck. Out of the sunshine, at night in her room,

I walk up and down, look at the bed, look at the writing table, look in the glass and am frightened of that girl with burning eyes, think, 'Will my candle last until it's light?' and then sit for a long time staring at the carpet – so long that it's only a fluke that one ever looks up again. And Oh God, this terrifying thought that one must die, and may be going to die. I have really suffered such AGONIES of loneliness and illness combined that I'll never be quite whole again. I don't think I'll ever believe that they won't recur – that some grinning Fate won't suggest that I go away by myself to get well of something.[4]

She was not exaggerating: Bruges, Bavaria, Bandol, Cornwall made a long litany, not yet completed.

Murry worked on at the War Office. Ottoline was still pressing the bailiff's cottage on them. The Woolfs were still printing *Prelude*. Murry went to dinner with them in June, and Virginia noted that he appeared 'pale as death, with gleaming eyes, & a crouching way at table that seemed to proclaim extreme hunger or despair'.[5] He told them that he had been near suicide at Christmas and had since kept going by worrying out a formula he called 'indifferentism' which involved keeping his conscience 'in two layers'.

Virginia sent Katherine letters, flowers and cigarettes. Privately she doubted whether *Prelude* would sell more than one hundred copies, but in July it was finally published, and Virginia noted her satisfaction: 'it has the living power, the detached existence of a work of art'.[6] Ottoline loyally sent a copy to Russell in prison. He did not care for it, and took the opportunity to warn Ottoline against Katherine's malice. Ottoline was not much moved by this tip, perhaps understandably; there was simply too much treacherous talk and behaviour in their circle to allow

* That Katherine understood this herself is obvious from an entry in her journal for 18 October 1920, in which she described a desperate spinster pretending that her doll is a love-child.

one to drop friends for that reason. But Virginia's estimate of Katherine's abilities suffered when she read her story 'Bliss' in the *English Review* in August. Virginia found it superficially smart, poor, cheap and badly written, or so she irritatedly wrote in her diary on first reading it; still, she did not allow this adverse judgement to spoil their friendship. Something about Katherine, so alien in background and character, so fixed on her work, drew and fascinated the older woman.

At the end of June, Murry went to Cornwall for a week's holiday. Katherine explained carefully in advance that she was taking a separate room for him, perhaps to reassure him that he would not be too intimately exposed to her tuberculosis, perhaps also to keep her pain from him. She asked Ida to be at Redcliffe Road to meet them when they returned together, evidently feeling it impossible to cope without her help; and from mid July until the end of August, she stayed in hot, unhealthy Chelsea, too ill to make a proposed visit to Virginia at Asheham, or to go to Garsington, where the Morrells had quarrelled with Murry temporarily over his unkind review of their protégé, Siegfried Sassoon. Sometimes she was feverish, sometimes she was unable to walk at all. A 'doctor' came to give her electric treatment for the pain in her joints. She told Ida, 'You see I am never one single hour without pain. If it's not my lungs it is (far more painful) my back. And then my legs *ache* . . .'[7]

Her own suffering doubtless affected her reaction to the news of her mother's death, received in mid August. She grieved, calling her 'a most exquisite, perfect little being – something between a star and a flower', a description which sits a trifle uneasily on the real woman who had dumped her in Bavaria to have a baby by herself, and even in her recently revised will confirmed her disinheritance. But Katherine insisted on Mrs Beauchamp's perfections of character to Brett, Virginia and Ottoline in turn. Approaching her own thirtieth birthday, and with the shadow of her own death in her mind, Katherine wanted to be reconciled to her memories of her mother. An idealized mother could be turned to as a model and a comforter; the process is similar to that shown by Proust, who makes his narrator's mother begin to identify with his dead grandmother. Katherine was overjoyed when her father told her later (in 1920), 'you're your mother again'. She consented to go and stay with her mother's sister Belle Trinder, in Tadworth, an unusual gesture of family feeling for her; and from Belle's she moved into Portland Villas.

It was probably Belle who alerted Harold Beauchamp to Katherine's condition, so that he arranged for Sydney Beauchamp, now a very successful doctor indeed, to make a professional call on her in October. In the course of the autumn she saw at least four doctors. The first specialist, summoned by Murry, impressed her by his intelligence, and told her that she must go into a sanatorium, not necessarily abroad, but simply to have the discipline and nursing which would allow her lungs to heal; her condition was 'serious but recoverable'. To Murry he said further that she had at most four years to live if she did not follow this advice. Ten days later, on her thirtieth birthday, came Sydney Beauchamp in his silk hat, who offered the consoling words, 'Well, dear, of course you won't make old bones,'[8] and gave the same advice about the sanatorium. By now she was feeling so ill, with 'a terrible boiling sensation' that she thought she might be dying. She turned to a doctor Stonham, recommended by Virginia; and he confirmed again that both her lungs were tubercular, and advised her to spend at least a year in Switzerland.

Still Katherine went on looking for a doctor, until she found one who gave her the advice she wanted to hear: Victor Sorapure, an Edinburgh-trained gynaecologist who had practised for some years in America and was now a consultant at Hampstead General Hospital. She saw him at the end of November. He was recommended by Anne Drey, and Katherine took to him because he allowed time to talk with her. 'He helped me not only to bear pain but suggested that perhaps bodily ill-health is necessary, a repairing process and he was always telling me to consider how man plays but a part in the history of the world.'[9] He also accepted her reluctance to go into a sanatorium as reasonable (he died of tuberculosis himself in 1933). Then he offered to treat her arthritis, and began a course of ferocious injections intended to relieve it. For a while she believed they helped. Ida misleadingly wrote in her memoir that Katherine was cured by Sorapure, but, since she was still suffering the same pains in 1919 and, indeed, right to the end of her life, the treatment cannot have been successful. The symptoms may have seemed less fierce for a while because, presumably at Sorapure's suggestion, she started regular doses of an opium-based medicine at this time too.

This is how she appeared to Virginia when she called at the Hampstead house in November:

Katherine was up but husky and feeble, crawling about the room like an old woman. How far she is ill, one cant say. She impresses one a little unfavourably at first – then more favourably. I think she has a kind of childlikeness somewhere which has been much disfigured, but still exists. Illness, she said, breaks down one's privacy so that one cant write – the long story she has written breathes nothing but hate. Murry and the Monster watch and wait on her, till she hates them both she trusts no one; she finds no 'reality'.*[10]

Ida also described the domestic side of life at Portland Villas as she saw it. She took Katherine breakfast and lunch on a tray, and brought meals to her visitors. Katherine had no compunction about degrading her to the status of a servant; she asked her to wait at table without introducing her, and gave orders over her head (Ida was meant to be the housekeeper) directly to the maids, Gertie and Violet, who came in daily, and the cook, who lived in but then had to be sacked for drinking. Ida lit the fires, dusted and polished, did the shopping, made clothes for Katherine and received her scoldings if lunch was late. During the day Katherine sat in her own white study, with a huge muff to keep her feet warm, a yellow-painted table to work on and two windows bringing in the afternoon sun. When she was in a good mood, she could be high-spirited. Murry's brother Richard, a frequent guest, remembered how one day, when the man next door played his gramophone in the garden, she knew all the operatic songs he put on, and supplied appropriate gestures at the window. Perhaps she thought of Garnet and the Moody-Manners. She liked music halls just as much, and struck Richard as a true entertainer and extrovert, 'very enmeshed with life'; he thought she and Gertler were similar in character. His account fits in well with Leonard Woolf's impressions of her:

By nature, I think, she was gay, cynical, amoral, ribald, witty. When we first knew her, she was extraordinarily amusing. I don't think anyone has ever made me laugh more than she did in those days. She would sit very upright on the edge of a chair or sofa and tell at immense length a kind of saga, of her experiences as an actress or of how and why Koteliansky howled like a dog in the room at the top of a building in Southampton Row. There was not the shadow of a gleam of a smile on her mask of a face, and the extraordinary funniness of the story was increased by the flashes of her astringent wit. I think

* 'The Monster' here is one of Katherine's many unkind names for Ida; nicknames were very much a Beauchamp habit, and Katherine used them systematically to express either affection or contempt. The story referred to as breathing hate is presumably '*Je ne parle pas français*', which Murry was proposing to print on the press he had bought in emulation of the Woolfs', and installed in the basement at Portland Villas.

that in some abstruse way Murry corrupted and perverted and destroyed Katherine both as a person and a writer. She was a very serious writer, but her gifts were those of an intense realist, with a superb sense of ironic humour and fundamental cynicism. She got enmeshed in the sticky sentimentality of Murry and wrote against the grain of her own nature. At the bottom of her mind she knew this, I think, and it enraged her. And that was why she was so often enraged against Murry. To see them together, particularly in their own house in Hampstead, made one acutely uncomfortable, for Katherine seemed to be always irritated with Murry ... Every now and then she would say *sotto voce* something bitter and biting.[11]

This is not the Katherine of the journal, or the Katherine Murry that Ida saw – which makes the testimony of these two disinterested witnesses all the more significant. With a different audience Katherine could forget her role as exquisite victim or domestic tyrant, forget her irritation and pain for a moment, and laugh and joke. She sometimes, privately, allowed herself to deplore Murry's sluggish and insensitive 'English' nature, writing in her journal that 'he is not warm, ardent, eager, full of quick response, careless, spendthrift of himself, vividly alive, high-spirited',[12] although after this catalogue of complaints she added firmly that it made no difference to her love for him. To a degree, they did enjoy the house together. They gave some parties, presided over from the sofa by Katherine, and old friends such as the Campbells, Kot and Gertler came to see her again. They kept cats, to which they were both deeply attached. Very occasionally, they might manage a short walk on the heath; and there were nights when they lay in bed together, reading poetry.

Katherine also had her hours of pleasure when she was alone in the house, with the sense that she, the Beauchamp family's Cinderella, had now achieved, after all, the dignity of a permanent home, a proper husband, servants, a position in life. When one of the cats came begging at lunchtime, she could give it cream in a silver spoon; and she enjoyed giving orders, to the cook or the shy new maid, and to Ida also, whom at this time she commanded to burn every letter she had ever sent her. Ida obeyed. But although she controlled her kingdom, happiness was rare at Portland Villas. Looking back, Katherine remembered the views from the windows on the stairs with pleasure, and the light 'like the light of a pale shell' in her room, but qualified her pleasure: 'It should have been a perfect little house: it never came to flower.'[13]

At Portland Villas the end of the war came without much celebration, but at Christmas they managed wine, crackers and charades, in which Kot and the Campbells tried to revive some of the old gaiety, and Murry wore a paper hat. A moment of jealousy flared at the new year, when Katherine called to Ida and Murry was 'very chagrined because I thought of her, and not only of him'.[14] Otherwise, the new year brought a refusal from Heinemann, which did not wish to publish a volume of Katherine's stories; but Murry was offered exactly the work he most enjoyed, the editorship, at £800 a year, of a weekly called the *Athenaeum* owned by the philanthropic Arthur Rowntree.

The offices were in Adelphi Terrace, down by the river, and Murry's first issue appeared in April. He appointed Aldous Huxley and another friend with a scientific education, J. W. N. Sullivan, as his assistants, and enlisted many impressive contributors, the poets Eliot and Valéry among them, as well as Russell, Forster and many of the Bloomsbury group. Katherine became the regular fiction reviewer. Apart from this she was writing nothing, though she did help Kot with his translations of Chekhov's letters, a process that involved no more than correcting his versions, since she knew no Russian – a disqualification shared by all Koteliansky's collaborators, who included Lawrence and the Woolfs. But Katherine could not be idle. 'Life without work – I would commit suicide,' she wrote in her journal in the summer.[15] She was proud of Murry and interested in the magazine, but found him unwilling to involve her, forgetting sometimes even to bring a copy home, or to mention that he had an interesting book in the house which she might like to read – and this when she could not get out to a bookshop herself: 'All this hurts me horribly, but I like to face it and see all round it. He ought not to have married. There never was a creature less fitted by nature for life with a woman.'[16]

She wrote frequently to her women friends, Anne and Ottoline – to whom she proposed a trip to Italy – and occasionally to Virginia. Many of these letters induce unease, because the tone seems forced towards something artificially literary, as though Katherine thought they might one day be adduced in evidence; and now that they are, they do suggest she was adopting poses to impress. To be fair, it must be added that the poses were taken up against a background of intermittent high fever, pain, spitting of blood and long courses of agonizing and unrewarding injections. Her courage is beyond question; it is her style that grates at times.

Harold Beauchamp arrived in London in August, with his youngest daughter, Jeanne, who was planning to stay in England, the last of the flock to abandon New Zealand for good. He had not seen Katherine since 1912, and his memoirs do not divulge what he thought, but tea at Portland Villas was obviously not a success. Murry was not prepared to feign appreciation of his father-in-law's jokes and anecdotes of business life, and the two men parted in mutual dislike. Whatever Katherine had hoped for from her father – displays of affection, offers of extra money to pay for medical treatment or comfortable holidays abroad – was not forthcoming. She decided she could not face another winter in London. Sorapure mysteriously advised against a sanatorium, and against Switzerland. Instead, he urged the Italian Riviera on her, a particularly bad suggestion, because the Italians had stringent public health measures against tuberculosis and did not tolerate infected patients in their hotels.

Before she left, she felt so frail that she sat down to write a will, without telling anyone, in the form of a letter to Murry which she left with Mr Kay. She bequeathed her manuscripts and any money to her husband, urging him to marry again after her death, and asked that Ida should dispose of her clothes. Then, accompanied by both legatees, she set off for Italy.

14

'A BROTHER ONE *LOVES*'

■

In October 1918 the friendship between her and Lawrence, which had been in abeyance apart from a few letters since 1916, was renewed when he called at Portland Villas, looking, Ida observed, 'like an old Italian picture of Christ'.[1] He had been through every sort of tribulation and humiliation since their last meeting, chased from Cornwall by the authorities on the grounds that Frieda was an enemy alien, unable to find a publisher for *Women in Love* (*The Rainbow*, of course, remained banned), often ill, forced to seek charity to find a roof over his head; he was currently living in a cottage in Derbyshire, had again been forced to apply to the Royal Literary Fund for a grant, and again called by the Army and declared fit to be conscripted for sedentary work, which he declared he would not submit to. He was writing nothing but essays and stories, and longing to go abroad again, to escape everything he had come to hate about England, its rejection of his work, its military machinery, its climate. His bond with Frieda was feeling the strain of the harsh times they had both been enduring too. She had gone down with 'flu during their visit to Hampstead; Lawrence called alone, and he and Katherine at once established a warm revival of their early affection. 'I loved him,' she wrote to Brett,

He was just his old, merry, rich self, laughing, describing things, giving you pictures, full of enthusiasm and joy in a future where we all become 'vaga-bonds' – we simply did not talk about people ... Oh, there is something so lovable about him and his eagerness, his passionate eagerness for life – that is what one loves so.[2]

Lawrence continued to call alone, and to be at his most charming. The physical change in Katherine, her weakness and emaciation, shocked him. He wrote to a friend, saying she had consumption, and expressing the hope that she might get better if only she could go abroad somewhere warm, once the war ended. He added, 'Mr Murry is quite flourishing – rather to my disgust, seeing she is so ill'.[3] Murry, coming in during one of his visits and finding them merry and sweet-tongued together, 'felt I weighed on them like a lump of lead'.[4] He probably did. 'Lawrence and Murry will never hit it off, they are both too proud, and Murry is too jealous,' was her comment in her journal:[5] something that needs to be borne in mind in all their later dealings.

As soon as Lawrence got back to Derbyshire, he sent her a copy of his play *Touch and Go*, wanting her opinion on it. Katherine's only recorded remark about it, that it is 'black with miners', sidesteps the fact that it contains scenes in which there are quite obvious references to her friendship with him.

The central theme of the play is concerned with industrial relations and a failed miners' strike, but the young mine-owner Gerald has a friend, Oliver, and an ex-mistress, Anabel Wrath, a sculptress who has lived in Paris and been part of what she calls 'a vicious triangle' with the two men. Oliver clearly speaks with Lawrence's voice, and Anabel with Katherine's. (It is perhaps the only interesting aspect of the play, which, unlike Lawrence's other dramatic works, is unperformably bad.)

Anabel tells Oliver that Gerald 'loved him far too well ever to love me altogether' and that while this undermined her relations with him, it did not prevent her from loving Oliver too, and trusting him: 'You seemed to be warm and protecting – like a brother, you know – but a brother one *loves*.'

'And then you hated me?' asks Oliver, to which Anabel replies that she came to hate both him and her lover 'almost to madness'. Madness and mad hatred were attributed to themselves by both Lawrence and Katherine at times,* and it seems fairly obvious that this dialogue is looking back at their Cornish days, and trying to put them in perspective. Oliver says of Anabel, 'How she hates the dark gods!': 'and yet they cast a spell over her' rejoins her cast-off lover.

Although Lawrence took *Touch and Go* perfectly seriously, his desire that Katherine should read it must have been at least partly for her personal reaction to Anabel; unfortunately, if she gave him one, it is lost with all her other letters to Lawrence who, unlike Murry, had no careful eye on posterity.

* See, for instance, Katherine's letter to Murry in November 1919.[6]

Lawrence also invited her to send him one of her stories now, but again there is no record of whether she did. He sent her his newly written *The Fox*, in which once again there is something familiar about the character of Ellen, with her 'wisps of crisp dark hair', her big, wide, dark eyes with their look which is 'strange, startled, shy and sardonic at once', her mouth 'pinched as if in pain and irony', the satirical flicker in her eye and 'dangerous satire in her voice'; all of this sounds much closer to Katherine than to Lawrence's country neighbour, the other inspiration for the story, which describes a three-cornered household in which a man and a woman vie for the love of the dark-eyed young woman. It is one of Lawrence's brilliantly dramatic tales, and Katherine liked it very much,[7] although the later version, done in 1921, with its stress on lesbianism and its violent dénouement, might have pleased her less.

The reason for dwelling on these instances of Lawrence's use of Katherine's appearance or conversation in his work is simply to stress how strongly she inhabited his imagination at this time, when he felt vulnerable and unhappy, and may help to explain the extreme bitterness of some of his remarks later when she clearly seemed to ally herself with Murry against him. He now embarked on a series of deeply affectionate and intimate letters to her in which he was clearly trying to put their friendship on a solid and permanent basis. He invited her to come and stay at Mountain Cottage, urging her to get better 'Quick – sharp'.[8] He suggested that the two of them should 'stand free and swear allegiance'.[9] He discussed his relations with Frieda and hers with Murry, warning her against allowing him to make her into a mother-figure, and adding, 'Frieda is the devouring mother. – It is awfully hard, once the sex relation has gone this way, to recover. If we don't recover, we die.'[10] Frieda, he went on, would not submit to his desire for male preeminence, hence their fight. He reaffirmed his belief in friendship, not only between man and man, but between man and woman too, and he invited her to show this letter to Murry, and suggested that they should both come to Derbyshire for Christmas. Katherine was almost certainly too frail to consider such a trip; he had warned her of the icy winds in the hills. In his next letter, he told her he had been on a visit home and seen a sick childhood friend, now dying (he did not add that it was of tuberculosis); in a passionate outburst full of fear for her and no doubt himself too, he wrote, 'Katherine – *on ne meurt pas*: I almost want to let it be reflexive *on ne se meurt pas*: *Point*! Be damned and blasted everything, and let the bloody world come to its end. But one does not die. *Jamais*.'[11]

At Christmas they exchanged gifts by post: he sent her a piece of Derbyshire fluorspar, the brightly coloured crystalline rock mined in the region, and she sent tangerines, a handkerchief, a wheatsheaf for Frieda. In the new year he kept writing, disconcerted by the gaps in her replies, thinking she was ill, sending her books and describing his walks in the snow, the tracks of birds and animals, details she must have enjoyed; he questioned Kot about her health, and expressed concern to other friends that she was only on the verge of existence. In February he had 'flu so badly himself that his own life was in danger, but at the end of March he was writing again, complaining at the difficulty of bringing the four of them together again, especially Murry: 'and if you must go his way, and if he will never really come our way – well!'[12] This same letter went on to describe a dream Lawrence had had; in which Katherine visited him and was quite cured of her consumption; the two of them went out together to look at the stars:

All the constellations were different, and I, who was looking for Orion, to show you, because he is rising now, was very puzzled by these thick, close brilliant new constellations. Then suddenly we saw one planet, so beautiful, a large, fearful, strong star, that we were both pierced by it, possessed, for a second. Then I said, 'That's Jupiter' – but I felt that it wasn't Jupiter – at least not the everyday Jupiter.

Ask Yung [*sic*] or Freud about it? – Never! – It was a star that blazed for a second on one's soul.

I wish it was spring for all of us.[13]

This splendid letter, in which Lawrence's joy in the world and his strong, biblical language were offered like a present to Katherine, would seem to seal the bond of friendship between these two for good; but nothing works out so simply in the real world, and two things intervened now.

One was that Katherine started writing to Frieda, 'would-be-witty letters' according to Lawrence, who was offended by this, after his proffered intimacy. The other was Murry's new position as editor of the *Athenaeum*, which put him in the position of patron, with the power to offer Lawrence work, and the income he desperately needed, or to withhold it. He took one article, and then turned down every single subsequent piece offered to him by Lawrence, whose desperate financial position he knew very well. Murry claimed later that Katherine agreed with his editorial decisions, which may or may not be true. She was certainly capable of being rude about Lawrence's work, especially to those who expected her to be, such as Ottoline and Murry. To no one else did she attack Lawrence, now or later, and even to Ottoline she confined herself to lamenting his lack of humour and the craziness of *Women in Love*, which she knew Ottoline loathed and resented already. Whether she pleaded his cause with Murry is another matter; she was ill and vulnerable, he was jealous and, as Frieda had already registered, in case of a real conflict Katherine would not break with Murry.

When Lawrence came to London in the summer, he did not call at Portland Villas again, and in August he complained that Murry had lost some of his manuscripts. His own state was one of increasing bitterness, and the spectacle of Murry, so comfortably established and now so dismissive of his efforts, was hard for him to bear. What most people would express as sorrow, anger or perhaps spite became from Lawrence an uncontrolled, childlike rage; and since Katherine had allied herself with Murry, and failed to respond to Lawrence's proffered friendship, she also became the object of his rage. In October, Koteliansky – who seems to have stirred things up at times – had a letter from Lawrence saying he hoped Katherine, now in Italy and complaining of a plague of mosquitoes, would be bitten to death. A few weeks later, however, he wrote her a perfectly friendly letter from Florence.

Then, when Murry went to spend Christmas with her, he took some of Lawrence's manuscripts with him and returned them to Lawrence from Katherine's address, implicating her in the rejection. It was this that brought Lawrence's outburst, in which he sent a letter to Murry, calling him a 'dirty little worm', and another to Katherine, telling her that he loathed her, found her revolting ('stewing in your consumption') and hoped she would die. Katherine forwarded the letter to Murry, urging him to tell Lawrence he would hit him in the face if they ever met again, and both of them wrote understandably furious retorts to Lawrence.* Silence then fell for a while, although Lawrence continued to malign 'the Murrys' to other people, and was particularly incensed when Murry had his wife's stories heaped with praise in his own magazine, the review being written by his assistant editor, Sullivan.

The striking thing about all this is that Katherine did not find Lawrence's outburst unforgivable and did not continue to hold it against him. Although circumstances meant they never met again, she under-

---

* Murry destroyed Lawrence's letter to Katherine, which prompts a question about what else may have been in it.

stood rage and cruel outbursts only too well from her own experience; she had also, after all, seen Lawrence raging against Frieda often enough; and just possibly she did not hold herself entirely blameless.

The depth of feeling between Lawrence and Katherine has been obscured by his spectacular rages and her occasional malicious remarks, which have, perhaps inevitably, attracted more attention than the underlying current of real affection and mutual interest. Yet there is so much to take into account: his fascination with her led him to incorporate her experience, conversation and physical appearance into his work. She, in turn, planned to imitate *Sons and Lovers* with an autobiographical novel of her own. For her, Lawrence had the warmth, the responsiveness to living things, the generosity of spirit that she could never find in Murry. Whatever irritation she may have felt at Lawrence's bad behaviour, or at shocking or uncongenial passages in his work, she acknowledged, over and over again, both that she loved him and that his writing was warm, breathing, living, vigorous and full of conviction, 'written by a living man'.[14]

Lawrence was someone she turned to in her imagination at crucial moments in her life, for example after her dream of dying (in December 1919) when she felt abandoned by Murry to her despair, and wrote in her journal, 'I'd like to write my books and spend some happy time with Jack (not very much faith withal) and see Lawrence in a sunny place and pick violets – all kinds of flowers'.[15] And in February 1922, when she was enduring awful suffering in Paris, she recalled to Brett the bluebells of the Cornish spring with Lawrence. Flowers and sunshine went with Lawrence. Murry, they both knew, was a doubter and a cold critic, counting the cost of everything. Lawrence and Katherine had much more in common, temperamentally, physically and in their circumstances. They were both real, imaginative writers (whereas Murry's efforts did not qualify him). Both were attacked and disabled by chronic illness, and both attempted to deny and ignore it. Both had moments when they doubted their own sanity. Both were aware of themselves as outsiders in the English literary world, and alert to condescension; while Murry, by virtue of his education and determined application, managed to penetrate it and become a power within it. Modestly as Murry sometimes acknowledged that his gifts were not to be compared with those of Lawrence or Katherine, they were gifts that put him in a position to make or break their reputations; and he was not always modest.

In January 1922 Katherine told a correspondent how Lawrence had once asked her to swear friendship for life:

At the time I was impatient with him. I thought it extravagant – fanatic. But when one considers what this world is like I understand perfectly why L. (especially being L.) made such claims ... I think, myself, it is pride which makes friendship most difficult. To submit, to bow down to the other, is not easy, but it must be done if one is to really understand the being of the other.[16]

During this last year of her life she thought of Lawrence a great deal, although he was away and out of touch (in Sicily, Germany, Italy, and then Ceylon and Australia). She expressed a vehement dislike of *The Lost Girl*, and refused to review it for the *Athenaeum*, although she was normally willing to say harsh things (instead Murry wrote a stinging attack of his own on the book). But when she came to read *Aaron's Rod*, Lawrence's next novel, she was delighted with it, and inscribed the following words in her copy:

There are certain things in this book I do not like. But they are not important, or really part of it. They are trivial, encrusted, they cling to it as snails to the underside of a leaf – no more, and perhaps they leave a little silvery trail, a smear that one shrinks from as from a kind of silliness. But apart from these things is the leaf, is the tree, firmly planted, deep thrusting, outspread, growing grandly, alive in every twig. All the time I read this book I felt it was feeding me.[17]

Perhaps the theme of the book, which describes a man abandoning his family and finding his own separate and independent fulfilment, spoke with especial resonance to her.

The quarrel was not breached. Lawrence would not have been pleased if he had heard, in 1921, that Katherine was writing for the *Sphere*, edited by Clement Shorter, one of the pack of reviewers responsible for the suppression of *The Rainbow*. He continued to snipe at 'the Murrys' from across the world, mostly to Koteliansky. But in August 1922 Katherine wrote Lawrence's name into her will, as she wanted him to have a book of hers. He was also one of those she thought might have understood what she enjoyed about the Gurdjieff Institute, where she spent the last months of her life (the other was E. M. Forster); only she thought Lawrence's pride might be a stumbling block. In this last autumn of her life she received with joy a card he sent her from Wellington, addressed to her c/o Ottoline and inscribed with a single word, '*Ricordi!*' She told Murry, 'Lawrence has reached Mexico and feels ever so lively'.[18] Koteliansky was probably her informant here, because he was trying to persuade Lawrence to write to her, and gave him news of her. In fact, Lawrence sent her greetings twice in December, through both Koteliansky and Murry, and in late November she encouraged Murry to write to him.[19]

The strongest proof that she had forgiven whatever there was to be forgiven Lawrence, and that her heart was full of tenderness for her old friend, comes in a letter to Murry, written just before she went to Fontainebleau in October: 'Yes, I care for Lawrence. I have thought of writing to him and trying to arrange a meeting after I leave Paris – suggesting that I join them until the spring.'[20] But by then it was no longer possible.

15

'A SENSE OF BEING LIKE'

■

Katherine, Ida and Murry had a long, exhausting journey across France in the September heat, stopping at Menton, at Mr Beauchamp's suggestion, to see his cousin Connie, who ran a nursing-home in England but spent her winters abroad with an elderly woman friend. Connie was interested in Katherine, and touched by her plight. After meeting her, they travelled on to San Remo. When they arrived, and the hotel staff observed Katherine's state, the manager explained that they could not have a tubercular person on the premises; in fact, they must pay for the fumigation of the rooms. He did, however, propose to them the use of a small villa nearby in Ospedaletti, for a low rent: the Casetta Deerholm. They had little choice but to take it, and here Murry left the two women and returned to England. Until pipes could be installed, all the water had to be fetched, and Ida had to master the use of a charcoal stove for cooking. The manager warned them to beware of possible intruders, and thoughtfully provided them with a revolver, just in case; Katherine, fascinated, took it into the garden to practise loading and firing. She determined to keep it (and she did too). Thus she and Ida settled into their isolation, the succession of hot days bringing swarms of insects – these were the ones Lawrence hoped would bite her to death – the sound of the sea crashing below striking a forlorn note, and Italy itself in a state of muttering crisis in the aftermath of the war and the rising power of the fascists.

The heat at least pleased Katherine. She planned to write a journal for publication, 'From the Casetta', to be an account of her six months' stay (she had told people in England she was going for two years, but secretly she and Murry had agreed that it was for the winter only). She noted the flowers and the butterflies, the wild thyme and rosemary on the hillside, the little cat that crept in one evening and purred for its meal; one afternoon she took the tram from Ospedaletti into San Remo, first class, with velvet-covered, iron-hard seats, and went shopping for fruit and brioches and china. Murry remembered her birthday, and sent her a small silver spoon, exactly the sort of present she delighted in. Lytton wrote her a kind letter, Ida gave her a bottle of the expensive scent she liked; even her father sent her a note, if not a present. But at the end of this auspicious October she ran out of the medicine Sorapure had given her, and could not get the same thing made up; immediately she became frightened and depressed, and began to hate Ida again.

Her father, whom she had expected to stay away for fear of infection, did now call on her, bringing his cousin Connie and her friend Jinnie Fullerton. They were not impressed by the Casetta. Mr Beauchamp took Katherine for a drive, picked her a bunch of wild flowers, gave her some cigarettes, and hugged her: 'to be held and kissed and called my precious child was almost too much ... it's having love present, close, warm, to be felt and returned'. This was what she missed and needed, or so she implied to Murry.[1] The reproach was obvious. A few days later, she described how she thought of the mornings in Hampstead when she woke before him and lay touching him with her hand while he slept, his dark head turned away, while the light grew just enough for her to pick out the figure in the Dürer print on the wall. Then, more than once, she told him how she envied Virginia, who had the safety and comfort of Leonard's perpetual presence and care; she could not help being jealous.

The weather turned cold. She told Murry,

Cold frightens me. It is ominous. I breathe it and deep down it's as though a knife softly pressed in my bosom had said 'Don't be too sure.' That's the fearful part of having been near death. One knows how easy it is to die. The barriers that are up for everybody else are down for you and you've only to slip through.[2]

And so the cross-currents of fear and hope and gaiety continued. When she felt well enough, she wrote detailed letters about the *Athenaeum*, criticizing the articles and making suggestions as well as sending her weekly reviews. She urged Murry to accept Ottoline's Christmas invitation. When Sorapure's medicine arrived, she rejoiced in its 'superb' effect. Sometimes, she said, she could not sleep at all, and then for days she was sleepy. At the end of November she was euphoric enough to write, 'we must have children, we must'.[3] In another breath, she accused Murry and Ida both of imagining her already dead; very often she would slip in a devastating remark of this kind, the rest of the letter apparently warm and loving. Her spirits rose and fell unpredictably, although the pronouncements of local doctors affected her deeply; one began by reassuring her that she would be cured in two years, explaining later that he was just trying to cheer her up because he saw she was depressed. Another, an Englishman, advised her to live comfortably and drink plenty of brandy or Marsala. Perhaps his advice was as good as any.

In December, she sent Murry a poem, written when she had a fever, she said, which accused him of abandoning her and predicted that his place would be taken by another husband: a husband called death. It is a dreadful poem in both style and content, and to Murry it was like 'a snake with a sting'. He was stricken, made immediate plans to come out to her for Christmas, and wrote to justify their separation in terms of the money he had to earn. Across this letter of his she scrawled scornful comments, and wrote back accusing him of caring too much for money and being unable to 'play the man'.[4] She took up the same theme in her journal, recalling how they had been like two men friends until disease turned her into a woman. Murry had stood it, she thought, because it was a romantic disease ('his love of a "romantic appearance" is immensely real'), but he had betrayed their love by his failure to accept that they could live together on what they might earn, away from London.

Even if Murry had some practical justification for his reluctance to leave his job, any fool could have seen that what Katherine wanted was for him to drop everything and stay with her. A mixture of blindness and wilful ignorance allowed him to make it obvious how much he preferred London to her company: he had his paper, and Waterlow as his lodger, and Forster and Russell dropping in, and Brett carrying him off to her studio, and Ottoline offering to sell him furniture, and important literary squabbles and puffs to busy himself with. When he did get to the Casetta for two weeks over Christmas, he was struck down with neuralgia, and when he left their letters became strained again. Katherine had 'heart attacks', fainting and weeping fits, and black depression. Then she sent him a story, 'The Man without a Temperament'; it contained another implied reproach, though a subtle one, for its hero has devoted himself to his invalid wife and is living out an intolerable existence in foreign hotels. His patience is admirable, but whatever love there had been between the two has been extinguished by the constraints of their way of life, which is bitterly contrasted with the blithe world of the fit. The husband in the story may tend his wife, fetch her shawl, kill a mosquito that has got inside her net, but he can do nothing to revive the energy and love they have lost; just as, in life, Murry was too sluggish and self-absorbed to distract or amuse Katherine into forgetting her illness for a while.

It took Murry another year before he could bring himself to try to play Leonard to Katherine's Virginia. Before that, in desperation she took up the suggestion of Connie Beauchamp in Menton, and decided to move there, where it was warmer and she could be looked after. The move was difficult – Italy was in turmoil, there was a postal strike, someone stole Katherine's overcoat and everything cost more than expected – and when she got to Menton she found Connie and Jinnie had decided to install her in a large private nursing-home rather than in their own Villa Flora. Ida was dispatched to a rented room, and for a few days Katherine luxuriated in the comfort and airiness of the place, the attentive nursing, massage and doctors; but then she grew suspicious of the atmosphere. It was full of elderly invalids, and cost more than she could possibly afford. She and Murry had another acrimonious exchange about money (and in the midst of this, Lawrence's attack reached her). Murry apologized for his meanness, explaining that there was 'a certain amount of real insensibility in me', and followed this up by telling her he had taken out a large life insurance policy, and sending her elaborate accounts.

This enraged Katherine, but, as always, she set aside her anger and determinedly built up the image of their perfect love once again. She had got herself out of the nursing-home and into Connie and Jinnie's Villa Flora, and here she began to enjoy herself as she had not for a long time, fussed over and spoilt by the two motherly women. They took her for outings in their big car along the corniche roads, and bought her frocks, hats and other presents. Murry found her letters false, he said, but they seem very natural in their expression of enjoyment of luxury and affection; Katherine was craving the comfort she remembered from her girlhood, remembering her mother's ability to set everything in order. In her illness, she was desperate for some pleasure and reassurance.

The fact that the two women were hoping, through all their mothering love, treats and shopping trips, to convert Katherine to their faith in Roman Catholicism did not really matter. She was perfectly prepared to flirt with the idea – indeed, for a day or two she thought she would convert, and wrote a secret letter to Ida to announce the fact – but the faith did not apparently take root, and Connie and Jinnie were disappointed. If Katherine worshipped at any shrines, they were pagan ones.

Another source of comfort now was the appearance of a very rich English couple, Sydney and Violet Schiff, aesthetes and patrons of the arts on holiday in France and eager to meet Katherine. Sydney wrote novels (later he translated the last section of Proust's *À la recherche du temps perdu*), Violet sang a little; her sister Ada Leverson had been a friend of Oscar Wilde; both Schiffs sought the company of writers and artists, and had given hospitality to Joyce and Wyndham Lewis as well as Proust, with perfect eclecticism. Katherine was grateful for their attentions, enjoyed being fetched by car for visits to their luxurious villa, and embarked on a warm friendship and literary correspondence with them.

She was also busy planning her summer in England with Murry. All through March and April her letters were full of proposals for the month's holiday they would take together, now in an inn at Beaulieu in the New Forest, where they would sail and picnic under the trees, now at a hotel in the wilds of north Devon. Murry was in the process of buying a cottage in Sussex, a gage of faith in their future; the gesture fell a little flat, since they could not have possession for over a year (and, in fact, never lived in it). For all his daily letters, with their protestations of love and longing, he was deeply enmeshed in his separate life, spending weekends at Garsington and finding Brett a flattering and congenial companion.

The four summer months in England did not turn out as she had planned and hoped. Whether through her physical frailty – 'I can't go anywhere except by car and I simply can't afford cars for long trips'[5] – or Murry's inertia, or a combination of the two, no holiday in the New Forest or Devon materialized. Ida made several plans to take her to the south coast, but they came to nothing. Instead, she sat, a virtual prisoner, in Portland Villas, while Murry pursued his editorial duties and spent a good deal of his spare time playing tennis with Brett, with whom he was now engaged in one of his ambiguous flirtations, simultaneously pressing his suit and declaring his loyalty to his wife. 'It's been chiefly the experience of your loving me that has made me realize how sacred is my marriage,' he wrote to her early in the year.[6] Katherine was upset and jealous when she realized the situation, but she struggled with her anger as best she could. Brett was torn in her feelings, but Murry was able to continue this particular dance without guilt, no doubt through his technique of keeping his conscience in two layers, as he had explained to the Woolfs.

The summer of 1920 was cold, or so it seemed to Katherine, and she had to endure vaccine treatment from Sorapure which made her feel iller than ever, without producing any evident benefit. One day Murry did take her out in a hired car to her bank, and they went on to the *Athenaeum* offices, but she felt out of place among his male colleagues and embarrassed him by trying to talk to them about the beauty of the south of France. The Schiffs took her to the theatre, and T. S. Eliot brought his wife Vivien to dinner; Katherine observed her with dislike and envy, noting how Eliot leaned towards her, 'admiring, listening, making the most of her': lucky Vivien.[7]

Her cousin Elizabeth, separated from Bertrand Russell's brother Francis,* also called on her, their first meeting since Katherine had taken her fiancé, George Bowden, to tea with her in 1909. The two cousins surveyed one another with some curiosity. No one could describe Elizabeth as a likeable woman: her ruthless egoism mixed with sentimentality, a blend that characterized many of the Beauchamp clan, prevented that. But she had a great capacity for hard work: she had borne five children, made a small fortune from her best-selling books and emerged the victor in her struggles with two consecutive aristocratic husbands, living a life of bold disregard for conventions of wifely and maternal behaviour. When she visited Katherine she was on the point of leaving for her Swiss chalet, where she habitually entertained smart guests and currently kept a young lover, A. S. Frere. Her success and independence must have seemed most enviable to Katherine. For her part, Elizabeth viewed her less robust cousin with genuine sympathy and admiration.

Another visitor was Virginia Woolf, who came despite a question in her own mind as to how welcome she was. But then the pattern of Katherine's friendship with Virginia was markedly one-sided. Virginia was always the wooer, Katherine – after an initial period of flirtatiousness in 1917 – elusive, difficult, unpredictable, unresponsive. It was Virginia who posted flowers and cigarettes to Katherine; who suggested to her

* Elizabeth had two husbands: Henning von Arnim, whom she married in 1891 and who died in 1910, and Earl Russell (Bertrand's elder brother), whom she married in 1916 and from whom she was now separated.

sister Vanessa in 1919 that she might let her Sussex house, Charleston, to Murry; who issued invitations to meals and weekends and wrote letters of affection and praise, whatever her private reservations. Virginia preserved Katherine's letters, whereas only two of the many she sent her survive. Virginia undoubtedly learnt both from Katherine's writing and from her criticism, changing her own direction as a writer and taking to heart Katherine's review of *Night and Day*, which appeared in the *Athenaeum* in November 1919: after this, none of her novels was cast again in the old conventional mould, none could have earned Katherine's gibe of being 'Miss Austen up-to-date ... extremely culti-vated, distinguished and brilliant, but above all – deliberate ... in the midst of our admiration it makes us feel old and chill: we had never thought to look upon its like again!'[8] Stung as she was by this verdict, Virginia accepted its justice and did not let it prevent her from seeking out Katherine as soon as she heard she was once more at Portland Villas. She valued the exchange of ideas and the intensity of their communion, even if she felt the friendship to be 'founded on quicksands':[9]

I find with Katherine what I don't find with the other clever women, a sense of ease and interest which is, I suppose, due to her caring so genuinely if so differently from the way I care, about our precious art. Though Katherine is now in the very heart of the professional world ... she is, & will always be I fancy, not the least of a hack.[10]

The affectionate relations established in 1919 had led Virginia to believe they had reached 'some kind of durable foundation', but the quicksands opened again when Katherine failed to write from abroad that winter or to make any move on her return. Yet as soon as they did meet, the spell was cast again. Virginia's accounts of her visits to Portland Villas during the summer of 1920 show her fascination with Katherine vividly, as well as providing a clear picture of the way life went on there, and Katherine's readiness to betray upon the shutting of a door. This is from a long entry for 31 May 1920:

I had my interview with K.M. on Friday. A steady discomposing formality & coldness at first. Enquiries about house & so on. No pleasure or excitement at seeing me. It struck me that she is of the cat kind: alien, composed, always solitary & observant. And then we talked about solitude, & I found her expressing my feelings as I never heard them expressed. Whereupon we fell into step, & as usual, talked as easily as though 8 months were minutes – till Murry came in with a pair of blue & pink Dresden candle pieces: 'How *very* nice' she said. 'But do fetch the candles.' 'Virginia, how *awful* what am I to say? He has spent £5 on them' she said, as he left the room. I see that they're often hostile. For one thing – Murry's writing. 'Did you like C. & A. [Murry's play *Cinnamon and Angelica*]?' No, I didn't. 'Neither did I. But I thought D. of an I. too dreadful – wrong – Its very difficult, often ...' [an essay called 'The Defeat of the Imagination'] Then Murry came back. We chatted as usual. Aldous was our butt ... But Murry going at length, K. & I once more got upon literature ... A queer effect she produces of someone apart, entirely self-centred; altogether concentrated upon her 'art': almost fierce to me about it ...[11]

Katherine went on to say flattering things about *Night and Day*; a piece of disingenuousness which pleased but also puzzled Virginia: there was, after all, the matter of the review. She concluded, 'Anyhow, once more as keenly as ever I feel a common certain understanding between us – a queer sense of being "like" – not only about literature – & I think it's independent of gratified vanity. I can talk straight out to her.'[12]

In June, she again noted the enjoyment of 'two hours' priceless talk – priceless in the sense that to no one else can I talk in the same disembodied way about writing; without altering my thought more than I alter it in writing here. (I except L. from this.)'[13] The last, parenthetic sentence is the most significant here: that Katherine was allowed an understanding and intimacy in conversation equal to Leonard's was an extraordinary tribute to the importance Virginia gave her. In August, she noted that she got 'the queerest sense of an echo coming back to me from her mind the second after I've spoken'.[14] The two women promised to write to one another, and Katherine said she would send her diary to Virginia from France.

'Shall we? Will she?' queried Virginia. 'If I were left to myself I should; being the simpler, more direct of the two.'[15] After Katherine's departure Virginia did write, and Katherine replied, telling her how much her visits had meant to her, and that 'You are the only woman with whom I long to talk work. There will never be another.'[16] It was a warm letter, and it ended, 'Farewell, dear friend (May I call you that)'; but though Virginia wrote again, Katherine neither wrote nor sent her diary as promised. Something made her suspicious. Perhaps it was a (well-founded) wariness of Bloomsbury gossip and malice. Perhaps it was professional jealousy.* Perhaps Katherine simply felt unequal to

---

* A letter from E. M. Forster to Sydney Waterlow in January 1921 indicates, albeit somewhat elliptically and obscurely, that Katherine could be just as jealous as Virginia over the question of their literary reputations: 'K.M. in one of my rare conversations with her complained that Virginia's art had no penumbra, was it her metaphor ran, a broken off piece of living stuff, and implied that her own was, or that if one implied it wasn't the evening would be a failure socially.'[17]

taking on another correspondent, and underestimated the degree of Virginia's attachment to her.

Katherine and Virginia admired in one another their professional dedication to writing. Both felt themselves to be writers first and foremost, everything else – their lives as women, social life, even success, although both craved it – was of lesser importance; and both took reviewing seriously as a corollary to their main work. Katherine praised the beauty of Virginia's prose, and was conscious of her range of knowledge; she could be sarcastic to Murry about 'those Hours in a Library', but she knew their value too. What she found lacking was immediacy, the thing she strove for in her own writing, and true human feeling; Katherine once said Virginia seized on beauty as though she were a bird rather than a person. It is a perceptive remark, for there is often a sense of remoteness about Virginia's observation.*

Both writers were intensely interested in the ambivalences of family life and feeling between men and women, parents and children. Both also had an affinity with animals: Virginia had a dog narrate one novel, and Katherine told Kot (among others) she wanted to write a story centred on a cat or kitten.[18] The immediacy of Katherine's writing, what Desmond MacCarthy praised as 'the bright sharp-cut circle of her extraordinarily vivid attention',[19] her ability to be there and make the reader be there alongside, made its impression on Virginia. *Jacob's Room*, her third novel, embarked on early in 1920, suggests that she had studied her friend's technique as well as pondering her review. Nothing about the new book resembles an Edwardian novel. Compared with *Night and Day*, it is overwhelming in its immediacy. There is no plot to speak of, but a series of impressionistic scenes, and a 'merging into things', as Katherine described it in a conversation reported by Virginia in August:

> I said how my own character seems to cut out a shape like a shadow in front of me [wrote Virginia]. This she understood ... and proved it by telling me that she thought this bad: one ought to merge into things. Her senses are amazingly acute.[20]

Of course Virginia knew other modernist writers (such as Eliot) and knew (and disliked) the work of Joyce and Dorothy Richardson; Katherine stood closer personally, and in her choice of themes. Both Virginia

---

* It must be remembered that Katherine died before Virginia's best work appeared; she did not read *Jacob's Room*, which was published two months before her death; *Mrs Dalloway*, *To the Lighthouse*, *The Waves*, *Between the Acts*, etc., all came after.

A. R. Orage, Katherine's mentor in 1910 and 1911, editor of the radical *New Age*, in which her early stories appeared

Beatrice Hastings, Orage's editorial adviser and mistress and, like Katherine, a writer and colonial separated from her husband

The budding author: Katherine in 1910

(left) John Middleton Murry with his little boy's look, in 1912, at the time Katherine invited him to become her lodger

(below) Katherine presiding at the Chaucer Mansions flat in 1913: the last days of the *Blue Review*, and the first meetings with Lawrence and Frieda

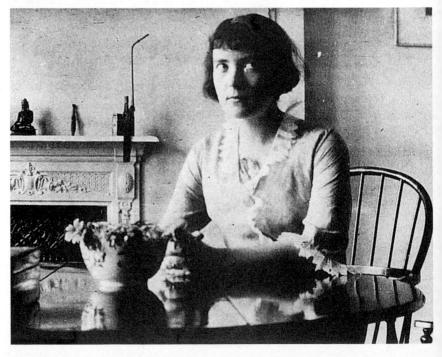

Lady Ottoline Morrell at home at Garsington

Francis Carco at the time of his friendship with
Murry and Katherine

(below) D. H. Lawrence and Frieda on their wedding day in 1914, with Katherine and Murry in the
Campbells' garden at Selwood Terrace

1910: Convalescent at Rottingdean

1911: The *New Age* contributor

1913: The successful young author

1915: Returning from the front in France

1916: In her St. John's Wood garden

1917: A dramatic studio portrait

THE CHANGING FACE OF K.M.

August 1919: Leaving for San Remo

(top left) 'A brother one *loves*': Lawrence in 1913

(top right) 'You are the only woman with whom I long to talk work': Virginia Woolf in the early 1920s

(bottom left) Murry on the terrace at the Villa Isola Bella: 'I *do* lament that he is not warm, ardent, eager, full of quick response, careless, spendthrift of himself, vividly alive, *high-spirited*. But it makes no difference to my love.'

(top) Ida's photograph of Isola Bella

(bottom left) The Chalet des Sapins at Sierre

(bottom right) Katherine standing in the garden at
Isola Bella: 'I get up at about 11. Go downstairs
until 12. Come up and lie on my bed until 5, when
I get back into it again.'

1921

and Katherine made the fragility of feeling, of happiness and life itself, into their subject; both felt a degree of antagonism for the male world of action (and for male sexuality); both turned to their childhoods and their dead to nourish their imaginations. *Jacob's Room* is an elegy for a lost brother just as 'Prelude' was planned to be; and *To the Lighthouse* (which reverted, five years later, to the seaside theme of the opening of *Jacob's Room*, using the same winking lighthouse, the same small boy who wants to preserve the skull of an animal, the same painter who represents the child's mother by a single, violet dab) is an elegy for a lost family. The seaside theme is paralleled in Katherine's 'At the Bay', although neither writer knew of the other's use of it.

Yet they remain very distinct. Virginia's writing is always reflective. Her people inhabit a world of social, cultural and historical connections; her houses and landscapes are rich in historical associations too. Katherine's characters often seem to inhabit a void; she excels, as MacCarthy said, 'in expressing a child's sense of things'. In Woolf, books and paintings become the emblems and props of feeling, which might sometimes seem precarious without them. Sandra Wentworth Williams, with her eye for young men and her distracted husband, has her volume of Chekhov stories and receives from Jacob his volume of Donne poems. A Mansfield character would not buy a copy of Fielding's *Tom Jones* as a means of approaching the young man she is in love with, as Fanny does in *Jacob's Room*; in Mansfield it is more likely to be clothes or flowers, ephemera, that carry symbolic meanings: a muff, a fur, a hat, a lace handkerchief.

Without any web of associations, conventions or history, Katherine's characters make their appearances quite boldly, equipped with nothing more than charm or absurdity or pathos, against their settings of railway trains, seaside houses, hotels, flats, park benches and far, unlabelled corners of the world. Like their creator, they may strike us as both pungently alive and vulnerable. Katherine often gives them broadly comic speech or thought patterns, whereas almost all Virginia's characters speak and think in well-formed sentences; they may be mildly satirized, but they do not lose their elegance; in the brothel, Laurette murmurs 'I used to ride' with the composure of a lady.

The element of mandarin that is always present in Virginia's work is quite absent from Katherine's. Where the cadences of their prose are most similar is in descriptions of the natural world.

'It suddenly gets cold. The sun seems to give less heat,' she said, looking about her, for it was bright enough, the grass still a soft deep green, the house starred in its greenery with purple passion flowers, and rooks dropping cool cries from the high blue. But something moved, flashed, turned a silver wing in the air. It was September after all, the middle of September, and past six in the evening.

The room was gay with morning light. The big french window on to the balcony was open and the palm outside flung its quivering spider-like shadow over the bedroom walls. Although their hotel did not face the front, at this early hour you could hear it breathing, and flying high on golden wings seagulls skimmed past. How peaceful the sky looked, as though it was smiling tenderly.

The first passage is from *To the Lighthouse*, the second from a fragment ('Such a Sweet Old Lady'), printed by Murry posthumously in *The Doves' Nest*; and the kinship is there, for all their general differences, in the shape of the sentences and the single image of menace dropped into each passage – such images being fundamental and characteristic to both their visions of the world.

Why did the friendship lapse before the end of Katherine's life? Evidently Virginia was hurt by her lack of response and, like many others, simply could not take in the severity of her illness. As late as August 1922, only months before Katherine's death, Virginia told Lytton Strachey that she had heard she was completely recovered. Without the excuse of disease, Katherine's tidal mood changes were less easy to overlook, and there were enough malicious gossips in both their circles to relay and exaggerate any slighting remark from one to the other. Katherine was stung by Bloomsbury, and knew Virginia could adopt a superior tone and crush her socially and intellectually if she chose. Virginia knew that Katherine was a liar and a flatterer. The figure of Murry did not help.

In the immediate aftermath of her death, Virginia wrote a long passage in her diary which is one attempt to sum up their relationship:

Katherine has been dead a week, & how far am I obeying her 'do not quite forget Katherine' which I read in one of her old letters? Am I already forgetting her? It is strange to trace the progress of one's feelings. Nelly said in her sensational way at breakfast on Friday 'Mrs Murry's dead! It says so in the paper!' At that one feels – what? A shock of relief? – a rival the less? Then confusion at feeling so little – then, gradually, blankness & disappointment; then a depression which I could not rouse myself from all that day. When I began to write, it seemed to me there was no point in writing. Katherine wont read it. Katherine's my rival no longer. More generously I felt, But though I can do this better than she could, where is she, who could do what I can't! Then, as usual with me, visual impressions kept coming & coming before me – always of Katherine putting on a white wreath, & leaving us, called away; made dignified, chosen. And then one pitied her. And one felt her reluctant to wear that wreath, which was an ice cold one. And she was only 33. And I could see her before me so exactly, & the room at Portland Villas. I go up. She gets up, very slowly, from her writing table. A glass of milk & a medicine bottle stood there. There were also piles of novels. Everything was very tidy, bright, & somehow like a dolls house. At once, or almost, we got out of shyness. She (it was summer) half lay on the sofa by the window. She had her look of a Japanese doll, with the fringe combed quite straight across her forehead. Sometimes we looked very steadfastly at each other, as though we had reached some durable relationship, independent of the changes of the body, through the eyes. Hers were beautiful eyes – rather doglike, brown, very wide apart, with a steady slow rather faithful & sad expression. Her nose was sharp, & a little vulgar. Her lips thin & hard. She wore short skirts & liked 'to have a line round her' she said. She looked very ill – very drawn, & moved languidly, drawing herself across the room, like some suffering animal. I suppose I have written down some of the things we said. Most days I think we reached that kind of certainty, in talk about books, or rather about our writings, which I thought had something durable about it. And then she was inscrutable. Did she care for me? Sometimes she would say so – would kiss me – would look at me as if (is this sentiment?) her eyes would like always to be faithful. She would promise never never to forget. That was what we said at the end of our last talk. She said she would send me her diary to read, & would write always. For our friendship was a real thing we said, looking at each other quite straight. It would always go on whatever happened. What happened was, I suppose, faultfindings & perhaps gossip. She never answered my letter. Yet I still feel, somehow that friendship persists. Still there are things about writing I think of & want to tell Katherine. If I had been in Paris & gone to her, she would have got up & in three minutes, we should have been talking again. Only I could not take the step. The surroundings – Murry & so on – & the small lies and treacheries, the perpetual playing & teasing, or whatever it was, cut away so much of the substance of friendship. One was too uncertain. And so one let it all go. Yet I certainly expected that we should meet again next summer, & start afresh. And I was jealous of her writing – the only writing I have ever been jealous of. This made it harder to write to her; & I saw in it, perhaps from jealousy, all the qualities I disliked in her ... I have the feeling that I shall think of her at intervals all through life. Probably we had something in common which I shall never find in anyone else ...[21]

Virginia wrote this wonderful, honest and honourable passage when she was ill herself, with a fever which in no way lessened her clarity of perception or expression. She was right in predicting that she would continue to be haunted by Katherine's ghost. In the winter of 1925, walking in Ken Wood with Leonard and depressed about Vita Sackville-West, with whom she was now in love, Virginia recorded how 'all this part of Hampstead recalls Katherine to me – that faint ghost with the steady eyes, the mocking lips'.[22] Possibly her discovery of erotic love for one of her own sex caused her to reconsider the feelings she had once had for Katherine, whose sexual ambiguity had been so firmly held in check when they knew one another.

In 1927 she reviewed Katherine's published *Journal* in the *Nation*, of which Leonard, always an admirer of Katherine, was literary editor. The article praised her for her 'sane, caustic, austere' attitude towards her work, and her lack of both vanity and jealousy, two sins Virginia was highly conscious of in herself. Four years later, in the summer of 1931, in answer to a question from Vita, she wrote this summing-up of her feeling for, and memories of Katherine:

We did not ever coalesce; but I was fascinated, and she respectful, only I thought her cheap, and she thought me priggish; and yet we were both compelled to meet simply in order to talk about writing. This we did by the hour. Only then she came out with a swarm of little stories, and I was jealous, no doubt; because they were so praised; but gave up reading them not on that account, but because of their cheap sharp sentimentality, which was all the worse, I thought, because she had, as you say, the zest and the resonance – I mean she could permeate one with her quality; and if one felt this cheap scent in it, it reeked in ones nostrils. But I must read her some day. Also, she was forever pursued by her dying; and had to press on through stages that should have taken years in ten minutes – so that our relationship became unreal also. And there was Murry squirming and oozing a sort of thick motor oil in the background – dinners with them were about the most unpleasant exhibitions, humanly speaking, I've ever been to. But the fact remains – I mean, that she had a quality I adored, and needed; I think her sharpness and reality – her having knocked about with prostitutes and so on, whereas I had always been respectable – was the thing I wanted then. I dream of her often – now thats an odd reflection – how one's relation with a person seems to be continued after death in dreams, and with some odd reality too.[23]

Virginia's testimony to her relationship with Katherine ('never again shall I have one like it'[24]) is of especial value and interest, because she was a friend and contemporary who faced some of the same problems, such as ill health and childlessness, and approached her work with the same dedication and professionalism; still more important, it is the testimony of a great writer. Virginia, like Lawrence, was devoid of sentimentality, so that, while her criticism is sharp, her love and praise ring with authority. Her Katherine, tricky and treacherous, burdened with the incubus of Murry (whom she nevertheless loves and depends on), utterly dedicated to the craft of writing although her stamina is broken by illness, seeking love and approval, but not so cravenly that she will write a false review, fascinating and inscrutable, fits remarkably well with everything that has been revealed about her since.

Two months before her own death, in 1941, Virginia was still recalling Katherine in her diary: a scene entirely to her credit, in which, taking the manuscript of *Ulysses* from the drawer at the Hogarth Press, Katherine began by mocking, and then stopped and exclaimed: 'But there's something in this.'[25]

16

'I AM A WRITER FIRST'

■

In September 1920, Katherine and Ida set off south once again and, against all the odds, hope rose once again at the prospect of change, France, sunshine, a new doctor. There was also the comfortable sense that she had earned £40 from a commercial publisher, Constable, as an advance on a new collection of stories, carefully arranged by Murry with his old friend from *Rhythm* days, Michael Sadleir,* who was now a director of the firm. This was the first substantial sum she had earned from her work.

Her journal entries for the long train-ride register pleasure and amusement in the journey itself, fellow passengers and passing landscape, the view from a station where they stopped:

> Breakfast Time. It grew hot. Everywhere the light quivered green–gold. The white soft road unrolled, with plane-trees casting a trembling shade. There were piles of pumpkins and gourds: outside the house the tomatoes were spread in the sun. Blue flowers and red flowers and tufts of deep purple flared in the road-side hedges. A young boy, carrying a branch, stumbled across a yellow field, followed by a brown high-stepping little goat. We bought figs for breakfast, immense thin-skinned ones. They broke in one's fingers and tasted of wine and honey.[1]

They travelled on to the Villa Isola Bella, another of Connie and Jinnie's places, standing at the end of their garden, just outside Menton. It was by far the most comfortable house she had yet established herself in in the south, and she revelled in its small luxuries, the velvet-covered furniture and gilt mirror, the silver teapot and supply of black dresses for the maid, the big mimosa in the garden, the tangerine tree, the sound of cicadas and frogs from the terrace, the sight of the sea, the smell of

---

* He changed his name from 'Sadler' to 'Sadleir' to distinguish himself from his father.

lemons, the lizards on the path. And as she grew iller ('I keep having fever ... fever and headache and nightmare pursue me. I must just keep dead quiet'[2]), she wrote more precisely and more wonderingly of the world about her:

> After lunch today we had a sudden tremendous thunderstorm, the drops of rain were as big as marguerite daisies – the whole sky was violet. I went out the very moment it was over – the sky was all glittering with broken light – the sun a huge splash of silver. The drops were like silver fishes hanging from the trees. I drank the rain from the peach leaves and then pulled a shower bath over my head. Every violet leaf was full.[3]

> The wind of the last days has scattered almost the last of the fig leaves and now through those candle-shaped boughs I love so much there is a beautiful glimpse of the old town. Some fowls are making no end of a noise. I've just been for a walk on my small boulevard and looking down below at the houses all bright in the sun and housewives washing their linen in great tubs of glittering water and flinging it over the orange trees to dry. Perhaps all human activity is beautiful in the sunlight.[4]

Behind the illness, and the heightened response to the world, Katherine had other worries. At about the time she was setting off, and with her new book (which was to be called *Bliss*) announced by Constable, her old lover Floryan Sobieniowski had approached Murry, now a figure of considerable repute in literary London, and suggested that it might be worth Katherine's while to pay him £40 for letters in his possession. He made some reference to 'good received'. The sum he asked for was the exact amount of Katherine's advance from her new publishers: £40.

All Murry's correspondence for this period has disappeared, destroyed either by Katherine or by himself, but some of her letters have survived, and we know that she insisted on the money being paid without an instant's hesitation. Ida gave her the necessary sum, since neither Katherine herself nor Murry seem to have had any to hand, and Katherine instructed Murry to take Floryan to a solicitor and get his sworn statement that he would in future leave her alone. She said she would give 'any money' to recover the letters: 'It's *not* a waste of £40.'[5] She also told Murry she would like the letters destroyed, but that he must do whatever he thought best. At the end of September he sent her a telegram to say he had them, and was posting them off with Floryan's 'signed declaration', but all through October they mysteriously failed to arrive. Finally, after many queries from Katherine, they reached her on 2 November, and she made no more reference to them.

The contents, and Murry's response to them, remain conjectural. Katherine's willingness to pay the blackmail may well have disconcerted him; and whether he read them himself or not, during the month in which he failed to send them, the whole episode may have made him look at his wife in a slightly different light. If they related to nothing more than a long-extinct love-affair, would Katherine have been so desperately worried about them as to hand over without protest her entire advance on *Bliss*? It is perhaps more likely that something in them threatened to damage her professional reputation: and the most likely area might be references to her old plagiarism of Chekhov's *'Spat' khochetsia'*, 'The Child-Who-Was-Tired' in her version. This would explain both her acute anxiety and Murry's subsequent behaviour to Floryan, which certainly requires explanation.

In January 1927, Murry acceded to Floryan's demand that he provide a letter of support for his application to the Royal Literary Fund, and wrote warmly recommending him as someone deserving of a grant. Why should Murry have done such a thing, knowing that Floryan had blackmailed his late wife quite ruthlessly, if the only hold the man had on him was that he had had a love-affair with her in 1909? But if Murry feared his power to muddy her carefully fostered reputation as a flawless creature, it becomes easier to understand: he had just reissued *In a German Pension* and was about to publish her *Journal*. In 1946, Floryan again approached Murry and the Royal Literary Fund, and Murry again wrote a letter of recommendation.

There is a further indication that Murry had some inkling of the matter of Katherine's plagiarism. In 1916, when Constance Garnett embarked on her thirteen-volume edition of Chekhov's stories in translation, Murry knew little of Chekhov, Katherine was virtually unknown and *In a German Pension* was largely forgotten; but as the Garnett volumes were issued steadily, year by year, and as Murry became known as a Chekhov critic, Katherine must have begun to wonder when *'Spat' khochetsia'* would be reached, and what he would think of it. In 1919, she wrote to Kot, denigrating Constance Garnett's translations, and suggesting he might rival and race her. In 1920, Murry heaped praises on Chekhov in his *Aspects of Literature*; in the winter of 1920, with the publication of *Bliss*, Katherine's own fame began to be established; one of the most influential reviews, that of Desmond MacCarthy, drew a particular parallel between her work and that of Chekhov. Early in 1921, she wrote to Constance Garnett, telling her what a wonderful translator she was, and from then on Murry praised Constance Garnett and Edward Garnett praised Murry as one of Chekhov's most understanding critics, especially for his perception of Chekhov's 'candour of soul' and 'pureness of heart'. Murry also took to drawing frequent comparisons between Chekhov and Katherine.

In February 1922, Murry wrote to Katherine, telling her that he had received two Chekhov volumes for review, both of which (he said) they had read before: *The Schoolmistress* and *The Schoolmaster*. In fact, the first of these had been in print for several years, and Murry had actually received *The Cook's Wedding* (vol. 12), which contained *'Spat' khochetsia'* ('Sleepy' in Constance Garnett's version). Murry reviewed the volume, his article appearing in both the English and American press in March and April respectively. Other reviewers commented on the particularly striking plot of 'Sleepy', but Murry's article was entirely devoted to general praise of Constance Garnett and a eulogy of Chekhov for his love of life, his truthfulness, his absence of didacticism, and so forth. Shortly after this, in May, Katherine instructed the firm of Pinker that she did not wish to have *In a German Pension* reissued. The grounds she gave were these:

About *In a German Pension*. I think it would be very unwise to republish it. Not only because it's a most inferior book (which it is) but I have, with my last book, begun to persuade the reviewers that I don't like ugliness for ugliness' sake. The intelligentzia [*sic*] might be kind enough to forgive youthful extravagance of expression and youthful disgust. But I don't want to write for them. And I really can't say to every ordinary reader 'Please excuse these horrid stories. I was only 20 at the time!'

But perhaps these reasons have too much sentiment in them. As a business proposition it would I am sure be bad. It would, quite rightly, provoke all those critics who have been good enough to let bygones be bygones in judging *The Garden Party*. It is true, *In a German Pension* had a very good press. But it was that unpleasant thing – a *succès scandale*.[6]

This curious chain of reasoning was her last word on the subject.

When attention was first drawn to the similarity between Chekhov's story and Katherine's, it was gently done. In 1935, Elisabeth Schneider suggested that it must have been 'unconscious memory' at work. Another critic, Ronald Sutherland, tried to demonstrate that Katherine had actually 'improved' on Chekhov. But in 1951, E. M. Almedingen, a Russian scholar, made the case squarely for plagiarism in *The Times Literary Supplement*, quoting long passages from her own translation of Chekhov alongside Katherine's story, and linking it with her reluctance to have *In a German Pension* reissued.

Her allegation drew an evasive reply from Murry, who then left the field to other combatants. A stalwart defence was put up by Sylvia Berkman ('careless rather than devious') and Antony Alpers, who claimed that Mansfield was neither 'furtive' nor 'ashamed of her youthful peccadilloes'; a curious statement from the biographer who himself did so much to show just how devious and deliberately misleading she could be.

A. E. Coppard also defended Katherine generously as an admired fellow artist, diluting the effect of his defence somewhat by adding that it had been 'common knowledge' twenty years earlier that the story had been plagiarized. Five years later, the Russian scholar Gilbert Phelps waxed sarcastic at the expense of Alpers's description of 'The Child-Who-Was-Tired' as a 'free adaptation' of Chekhov.[7] By then the case for plagiarism had been thoroughly and unanswerably established by those in the best position to make it, i.e., readers of the original Russian.

Mimicry and plagiarism are close cousins, and many writers have testified to how much they have learnt from the first and how easy it is to fall into the second. In Katherine's case it was a quite minor and forgivable action: she had not copied the story so much as used it. Nevertheless, it must have haunted her, particularly as she lived alongside Murry's perpetual insistence on her truth and purity, her exquisite fastidiousness and her kinship with that other true and pure writer, Chekhov. For the same sin of plagiarism, Murry had turned against his idol Frank Harris.

Secretive as she was, she could not bear to be caught at any sort of disadvantage, exposed to mockery, vulnerable to gossip. The fear of exposure must have nagged and tormented her like a sharp pebble in her shoe. Hence, no doubt, her willingness to pay off Floryan, even though she and Ida were chronically short of money. Hence too, no doubt, Murry's subsequent generosity to the wretched Pole.

If further evidence as to the character of Floryan is needed, one has only to turn to a letter addressed to him by Bernard Shaw in 1924, in which he says he will never consent to see his Polish translator again if he can possibly help it: 'it costs me too much'. His letter of dismissal ends,

'Farewell, Floryan. God send you safe to Poland, and keep you there!'[8]

Floryan did not, however, return to Poland for many years; and after World War II, with the sufferings of all the Poles in mind, Shaw relented to him. In his old age, Floryan gave an interview to *Zycie Literackie*, a Warsaw literary weekly, in which he spoke at length about his association with Shaw; but he remained entirely silent on the subject of his friendship with Katherine Mansfield.

Despite the trouble with Floryan, Katherine worked throughout the autumn at the Villa Isola Bella with great intensity. To begin with there were the parcels of novels which arrived regularly from Murry — sometimes five in a batch — which she dealt with in a weekly piece, posted off punctiliously whatever her state of health. Not many of the books were worth the effort she put into them, but she turned out readable enough reviews. They are light-hearted and glancing, but fearless in mocking or chiding fashionable writers: Hugh Walpole, John Galsworthy, Gertrude Stein and Edith Wharton were all treated to some astringent words. In addition, she would sometimes take the trouble to go through the latest issue of the *Athenaeum* in a letter to Murry, making criticisms of each article, and suggesting ways in which it might be improved (for it was not doing well).

When Murry failed to pay her for her reviews, or when he forgot her birthday, she registered hurt; but then by the next post she would be reassuring him of her love, and wistfully expressing her hopes that he would soon join her. However often he disappointed her, it was still necessary for her to be able to draw on a vision of him as the ideal lover, with 'a far nobler and stronger nature' than her own.[9] The strain of idealizing him must have been considerable at the best of times; and, in fact, he was now in the throes of another entanglement, this time with the glamorous and forceful Princess Bibesco (née Elizabeth Asquith), who had literary as well as romantic designs on him, for she too wrote short stories. But for the moment Katherine did not know about this.

The villa and garden gave her great joy: 'the first real home of my own I've ever loved',[10] and she was devoted to her cook Marie, for whom food was a pleasure and an art. On sunny days she had a *chaise-longue* on the terrace where she read and wrote, taking to her bed in early evening, but often working into the night inside the mosquito nets. Her health was not improving, and in the middle of October she saw a new doctor, Bouchage, 'a very decent, intelligent soul' who insisted on going carefully through her whole medical history.* While he was looking into her secrets, she was also observing him. She divined that he too was tubercular:

I recognized his smile – just the least shade too bright ... his air of being a touch more vividly alive than other people – the gleam – the faint glitter on the plant that the frost has laid finger on. ... He is only about thirty-three ...[11]

His questions about her early life may have helped to prompt some musing in a letter to Murry:

I've acted my sins, and then excused them or put them away with 'it doesn't do to think about these things' or (more often) 'it was all experience'. But it hasn't all been experience. There is waste and destruction too.[12]

The next day she described dreams she has had, sinister, surreal fantasies of guilt and corruption – which is, no doubt, what they were – in which she was pursued by vile, drunken people led by Beatrice Hastings, who screamed '*Femme marquée*' at her. As this first dream went on, she found herself in a theatre in Piccadilly Circus, the actors beginning to fail and drift away until the performance was interrupted by an iron curtain falling. Outside, it was the end of the world, a huge crowd standing under a greenish sky from which soft, fine ash fell, while Salvation Army people with boxes of tracts asked her, 'Are you corrupted?' In another dream, Oscar Wilde appeared with long greasy hair, joking one minute, sobbing the next. Perhaps the dreams were a way of telling Murry, who never asked Katherine anything about herself and never showed any curiosity about her past, something real about herself, something different from the child-wife he wished to believe in.

At the end of October, in a burst of surprising energy, she began to write stories again. Almost all were built around the figures of women who find themselves at the mercy of monsters of one sort or another, whether mothers or fathers, husbands or employers (only in 'Poison' is the man presented as the victim of the woman). They are stories of great intensity, finely and deliberately paced and finished, though some were written at a single sitting, in an almost hallucinatory state. When one was completed, Ida might be summoned in the middle of the night to provide tea and sandwiches, an experience both women enjoyed. Some of the characters are drawn in brilliant caricature, some – the colonel's daughters, the 'young girl' – handled gently, and although the themes of vulnerability and isolation may relate to Katherine's sense of her own

* See p. 77 above.

situation, there is nothing self-pitying about them. They are impersonal, hard-edged, the work of a true writer, not a complaining woman. In 'The Daughters of the Late Colonel', in which Ida proudly fancied herself satirized, Katherine's ear for speech rhythms catches the fluttering self-effacement of the middle-aged spinsters who have been terrorized by their father all their lives, and have no idea how to live when at last he dies, with beautiful accuracy. Some – 'Miss Brill', 'The Lady's Maid', 'The Life of Ma Parker' – were conceived virtually as dramatic monologues; Katherine never lost her interest in performance, and as late as 1922 she wrote to Ida:

I intend, next Spring, to go to London, take the Bechstein Hall and give readings of my stories. I've always wanted to do this and of course it would be a great advertisement. Dickens used to do it. He knew his people just as I know old 'Ma Parker's' voice and the Lady's Maid.[13]

Katherine was now quarrelling with Murry by post again, the ostensible reason being his giving Constable a photograph she disliked for the jacket of her forthcoming book; but she was also annoyed by his failure to take time to discuss her work with her. 'I don't want dismissing as a masterpiece,'[14] she chided him sharply, and pertinently, for he was all too prone to greet her stories with a few exclamatory, flattering phrases, and leave it at that. She decided to approach an agent to act for her instead of Murry. J. B. Pinker, who had turned her down in 1912, agreed this time to take her on. He was one of the most successful of the relatively new tribe of literary agents; Arnold Bennett and Joseph Conrad were among his grateful clients, Lawrence and Wells among the ungrateful. Pinker enjoyed fostering new talent. He had an office in New York as well as London, and he set about helping Katherine to make money from her work at last.*

In December, Dr Bouchage insisted that she must at least stop the chore of reviewing, because her health simply would not stand the amount of work. She had developed a tubercular gland in her neck, which pressed painfully on an artery, and had to be lanced at regular intervals to let out large quantities of pus. Again she complained that she could do virtually no walking at all. From a medical point of view, what she needed now was rest, a simple routine and calm. Instead, a row blew up over Bibesco. Katherine did her best to be tolerant and

* Katherine never met her agent. J. B. Pinker died in New York in February 1922; his son Eric continued the business, but it crashed in the late 1930s.

wrote Murry a generous letter, telling him she knew how attractive he was to women, teasing him gently:

there is even a strong dash of the lady-killer in you! And think of the way you look in a glass if a glass is in the room – you return and return to it; it's like a woman to you – I have often noticed that ...[15]

She went on to say, '*Do feel free*. I mean that.' But she didn't mean it, of course, and when he committed the cardinal sin of sending her one of her rival's stories to read, she refused to, and raged to Ida. Murry wrote blubberingly to express his fear that he had contributed to the deterioration of her health, and she froze him in her grandest manner by return:

I have of you what I want – a relationship which is unique but it is not what the world understands by marriage. That is to say I do not in any way depend on you, neither can you shake me ... I am a writer first.[16]

As always, part of her meant it, part of her believed she was a pioneer in a new form of marriage. Her story 'The Stranger', written at this time, is full of distaste for the intimacies and exclusivities of marriage, showing a possessive and insistent husband suffering from his wife's elusiveness and interest in other people. Lately too she knew that Ida's ministrations had done more to allow her to write than Murry had ever done. Yet she was vulnerable, and he could shake her to the core. Her creed of freedom meant freedom for her to withdraw and make other arrangements, not for him. The private cosiness of marriage seemed an irresistibly attractive protection against the world at times.

Bliss (the book) appeared in December; so did Murry, for his Christmas visit, in a sheepish state. Things were soon patched over, after a fashion. Seeing her frailty, guilty at his own, and knowing that the *Athenaeum* was, in any case, failing, he decided to give it up and settle for a while at Isola Bella. He had been invited to lecture at Oxford in the spring, and needed to prepare his material.

First he returned to London to wind up the magazine and explain how things stood to his friends. Katherine was ill with fever and pain throughout much of this time, but her book was getting a good reception, in particular a magnificent long review from Virginia Woolf's friend Desmond MacCarthy in the *New Statesman*. In January, Knopf published the collection in New York.

Murry returned to Menton, and Ida set off for London in turn to clear out Portland Villas. Katherine wrote regretting the house, complaining of Murry's meanness, complaining that Bouchage was no longer satisfactory or helpful and had told her she must leave the Riviera. She was worried about money, and angry at a letter to Murry she had intercepted:

> Elizabeth Bibesco has shown signs of a life again. A letter yesterday begging him to resist Katherine. 'You have withstood her so gallantly so far how can you give way now.' And 'you swore nothing on earth should ever come between us'. From the letter I feel they are wonderfully suited and I hope he will go on with the affair. He *wants to*. 'How can I exist without your literary advice,' she asks. That is a very fascinating question. I shall write to the silly little creature and tell her I have no desire to come between them only she must not make love to him while he is living with me, because that is undignified. He'll never break off these affairs, tho', and I don't see why he should ... I wish he'd take one *on* really seriously – and leave me. Every day I long more to be alone.
>
> My life is the same, I get up at about 11. Go downstairs until 2. Come up and lie on my bed until 5 when I get back into it again.[17]

Prompted, perhaps, by the thought of Murry being so free with his literary counsels to others, she took up her pen again and wrote to her own literary master, Orage, telling him how grateful she was for what he had taught her about writing in the old days. The letter is obviously sincere, and at one stroke annihilates Katherine's argument to Murry that she considered *In a German Pension* unworthy to be republished, for, of all her collections, it most clearly bears the stamp of Orage's coaching. 'You taught me to write, you taught me to think; you showed me what there was to be done and what not to do,' she wrote to him in February.[18]

Later she sent a stinging rebuke to Elizabeth Bibesco, couched in terms that demonstrate what a formidable opponent she could be in straight combat with another woman. No one could possibly suspect from this letter that Katherine had once been a Bohemian and a merry adultress herself; the queenly tone of the rebuke may well have been an echo of the voice in which her mother had addressed her in those earlier years.

> Dear Princess Bibesco,
> I am afraid you must stop writing these little love letters to my husband

while he and I live together. It is one of the things which is not done in our world.

You are very young. Won't you ask your husband to explain to you the impossibility of such a situation.

Please do not make me have to write to you again. I do not like scolding people and I simply hate having to teach them manners.

Yours sincerely,
Katherine Mansfield.[19]

(The existence of a typed copy of this letter in a university library prompts the speculation that Katherine gave one to Ida; it seems scarcely likely that the Princess or Murry would have distributed copies.)

It marked a bad end to a bad winter for Katherine, but at least she had established a fundamental fact about herself at Isola Bella. It was that her writing mattered to her more than anything else: 'more even than talking or laughing or being happy I want to write'.[20] Nothing else was measured in the same scale. Shifty husband, failing health, the blackmail of an old lover and the treachery of other women, all these could be put aside with the brave and steely truth she had now set up as her device: 'I am a writer first.'

17

'READ AS MUCH LOVE AS YOU LIKE INTO THIS LETTER'

■

In May Murry returned to England, Ida arrived and the two women left the Mediterranean by train for Geneva. They alighted first at a hotel above Montreux, where Katherine pretended to the management to be suffering from nothing more than a weak heart. She was cheerful enough to mock the Swiss, as travellers do, for their cleanliness and respectability, their thick ankles, broad bottoms and large appetites, even their oversized bunches of flowers. As for her, she told her regular and affectionate correspondent Ottoline, 'on my bed at night there is a copy of Shakespeare, a copy of Chaucer, an automatic pistol and a black muslin fan. This is my whole little world.'[1] There was a touch of self-conscious and pathetic dramatization about this. The truth was, she was pleased and excited by the change of scene, the delicious mountain air, the spectacular scenery, even by hearing the German language spoken again, for which she felt a nostalgic affection from her Bavarian days.

Travelling further into the mountains up the valley of the Rhone to Sierre, where she had an appointment with an English doctor, she became more and more responsive to the beauty of the countryside and the old villages with their wooden houses, where the people still wore peasant costume. Her cousin Elizabeth had her chalet at Randogne, and the whole of that south-facing slope of the Alps was famous as a health resort. Katherine later said it was depressing to see so many obviously tubercular people about, but at first it seemed that now, at last, she had found the right place, and she wrote ecstatically to Murry about the possibility of renting a small wooden chalet of their own, where they could work together, comforted by a big white china stove in winter, with a kindly peasant woman to bring them coffee.

What actually happened at Sierre was that the doctor put her straight into a clinic. She refused to stay in for more than one night, and the doctor offered her his mother's chalet, which was empty, as an alternative. It stood higher still, under the glaciers, at Montana-sur-Sierre, with the pine forests standing on all sides: the sort of place where you can believe you might live for ever.

Murry wrote to say he was enthusiastic about the chalet and ready to live in Sierre for as long as she liked. His lectures were well received in Oxford; in one, 'The Process of Creative Style', he cited his wife's work, quoting from 'Prelude' as an example of true descriptive writing, alongside passages of Hardy and Shakespeare; and in a private letter to her he compared 'The Daughters of the Late Colonel' to Chaucer and Shakespeare. ('It's *fairy*. There's nothing been done to touch it these dozen years.') It seems unlikely that critical commentary of this kind can have pleased Katherine very much, however ill she might be feeling. At the same time, Murry was writing a long article for the *Athenaeum* in which he attacked a translation by Koteliansky and Leonard Woolf of Chekhov's notebooks, saying it was

almost a crime to make public fragments of an author's manuscripts which he obviously did not mean to show the world ... a tendency that is already much too prevalent among those who meddle with letters – the tendency to approach an author by the backstairs.[2]

When Katherine wrote to express her disappointment over the new volume of Chekhov stories from Constance Garnett, Murry agreed, and pointed out that 'poor old Chekhov' was probably writing for money, would doubtless have disowned half his stories if he'd had the chance, and had suffered from having them gathered by impious hands after his death. Of course, he went on, 'he is lemonade compared to Tolstoy'. Chekhov, he added, could never get the whole of himself into anything he wrote; whereas Katherine could, and he and she were going to sit down and write really big novels together.

The Woolfs and Koteliansky were, not surprisingly, annoyed by Murry's attack. As it happened, Virginia fell seriously ill for two months at this time, and when she recovered she read some of the stories in *Bliss*; she had already disliked the title story, and now she dismissed them as clever and disagreeable, leaving her feeling she must 'rinse out' her mind. For the time being, she allowed her jealousy of Katherine's success full rein.

When Murry arrived in Switzerland in June, they moved into the

Chalet des Sapins, perched at 5,000 feet among the pines, so high that patches of snow still lay about, like drying linen, wrote Katherine. She insisted on taking the room at the very top of the house, two floors above the bathroom, but Ida did not mind carrying jugs and basins of hot water up and down, even when she moved into lodgings in the village to give the other two more privacy. A routine was established that suited both Katherine and Murry very well. They read and wrote, sitting on their balconies as birds flew past, bright pots of flowers beside them and the forest and mountains all around. Katherine wrote to Brett that they had no intention of returning to England for years; here were woods and streams and the sound of bells in the air, golden sunshine with only occasional days of white mist, nights of planning future travel and future homes.

There were good doctors too, even if no doctor would tell Katherine what she wanted to hear: that she might yet be cured. In spite of her airily cheerful account of their life to Brett, there were bleaker moments when she told her cousin she thought Murry should leave her and find himself a healthy wife, and have children. Still, he was content for the moment. They read Proust together, and Jane Austen, whose ability to make plots Katherine admired: 'She makes modern episodic people like me, as far as I go, look very incompetent ninnies.'[3] Modest as she was, *Bliss* was enjoying success, the publication in May of 'The Daughters of the Late Colonel' had caused a stir (including a compliment from Thomas Hardy) and Pinker's efforts meant that her work was in great demand from magazines. As Antony Alpers has pointed out, this was not all to the good, since she felt obliged to deliver stories to deadlines, and passed some inferior work; nevertheless, the encouragement was a spur, and she responded by working for hours at a stretch and, despite a recurrence of her tubercular gland, the loss of teeth and all the horrors of breathlessness and pain, she produced another group of admirable stories.

Murry was also working on a second novel (chiefly interesting, his biographer F. A. Lea notes, as evidence that he had no talent in the direction of fiction any more than poetry). He was also reviewing books, and in late July a copy of Lawrence's *Women in Love*, which had finally found a publisher, arrived for him. Although Katherine wrote 'Really! Really! Really!' to Ottoline, knowing her intense dislike of the book for its libellous portrait of herself, her real response to it is not known. Murry wrote a review attacking it for its 'sub-human and bestial' aspect and, while praising Lawrence as a writer whose gifts were valuable, condemned him for here 'murdering' his gift in the service of a search for 'sensual mindless mysteries'. Murry, in short, saw *Women in Love* as a catastrophe (his review appeared in the *Athenaeum*, 13 August 1921). Since then, the novel has been read as a triumphant attack on the values of twentieth-century civilization by some, though more commonly, perhaps, as a very mixed offering in which passages of absurdity alternate with brilliant descriptive and dramatic writing. Few readers take Lawrence's sexual message to heart, either literally or allegorically; few have even attempted to decipher it. But, however ridiculous, or bathetic, or plain incomprehensible it becomes in certain sections – and however hard it is to understand why Birkin and Ursula enjoy 'good' sex, while Gerald and Gudrun are stuck with the bad kind – Murry's talk of bestiality misses both what is good and what is bad in the book.

In a letter to Brett in August, Katherine remarked that Lawrence had 'got it all wrong' in his depiction of 'tortured, satanic love'; but she prefaced this remark with praise: 'What makes Lawrence a *real* writer is his passion. Without passion one writes in the air or on the sand of the seashore.'[4] She went on to criticize his view of love and put in its place a 'religion' of love between human lovers, what she called an act of faith which replaced God, now that God no longer existed for us: 'we must feel that we are known, that our hearts are known as God knew us'. This, recalling Murry's claim ('Lo! I have made Love all my religion'), strikes one as both sad and artificial in the light of the actual relations between them. Just as Lawrence's declarations about love and the necessity for male dominance read with a hollow ring when one considers the state of affairs between him and Frieda (who became increasingly dominant throughout their life together), so Katherine's talk of being known by a lover as by God comes oddly from a woman whose husband was so oddly content not to know her.

The stories Katherine was writing now were little concerned with love except in its negative aspects. 'At the Bay' shows a mother brooding on her inability to love her children, a young girl drawn by vanity and boredom to risk a flirtation with a married man who proves to be merely predatory and sinister, very like the man in her early story 'The Swing of the Pendulum'. 'The Doll's House' is a study of the cruelty of petty snobbery taught to children by their families. 'Her First Ball' shows a girl falling into a black hole of despair, opened by a cynical dancing partner, in the middle of what should be an experience of unthinking enjoyment. 'The Garden Party' is about a crass and disunited family and the momentarily shattering experience of witnessing death in another family, again built around an innocent young woman. 'A Married Man's Story', a powerful, unfinished piece, is full of talk of poison, unhappiness and treachery; and it is hard to read its opening passage, in which a coldly withdrawn husband meditates on his sense of estrangement from his wistful wife, without one's mind slipping towards the evening scene in the Murry household; the man's account of his sense of isolation as a child also has obvious parallels with Murry on his own childhood. Even the most tender section of 'At the Bay' has the child Kezia asking her grandmother about a dead uncle, which brings her face to face with the unendurable notion of her grandmother's death. The same melancholy pervades 'Honeymoon', ostensibly a light-hearted sketch set on the Riviera but shadowed by the presence of suffering and death in the shape of a spectral Spanish singer. And 'The Voyage', a flawless evocation of a child's consciousness, in which a little girl takes an overnight boat-trip with her grandmother, is built around the obliquely referred to death of the child's mother. The surface of these stories is calm and even bright, but their theme is mortality, and even the joy in them is like Keats's joy, 'whose hand is ever at his lips/Bidding adieu'; and it is this precariousness that gives them their stinging clarity.

On a bad day, Katherine was too weak to raise her head from the pillow; on a good one, she was up at seven-thirty and able to get herself out – just – as far as the trees surrounding the house, and sit on a log in the sunshine, enjoying the sense of being alone. Murry might go flower-finding, bringing her back specimens, and she might play the piano for a while; at other times they read Shakespeare aloud together, and her notebooks are full of comments on the plays which show how deeply attentive she was to the economy of their language, and the way a pictorial effect is produced in a few words, two things she, as a writer, was especially concerned with: all Katherine's reading was that of a modest apprentice to the writer's trade. It is one of the most attractive things about her. She understood the difficulty, and appreciated the achievement, all the more.

Since they seemed so settled in Montana, Katherine asked Ida to go to London in August to collect her winter clothes and her cat, Wingly; Katherine was delighted to have her pet, and lavished love and attention on him. When, however, Ida decided she must make a second short visit to London to see her sister, who was expecting a baby, and proposed to act as escort to an English girl on the journey back to Switzerland, there was an explosion of rage from Katherine.

You're the greatest *flirt*, I ever have met, a real *flirt*, I do wish you weren't. With all my heart I do. It seems so utterly indecent at our age to be still all aflutter at every possible glance ... I am not going to flirt back, Miss, and say how I want you as part of my life and can't really imagine being without you. The ties that bind us! Heavens. They are so strong that you'd bleed to death if you really cut away. But *don't* – Oh please don't make me have to protest ... You can, in spite of my rages, read as much love as you like into this letter. You won't read more than is there.[5]

As far as flirtatiousness goes, it would be hard to improve on this angry example of the genre, and it marks one of the very few occasions on which Katherine seemed to doubt Ida's total loyalty, and pulled out the stops accordingly. But there was no need for her outburst: Ida returned quite unscathed and unchanged by her trip to London on her own business.

She found the winter approaching, and the period of remission in Katherine's symptoms giving way to new onslaughts of fever and pain. Murry was happy in Switzerland; he was able to work well, he enjoyed the company of Cousin Elizabeth and her guests down the hill, he was learning skating and skiing with great pleasure, and he believed that they had found the best possible situation for Katherine. But she was growing restless. In October, she heard from Koteliansky, with whom she was determinedly rebuilding her friendship, of another Russian exile, a Dr Manoukhin who was now in Paris claiming to be able to cure tuberculosis by irradiating the spleen with X-rays. The treatment was said to have been effective for many thousands of Russian soldiers (a point which was hard to check) and it was not unreasonable to ask herself if it might work in her case. She also began to consider the possibility of curing her diseased body by mental and spiritual means, and the names of other oriental gurus began to be mentioned: Piotr Ouspensky, author of mystical books, who arrived in London from the east in September, and immediately impressed Orage; and trailing behind him news of another still, the Greek-Armenian George Gurdjieff.

Murry, though not adverse to mystical ideas and experiences, was utterly opposed to Katherine seeking help from Manoukhin; but Katherine had another ally to hand, and she enlisted a willing Ida to make the necessary telephone calls to Paris. Once Christmas was over, for which Ida also organized the tree, pudding, crackers and presents, she went down the mountain to buy the tickets; and in the face of Murry's set disapproval, she escorted Katherine to Paris at the end of January, settled her in the Victoria Palace Hotel in Montparnasse, trudged around looking for an alternative hotel when Katherine complained it was sordid, visited agents in the hope of finding a flat to rent and performed her usual task of acting as lady's maid. Katherine was understandably nervous; she felt ill and exhausted, she quarrelled with Ida. When she set off to see Manoukhin she went first to the wrong house, where the sound of 'scampering and laughter inside' as she rang the bell seemed ominous; and when she found the right one, and he told her (through an interpreter) that he could cure her completely, she was wise enough not to believe him.

The next day she decided, or half decided, to trust him after all: 'I have the feeling that M. is a really good man. I also have a sneaking feeling ... that he is a kind of unscrupulous impostor'.[6] Even to Murry she sounded an only partially optimistic note. The action of the X-rays, she explained, would be like that of the sun, only more concentrated: it made them sound delightful. Manoukhin and his French partner had gone into her medical condition – heart and rheumatism as well as lungs – and were confident of a total cure. Privately she noted acute pain from 'sciatica' (another name for her rheumatism). 'Put it on record,' she wrote, 'in case it ever goes. What a pain it is. Remember to give it to someone in a story one day.'[7]

Despite her misgivings, she made up her mind to begin the treatment at once. It was expensive, 300 francs for each session. There were to be fifteen initial sessions, she told Murry, who was busy examining his conscience in scrupulous detail at the chalet to decide whether to remain and get on with his work or join her in Paris. 'I see myself,' she wrote to him with bleak humour, 'after fifteen goes, apologizing to them for not being cured.'

Ida was taking things too tragically for her, she thought of sending for Brett instead, and categorically forbade Murry to come. This, of course, brought him to heel at once, and Ida was sent back to Montana, pursued by contrite letters from Katherine, confessing that she had behaved like a fiend, 'but ignore all that. Remember that through it all I love you and understand. That is always true.'[8] This was soon followed by a suggested plan for their future lives in which she would spend six months a year with Murry in England, and six abroad with Ida, during which Katherine would work but they would enjoy many idyllic pleasures together:

tea in a forest, cold chicken on a rock by the sea ... concerts in public gardens, sea-bathing in Corsica and any other pretty little kick-shaws we have a mind to ... For we must be happy. No failures. No makeshifts. Blissful happiness. Anything else is somehow disgusting.[9]

In her next letter, this charming picture was cancelled, and she explained that Ida's very readiness to help her prevented her from making any effort herself; at the same time she asked her to make her some hand-sewn knickers (delicately referred to as *pantalons*) out of material Brett was sending her. In the next letter she reminded her to get the patterns for the knickers.

In their two rooms at the end of a dark little corridor in the Victoria Palace, she and Murry played chess together, drank bowls of tea, ate what Murry managed to bring back from his shopping expeditions, and worked as best they could. Katherine produced 'The Fly', one of her most famous stories, a bitterly painful and perhaps too obviously symbolic story of a bereaved father and a struggling, doomed creature. In England, *The Garden Party* was published by Constable, sold out and went into a second and then a third edition. Sydney Schiff brought James Joyce to tea with the Murrys and, although Katherine had mixed feelings about *Ulysses*, she struck Joyce as understanding the book better than her husband. She was beginning to be a celebrity, receiving letters from admirers and requests for foreign editions of her work. At the same time the forefront of her life was the treatment, which turned out to be less pleasant than a concentrated sunbath:

one burns with heat in one's hands and feet and bones ... Then one's head begins to pound ... if I were a proper martyr I should begin to have that awful smile that martyrs in the flames put on when they begin to sizzle![10]

she wrote gallantly to Brett at the end of March. Then she began to put on some weight, and allowed herself a flicker of hope. For a spell in May she was well enough to go out for pleasure, to the Louvre, to some literary dinners; but when Ida called in on her way through Paris to London, she registered a doubt as to whether things were quite as good as Katherine claimed.

As soon as Ida reached England, where she was planning to set up a teashop with a friend, she had a letter from Katherine which ended with the words,

the old feeling is coming back – an ache, a longing – a feeling that I can't be satisfied unless I know you are *near*. Not on my account; not because I need you – but because in my horrid, odious, intolerable way I love you and am yours ever.[11]

Within a week, having travelled back to Switzerland with Murry, who disastrously mislaid tickets and luggage, Katherine followed this up with a secret note. Apparently he could not begin to understand how ill she was, and would Ida help her to deceive him by 'proposing' to return to help: 'the truth is I can't really work unless I know you are there'. Ida immediately wrote that she would drop all her other plans and come. Katherine warned her that she would behave no better, but that Ida should 'try and believe and keep on believing without signs from me that I do love you and want you for my wife'.[12] The word 'wife' now seemed so right that she used it in her next letter to Brett, apropos Ida's arrival: 'the relief to have her is *so* great that I'll never say another word of impatience. I don't deserve such a wife.'[13]

Katherine sometimes spoke of herself as being more man than woman in her relations with Murry, in the sense that she took her own decisions and ran her own financial, professional and emotional affairs and did not depend on him. Whatever sexual attraction there was in the first place seems to have drained away pretty thoroughly, leaving Katherine, at any rate, as a being desexed by her illness and his incapacity. Equally, whatever incipient eroticism there may have been in the relationship with Ida (and I do not believe there was much), it was buried very deep by Katherine's determined rejection of lesbianism and by Ida's innocence. When she spoke of Ida as her 'wife', it was not, obviously, in a sexual sense, but in profound acknowledgement of her as a constant and indispensable figure in her life, often irritating when present, haunting the imagination when not, slighted for other, more fascinating rivals but yet offering attentions no one else could ultimately match: an exasperating, and triumphant, patient Griselda of the twentieth century.

I have suggested earlier that Katherine found in her exactly the mothering she never had from Mrs Beauchamp, and craved all her life: a warm, uncritical, generous and self-sacrificing devotion. Her rages against Ida were the rages of an angry infant; indeed, their whole story is a perfect illustration of the way in which one type of human relationship mimics and becomes a paradigm of another. Despite her claim to manly independence, Katherine also loved to be fussed over, given presents and flowers, have her clothes made by hand, offered delicious little meals on trays, all the attentions a child enjoys from an indulgent mother. Ida performed these functions, catered to Katherine's sometimes outrageous whims and summonses, cared for her physically and sympathized with her indignation against the meannesses and treacheries of others, whether family, friends or lovers. She was rewarded by knowing that her idol relied on her as on no one else. No doubt she derived considerable sly satisfaction from the spectacle of Murry perpetually berated for his lack of generosity, his coldness and unsatisfactory behaviour, even though he was always forgiven and reinstated. Ida learned to accept that Katherine loved him quite as much as she hated him, and that he was too deeply woven into her life to be cast off. She also knew that her own intimacy was older and deeper, that she and Katherine had shared more profound experiences than Murry had ever known, that Katherine trusted her with more than she trusted him; and whereas Murry would sometimes complain, absent himself, criticize or sulk, Ida had the terrific strength of the all-tolerant.

With the arrival of Ida, Katherine now once more resolved to part from Murry. 'We agreed that we had a depressing effect on one another,' he wrote in his notes to her letters, but it seems unlikely he would have been responsible for the break at this stage. She and Ida moved to the Hôtel Château Belle Vue in the lower part of Sierre, where Brett came to join them for a time, while Murry stayed at Randogne, having long talks with Elizabeth and visiting Katherine at weekends.* The heat made her increasingly listless and, although she still struggled to write, she produced nothing to match her work of the previous season.†

Early in August, she prepared two documents. The first was a private letter to Murry, which she deposited with her bank, leaving him all her

---

* According to Karen Usborne's study of 'Elizabeth', her companion A. S. Frere heard Murry telling her that Katherine had contracted syphilis after her visit to Carco at the front in 1915, when she is alleged to have had her hair cropped like a soldier's and visited the trenches in uniform. Apart from the fact that she did come back with her hair cropped very short, this seems an unreliable bit of reporting by someone known to be hostile to Katherine, as Frere was; but it may be a garbled version of Katherine's gonorrhoea, which very possibly flared up again as a result of the Carco episode. It does suggest that Murry spoke of his wife in less exalted terms during her lifetime than later.

† The fragmentary 'The Doves' Nest', which reads like pale imitation of a Henry James story, and 'The Canary', written as a present for Brett, and perhaps best left at that, for it is one of Katherine's handful of truly mawkish efforts.

manuscripts to do with as he pleased: 'destroy all you do not use. Please destroy all letters you do not wish to keep and all papers,' she instructed him, with just that ambiguity that so often appears when people are giving final instructions. It was a deeply loving letter, affirming her positive feelings for her husband, and undoubtedly intended to console him after her death, which it did.

A week later, she asked Ida to help her compose her formal will, discussing each bequest with her, and urging her laughingly to accept any money Murry might ever offer her ('don't hesitate'), his stinginess being an old joke between them. In this document she urged him much more directly to publish as little as possible of her remaining manuscripts, and to 'tear up and burn as much as possible'.[14] Had she given the instruction to Ida, there is no doubt that it would have been carried out, and we should now know less about her, and less of her writing; but it is also worth reflecting that she could have destroyed her papers herself and insisted on Murry returning her letters, had she really been set on their destruction.

18

'I WANT TO *WORK*'

∎

Katherine's next move was to wire Brett, back in her house in Hampstead, asking if she might come and stay. She wanted to see Orage; she wanted to see Koteliansky; and she wanted to see her father, once again on a visit 'Home'. Knowing his fear of disease, she explained to him in a letter that she was now entirely free of consumption, a very bold lie under the circumstances.

Ida and Murry both travelled with her this time. Katherine was installed on the first floor of Brett's Pond Street house, and quickly made herself a card to hang on her door against visitors, with either 'Out' or 'Working' inscribed on it. After a few days in the house next door, Murry went to Garsington, and then to friends in Sussex; Ida stayed in Chiswick, from which she travelled daily to Hampstead in case Katherine needed anything.

Frail as she was – one flight of stairs made her gasp for ten minutes, according to Brett – she maintained a hectic schedule, seeing the people she had come to see and several others; Dr Sorapure, who seems to have been his usual reassuring self, her old friend Anne Drey and an even older, childhood friend, Marion Ruddick. She saw her father twice ('This was the last time I saw Kathleen' is her father's entire comment in his memoirs) and her sisters Chaddie and Jeanne. Edward Garnett was eager to take both Murrys to meet his wife Constance in Kent, but this plan dwindled to a *tête-à-tête* luncheon in London between Garnett and Katherine.*

Orage was an early caller, and took her to hear Ouspensky lecture on

---

* Constance Garnett expressed some alarm at the prospect of entertaining Katherine on the grounds that she might be bored and 'I should fancy her rather a difficult person, very what used to be called *fin de siècle* and decadent'.[1]

his own and Gurdjieff's ideas as to how human beings might change themselves. Orage was ripe for conviction, and carried Katherine with him. When the Schiffs invited her to lunch to meet Wyndham Lewis, she was deeply offended by his jeering abuse of Gurdjieff as a 'psychic shark', and wrote scolding him and the Schiffs.

She had begun the irradiation treatments again, with a Harley Street man using Manoukhin's technique, but this time there was no perceptible benefit. Still, she saw her cousin Charlotte (Elizabeth's elder sister) and her brother-in-law Richard, for whom she felt great affection, and several of Murry's old colleagues from the *Athenaeum*; but she put off Ottoline and had no contact with any Bloomsbury friends. She made one visit to Murry in Sussex at the beginning of September, and they agreed tentatively that she might return to stay there in the spring. On the other hand, she told a young literary admirer (William Gerhardie, whose first novel she had recommended to a publisher) that she was planning to go to Lake Garda; she also said she was intending to write a play. When Kot called, they discussed the quarrel between Murry and Lawrence; Katherine defended Murry's hostile review of *Women in Love*, though not the manner in which he expressed his dislike of the book, adding, 'You know I am deeply sorry for Murry; he is like a man under a curse.'[2] Koteliansky urged Katherine to work, as a way of facing pain and suffering, but she said she could no longer write.

At the end of September, Orage announced that he was quitting the editorship of the *New Age*. On 2 October, once more accompanied by Ida, and seen off by Brett, Katherine set off for the Continent again; and once again, the sheer fact of travelling elated her:

We had a divine crossing, very still silvery sea with gulls moving on the waves like the lights in a pearl. It was fiery hot in Calais – Whoof! It was blazing. And there were old women with pears to sell wherever you looked ... old hands holding up satiny baskets. So beautiful. English ladies trying to eat them through their veils. So awful. The way to Paris was lovely too. All the country just brushed over with light gold, and white oxen ploughing and a man riding a horse into a big dark pond. Paris too very warm and shadowy ...[3]

She and Ida went back to their old haunt of 1918, the Select Hôtel by the Sorbonne, taking cheap attic-rooms up five flights of stairs, but with wonderful views over the roofs of the university with its monumental statues of 'large grave gentlemen in marble bath gowns'.

She went for a few sessions with Manoukhin, but they made her feel so ill with the pounding of her heart that she gave them up, although Ida obstinately believed the treatment had arrested the disease.

On her thirty-fourth birthday, 14 October, Katherine wrote at length in her journal, half intending to send her confession to Murry (but she didn't):

I have been thinking this morning until it seems I may get things straightened out if I try to write ... where I am.

Ever since I came to Paris I have been as ill as ever. In fact, yesterday I thought I was dying. It is not imagination. My heart is so exhausted and so tied up that I can only walk to the taxi and back. I get up at midi and go to bed at 5.30. I try to 'work' by fits and starts but the time has gone by. I cannot work ...

My spirit is nearly dead. My spring of life is so starved that it's just not dry. Nearly all my improved health is pretence – acting ...[4]

From this she justified her decision to try a different sort of healing with Gurdjieff. She rejected Murry's objections, saying that he knew nothing of the ill person she was, but only a fantasy of what she might be if she got better. The very risk involved in entrusting herself to Gurdjieff, who might be a charlatan, now seemed preferable to any other course she could think of, since her one quest was health:

By health I mean the power to live a full, adult, living, breathing life in close contact with what I love – the earth and the wonders thereof – the sea – the sun. All that we mean when we speak of the external world. I want to enter into it, to be part of it, to live in it, to learn from it, to lose all that is superficial and acquired in me and to become a conscious, direct human being. I want, by understanding myself, to understand others. I want to be all that I am capable of becoming so that I may be (and here I have stopped and waited and waited and it's no good – there's only one phrase will do) *a child of the sun*. About helping others, about carrying a light and so on, it seems false to say a single word. Let it be that. *A child of the sun*.

Then I want to *work*. At what? I want so to live that I work with my hands and my feeling and my brain. I want a garden, a small house, grass, animals, books, pictures, music. And out of this, the expression of this, I want to be writing. (Though I may write about cabmen. That's no matter.)

But warm, eager, living life – to be rooted in life – to learn, to desire to know, to feel, to think, to act. That is what I want.[5]

With this in mind, she submitted herself to an examination by Orage's friend Dr Young, who had himself abandoned his practice to join

Gurdjieff, and received permission to go, accompanied by Ida, to Fontainebleau where he was installed.

The background to George Gurdjieff's Institute for the Harmonious Development of Man, the sonorous but not over-precise name bestowed on the enterprise at Fontainebleau, was not a simple one. Gurdjieff had advanced his theories about the way in which human character could be remoulded in Russia, where such cults were popular in the almost apocalyptic atmosphere of the years leading up to World War I and the Revolution. He had been driven west by the civil war. His father was a Greek carpenter, reputed to have been once a rich herdsman, but fallen on hard times. His mother was Armenian, and he was born some time in the 1870s in a territory disputed between Georgia and Armenia, somewhere east of Mount Ararat. He was a clever boy and was selected for a good education at a cathedral school, and then as a young man appears to have set off on his travels east, seeking holy masters, possibly spying, and picking up a living as a carpet salesman and odd-job man: he was shrewd and practical, never at a loss, a spellbinder. When he felt he had travelled and learned enough, he set up as a 'master' himself, working that area where revivalist preachers and advertising men meet, and immediately attracted disciples. He was not an ascetic, but a gross drinker, eater and fornicator, a big, strong man possessed of great authority; people who put themselves in his hands felt secure, despite his caprices, through the sheer power of his personality.

Ouspensky, who was purely Russian, took up his ideas and began to lecture on them; the two men met in Istanbul in 1920. Then Ouspensky, who could speak English, attracted the attention of Lady Rothermere, the enormously wealthy wife of the newspaper proprietor, who summoned him to London (expenses paid). In 1921 both T. S. Eliot and Orage attended lectures and seances with Ouspensky, and Orage and Lady Rothermere became interested in what he had to say about Gurdjieff, who was now in Germany. He arrived in London also, early in 1922. The fact that he knew no western languages at all seems, if anything, to have added to his allure, for he quickly surpassed Ouspensky in popularity. Plans to establish his Institute in Hampstead were prevented by the Home Office, where he was suspected of being a spy; and, in any case, after a short spell in England, he himself expressed a preference for life in Paris.

In October 1922, the beneficent Lady Rothermere, with a good part of the profits from the *Daily Mail* and *Mirror* to play with, used them to become patroness of two ventures that might have surprised their readers, one being a quarterly literary magazine, the *Criterion*, edited by T. S. Eliot, the other the Gurdjieff Institute for the Harmonious Development of Man. It was set up on a large estate known as Le Prieuré, at Avon, near Fontainebleau, in the lovely wooded country south of Paris. Gurdjieff claimed that he raised most of the money for the rent himself, by treating drug addicts with hypnosis, by speculating in oil shares, and by setting up two profitable restaurants in Montmartre; but Lady Rothermere's contribution was probably more significant.

Once a monastery, as its name suggests, Le Prieuré had been converted into a private mansion in the early nineteenth century. Since the war it had been standing empty, its huge park and buildings both much neglected. Gurdjieff arrived there for the first time on 1 October – he had taken the place sight unseen – and, with about one hundred disciples, set about stocking the farm and making the place habitable. The most comfortable parts of Le Prieuré were used by Gurdjieff himself and important visitors such as Lady Rothermere, and, accordingly, were known as 'The Ritz'. Gurdjieff appointed servants for himself among the disciples; his personal habits were disgusting, and his bedroom and bathroom frequently needed the walls washing down (according to one of his most affectionate pupils, who performed this function as a boy*). Most of the disciples lived in small estate cottages or in comfortless, unheated rooms, which they no doubt welcomed, seeing the cold and inconvenience as part of their testing. They were set to work at once on building a huge oriental 'tent' out of an aeroplane hangar frame, complete with a throne for the master and lined with carpets from Bokhara and Baluchistan. It was to be a place for ritual dancing, meetings and holy observances. People's personalities were to be 'broken down' through severe manual work, compulsory oriental dancing and special tests, some of which resembled children's games: one called 'Stop', for instance, involved remaining absolutely motionless, whatever you were doing, at the command of the master. Orage was ordered to give up smoking and set to hard digging; not surprisingly, his health improved noticeably.

Gurdjieff's creed was that civilization had thrown men and women out of balance, so that the physical, the emotional and the intellectual parts had ceased to work in accord. It is an idea that appeals to many people, and, indeed, has an obvious element of truth in it. Whether

---

* Fritz Peters, an American who has given a wonderful account of Le Prieuré and the methods of the master in *Gurdjieff* (Wildwood House, London, 1976).

Gurdjieff's methods for righting the internal balance of his disciples had much, or any, merit is another matter. Since the whole thing depended on his personality, and made no scientific claims (as psychoanalysis did) or cosmological and moral claims (as most brands of Christianity did), it remained an amateur, ramshackle affair, and although Gurdjieff aroused passionate hate as well as love, his system seems to have done little lasting damage, and obviously allowed some people to change direction in a way that seemed helpful to them.

For Katherine, Orage's enthusiasm and her feeling that she must find something, if not a miracle at least another change of direction before her time ran out, was decisive. There can be no doubt that she knew she was nearing the end. She could not work, she had grown dissatisfied with the scale and quality of the work she had already done, 'little stories like birds bred in cages' she described them to Orage. 'Love', Murry's religion of love, had also failed her utterly. Ida's love, loyal and precious as it was, was that of a subject, not an exchange between equals, and she knew that was, in the end, not right for either of them. Her family was close only in her dreams: dead brother, dead mother, unloved and envied sisters, father so much more satisfactory as a creature of fantasy than in reality. Gurdjieff and his Russian disciples seemed to offer the attraction of a large, exotic, extended family, and one that had faith in its own busy activities and might make a place for her without subjecting her to special treatment or nursing; something positive in place of doctors, weakness, despair.

Katherine and Ida arrived at Le Prieuré together on 16 October for an exploratory visit. Ida was now the diary keeper:

A drive in the sharp air through an avenue of immense trees, arriving at an old château, long and low, with a fountain playing into a round basin in a large courtyard, the flower beds full of crimson flowers and golden autumn leaves.[6]

Katherine was given a pleasant room, with a mattress on the floor for Ida, and the next day Gurdjieff said she might stay for two weeks 'under observation'. All the evidence suggests that he was behaving kindly towards a woman who was clearly dying; there was little question of any cure being offered. Ida was sent back to Paris to collect Katherine's things, and then given her last dismissal: or rather, in the long comedy of their association, a semi-dismissal.

For while Katherine urged her towards independence, and affirmed her own happiness and self-sufficiency: 'If you love me as you imagine you do how could you make such a moan because I was no longer helpless,'[7] she scolded her briskly; at the same time, she still needed the old Ida. Her very next letter was an urgent plea for help again, as all her underclothes had been stolen from the laundry. Would Ida go to several shops in Paris for different items, about which she was most particular, and in addition quickly make her some 'tops', a shawl and a nightdress? This was followed up with more requests for things to be packed up and sent to her. Then she began to suggest that it would be a good idea for Ida and Murry to settle down together somewhere, perhaps on a farm. In fact, Ida found herself a farm to work on in Normandy.

Thus did Katherine 'release' Ida, and at her death a long, affectionate and wistful letter to her lay unposted on her table: Ida, obeying Katherine's injunctions to become independent, had not written as often as she would like: 'Write and tell me how you are will you? Dear Ida?'[8] Katherine remained, until Ida's own death at ninety, the beloved idol, brilliant and beautiful, her sins excusable on the grounds of pain and illness, her friendship an unbreakable bond: 'just as she expressed herself in writing, so I expressed myself in service.'[9]

Eager as she was to enter into the life of the commune, Katherine was offered, and took, the job of peeling vegetables in the kitchen. It was something she had done very little of in her life, and it spoilt her hands, but she did not complain; in fact, she boasted that she was able to do it rather than staying in bed and having special meals brought to her on trays. Across the impenetrable language barrier, she felt drawn to the Russians in the group, and they found her attractive and touching, with her burning bright eyes, her frailty and enthusiasm. She watched the dancing and the farm activities such as pig-killing and the delivery of a calf; she made her own bed, kindled her own fire and washed in cold water.

Her letters to Murry were still full of fantasy, only the fantasy had changed. Instead of the lovers' houses and children, she talked of how she was going to learn carpentry and farm work; already she was learning to weave carpets, and was about to be put in charge of the cows Gurdjieff had acquired; in fact, she was told to sit on a platform above the cowshed, following an old peasant remedy for tuberculosis. As time went by, she mentioned, without complaint, the difficulty in getting a bath or even a warm wash, and the intense cold, which made her stay in her fur coat: 'I gird it on like my heavenly armour and wear it ever night and day'.[10]

(Anyone who has ever tried to scrape carrots in a fur coat will know what this means.) She spoke enthusiastically of the friendly atmosphere and Gurdjieff's wisdom, but she could not as yet say she had made many friends, although she was learning Russian. When Murry suggested a visit, she put him off; but then she had always done this, even when she most wanted him to come. Now she was obviously worried that he might judge the place, where meals were at all hours, the men looked like brigands, and she spent many hours sitting alone in her room or in the cowshed.

She had, of course, one old friend to talk to: Orage, who said in the brief article he wrote in 1932 that he saw her almost every day at Le Prieuré. His account is dull and stilted, but worth pondering. He explains that she entered the Institute in order to undergo a process of self-training; that she had become dissatisfied with her work, and spoke of the need for literature to be more than didactic or aesthetic. Sometimes, he says, she claimed to have lost all interest in literature; at others she talked of working on new stories, and of having a contract for a book which she must honour.

One day she sent for him to tell him she had a new idea, which was that she should present good characters attractively. Hitherto she went on, she had been a camera, but a selective camera. She wanted to write stories that would 'first see life different and then make it different'.[11] She showed Orage fragments of stories begun, but then destroyed them. So far her words, or her words as reported, are sadly too vague and general to be of interest. When she came to outline to him a plan for a story she was considering, at once she becomes interesting.

It was to be about a married couple, both writers (Orage's unhappy phrase is 'jointly competing for the divine laurel'). 'One, or perhaps both of them, have had previous affairs, the remains of which still linger like ghosts in the new home. Both wish to forget but the ghosts still walk.'[12] To Orage's question as to whether their exercise in ghost-laying would have a happy ending, she answered, 'Not by any means. The problem might prove too big.'[13] Orage's report carries the sad, but hardly surprising, confirmation that Katherine's imagination remained haunted by the effects of her secret early experiences upon her subsequent life, and by the bitter lesson that she could not simply write off her adventures and tragedies to experience, but had to live with their grim after-effects as surely as the Alving family in Ibsen's *Ghosts*. Behind the talk with Orage there is a sense that she is groping towards confession and expiation instead of secrecy: a secrecy which must have been, at times, as great a torture as any disease.

In November, Gurdjieff decreed that Katherine should be moved into a tiny, uncomfortable room, without carpets. She told Murry it was warm, but the list of words for which she wanted Russian equivalents suggests otherwise: 'I am cold. Bring paper to light a fire. Paper. Cinders. Wood. Matches. Flame. Smoke. Strong. Strength. Light a fire. No more fire. Because there is no more fire ...' The conditions were obviously too much for her to bear, and she was moved back into her old, comfortable room just before Christmas. She gathered the commune's children to make paper flowers for the festivities, and prepared to deliver some recitations of her work on Christmas Day itself.

On 31 December she wrote loving letters to her father and her cousin Elizabeth; and to Murry, whom she had hitherto forbidden to visit her, at least until the spring, she now sent a pressing invitation to come within a week or so. January 8 or 9 was the suggested date, to which Gurdjieff had given his personal blessing. In fact, he wanted Murry to see his new theatre, which was to be opened on 13 January. Katherine told Murry exactly what clothes he was to bring, and asked him to include some shoes and a jacket for her in his luggage. 'I hope you will decide to come, my dearest. Let me know as soon as you can, won't you?'[14]

Murry arrived on the afternoon of 9 January. He found her 'very pale, but radiant'. They talked together in her room, and she explained that she had

perhaps now gained all that it had to give her, and that she might be leaving very soon. When she did, she would like to live with me in extreme simplicity in a small cottage in England, and she would like me to cultivate the land.[15]

She then introduced him to various other inmates, including Orage, whom Murry had not seen for many years, the English doctor James Young and Olga Ivanovna (who later became Mrs Frank Lloyd Wright, and ran her own very strictly organized community in America).

Murry's impression was that they all seemed serious, simple and also exhausted from their prolonged manual labours preparing the theatre. He himself lent a hand in painting coloured patterns on the windows. In the evening he and Katherine sat in the salon; at about ten she said she would go to bed. Her room was on the first floor. As she went up the stairs, she began to cough. Murry took her arm to help her. In her room, her cough became worse and 'suddenly a great gush of blood poured from her mouth. It seemed to be suffocating her. She gasped out "I believe ... I'm going to die."'[16] Murry put her on the bed and rushed for a doctor. The two who came immediately pushed him out of the room, although, as he always remembered, 'her eyes were imploring me'. A few minutes later, and she was dead.

19

'WHAT IS GOING TO HAPPEN TO US ALL?'

■

Murry sent a telegram to Ida at once, and she arrived on the following day. Both she and Murry said they felt Katherine had benefited from her time at the Institute, bizarre as it was, and despite her death. Both must have known in their hearts that her death was, in any case, inevitable and close; perhaps it had been as well for her to spend her last weeks engaged in something she felt enthusiastic about rather than simply waiting for the end. It's a view one can share, whatever reservations may be entertained about Gurdjieff and his entourage.

The funeral took place in the Protestant Church in Fontainebleau, and was attended by Murry, Ida, Orage, Brett and Katherine's sisters Chaddie and Jeanne; Koteliansky, refused permission to travel, mourned at home in Acacia Road. Ida threw marigolds on to the coffin, and travelled back to England with a distraught Murry.

In Wellington, Harold Beauchamp had just been honoured for his services to the Bank of New Zealand with a knighthood in the New Year's honours list, a fact that figured prominently in Katherine's obituary notice in *The Times* (which also placed her marriage to Murry in 1912). Beauchamp took as his motto *Verité sans peur*. With the growth of Katherine's fame he began to change his view of her, exactly as she had predicted. All the same, when Sir Harold came to write his memoirs, he was cautious enough to call in a 'literary expert' to write the chapter devoted to her, as though he did not trust himself to speak of her.

At Garsington, Ottoline sat down to write a memoir of her dead friend, which she read out to an invited group one evening by candlelight. It has not survived, and her friendship with Murry lapsed. Brett began a grieving diary addressed to Katherine (or 'Dearest Tig'); soon it became the repository of the details of her affair with Murry, who had no compunction about either seducing or dropping this forty-year-old virgin. Fortunately, the blood of the Eshers ran strongly in her veins, she showed great fortitude and found a new idol in Lawrence shortly afterwards.

Ida became, for a time, companion and housekeeper to Katherine's cousin Elizabeth; but she could not be handed on like a useful piece of furniture, and soon she settled alone in a cottage in the New Forest, a tiny, remote place where she lived out her long life with few disturbances beyond the occasional literary sleuth struggling up the overgrown path. When she came to write her book about Katherine, fifty years later, her memory was dim, but the power of Katherine's personality was not. She gave her the uncritical devotion of a perfect widow: in its pages, Katherine is always either a victim – of family, of lovers, of illness – or an idol, brilliant and irresistible in all her whims.

It took the news of Katherine's death to mend the quarrel between Murry and Lawrence, who wrote grieving from New Mexico,

> Yes, I always knew a bond in my heart. Feel a fear where the bond is broken now. Feel as if old moorings were breaking all. What is going to happen to us all? Perhaps it is good for Katherine not to have to see the next phase. We will unite up again when I come to England. It has been a savage enough pilgrimage these last four years. Perhaps K. has taken the only way for her.[1]

After this, Lawrence wrote regularly to Murry again, even inviting him to look for a country house where they might settle near one another, and offering to contribute to the new magazine Murry was setting up, the *Adelphi*, with a reconciled Koteliansky as business manager; this was not out of any need for money, for Lawrence's financial position was at last secure, thanks to sales of his books in America. An uneasy peace was reached, and when Frieda travelled to England alone in the summer, Lawrence asked Murry to look after her.

Murry sent Lawrence a copy of *The Doves' Nest*, a volume consisting of a few finished stories of Katherine's ('The Doll's House', 'The Fly', 'Honeymoon', 'A Cup of Tea') but mostly fragments. At this, Lawrence scolded Murry for making excessive claims for her work: 'Poor Katherine, she is delicate and touching. – But not Great! Why say great?'[2] He complained to another correspondent, in his most acerbic tone, of Murry's cheek in asking the public to buy Katherine's 'waste-paper basket'.[3] He did not know about her request to Murry in her will; nor did Murry ever give him one of Katherine's books, as she had requested, or apparently even bother to tell him of the bequest. Lawrence was irritated by the puffing. He was not an attentive or generous reader of his contemporaries, but he was ready to admire certain strengths in Katherine's work; only not at Murry's bidding. 'She was a good writer they made out to be a genius,' he said in 1925. 'Katherine knew better herself but her husband, J. M. Murry, made capital out of her death.'[4]

Still, the links between the old foursome of 1913 remained tenacious. It appears that Frieda tried to seduce Murry in the summer of 1923 and, although she did not succeed, Lawrence was angry and jealous enough to write a series of stories in the 1920s in which he systematically humiliated and sometimes killed off a figure modelled on Murry. In one, the faun-like hero is visiting the dead body of his beautiful young wife in a foreign convent (shades of Le Prieuré); he finds himself, through his display of grief, magically and irresistibly forced to smile. Presently, the attendant nuns notice that the corpse too has broken out into a smile: a cynical, Katherine-like one.

In another story, as the hero wanders Murry-like from one woman to another in Hampstead, he is struck dead by the god Pan; and, in the oddest of all, another Murry-figure becomes the second husband of a widow whose first (a self-portrait by Lawrence) returns to haunt the guilty couple. The story culminates in the mysterious death of the second husband and the first husband's triumphant, ghostly, sexual repossession of his wife. For good measure, she is given the name of 'Katharine'. It does not take a Dr Eder to read the significance of these works.

Murry struck back in his own way after Lawrence's death, both by writing *Son of Woman*, which purports to praise but, in fact, denigrates him, often in crudely sexual terms; and by becoming Frieda's lover, briefly. No ghost appeared to strike him down. By the 1950s he and Frieda were corresponding warmly and nostalgically about the golden past.

Lawrence was not the only one who thought Murry's zeal on Katherine's behalf excessive. Although T. S. Eliot sent a letter of condolence in January, saying he would be writing a critical article on her work, in June he wrote to his assistant on the *Criterion*, Richard Aldington, asking him to get 'a copy of Katherine Mansfield's book for me when it comes out. I think her inflated reputation ought to be dealt with.'[5] The article was not apparently written. Another friend of the Murrys, Sylvia Lynd, also spoke of Murry 'boiling Katherine's bones to make soup'.[6]

It is true that Murry did boil the bones, puffing and promoting Katherine's work through his own magazine, and running with Constable a well-organized and enormously successful publishing campaign in which segments of her work, fragments of stories, reissues, scraps of letters and pieces of journal (followed by 'definitive' versions of the same) were issued to the public all through the 1920s, and indeed into the 1950s. The pathos of her early death undoubtedly gave her work an extra appeal – people love to dwell on the words of the dying – but that alone would not account for its popularity, in England and America, France, Germany and in most countries touched by English culture.

What did make her so popular? It was not only the delicacy, charm and pathos attributed to her by Lawrence. The sharp impersonality, the clarity and concision of the best stories made them genuinely startling. Her voice was the voice of modernity, bright, short-winded, sometimes whimsical, often ambiguous, with no claim to wisdom and no time for the scene-setting of the classical novelists. Her territory was that of the fragile emotions, half-understood feelings, the fine edge between the ridiculous and the pathetic; she could render the vulnerability of the young, the sad stirrings of the sick, the jealous, the powerless, those who make animals or inanimate objects the focus of their feelings. Other writers studied her approvingly for 'her economy, the boldness of her comic gift, her speed, her dramatic changes of the point of interest, her power to dissolve and reassemble a character and situation by a few lines.'[7] The decades may have taken some of the shine off the originality of her method, but they have not robbed the stories of their vigour. Even those who dislike them acknowledge that there is something pungently alive in them.

Katherine's assessment of her own work was modest. Like all writers, she was pleased when she was praised and hurt by unkind criticism or dismissal; but she reproached Murry with overpraising her: 'I don't want dismissing as a masterpiece'. Her success meant a great deal to her, and she was businesslike in her letters to the Pinker agency. She saw herself as a professional, writing for money, always trying to learn from the work of other writers, aware of her own limitations and dissatisfied with her own best efforts. She noted in her journal, for instance, that 'The Garden Party', one of her most admired stories, 'is a moderately successful story, that's all'.[8] She accepted modestly enough Gerhardie telling her he did not like 'The Fly', though he was younger than her, and unpublished himself. Murry's claim that she was a genius would have seemed bizarre to her, accompanied as it was by his publication of negligible and discarded scraps and obviously private letters. She would not have been pleased either by his denigration of the meticulous professionalism she took so seriously, when he wrote that 'there was no difference between her casual and her deliberate utterances; ... her art was not really distinct from her life; ... she was never what we understand by a professional writer'.[9] Unable to control her while she lived, Murry could not resist manipulating her after her death to fit the pattern he preferred.

Although Katherine and Murry often presented their relationship as the most important element in both their lives – and it did absorb a huge amount of their energy – there is a sense in which neither sought true understanding of the other. For each of them, the other became a symbolic figure very early on: she the good, suffering, spontaneous genius, he the ideally beautiful scholar–lover without whom neither life nor death could be properly contemplated. Each settled to a dream-version of the other. Murry, being the more self-absorbed of the two, was entirely content to live with a woman whose history he ignored and whose inner life he denied; and she, with her desperate desire for secrecy, was in some degree satisfied by this, even though, in the long run, it left her isolated and frightened in her perfectly protected privacy.

Katherine was outstandingly gifted, original and ambitious to develop her gifts. She needed time, freedom and tolerable living conditions in which to work; the pity was that she never found all at once. Had she done so, it is not unreasonable to think she could have grown into a major writer. As it was, she spent the best part of her energy battling against her family and its expectations of her; against her ruined health; against her resentment of Murry's inadequacies and still more, perhaps, against his vision of her and her role as an artist in his romantic pantheon; against her fears and hugely exaggerated feelings of guilt.

The iconized, sanitized, flawless Katherine insisted on by Murry must have increased the panic anxiety she felt at any threat to expose the secrets of her youth. Today, ironically, we have ceased to want our artists to be virtuous, and rather favour a history of dubious deeds as a basis for the creative life. Katherine, alive to irony, might laugh at the change in attitude; but she would probably hate to have our sympathy.

Yet she deserves it, for it was largely through her adventurous spirit, her eagerness to grasp at experience and to succeed in her work, that she became ensnared in disaster. Her short life, so modern and busy, has the shape of a classic tragedy.

At her least likeable, she adopted sentimental postures, and used them as a shield for treacherous malice. Yet how much there is that is admirable about her. She was always more interested in the external world than in her own suffering. She was a worker to her bones, and prized the effort required by craft. She fought, bravely, stubbornly, tenaciously, against two terrifying and incurable diseases that finally destroyed her. If she was never a saint, she was certainly a martyr, and a heroine in her recklessness, her dedication and her courage.

NOTES

■

1 'THE FAVOURITE OF THE GODS'

1. *The Diary of Virginia Woolf: 1925–30*, 7 December 1925, ed. Anne Olivier Bell (Hogarth Press, London, 1980), vol. III, p. 50.
2. J. M. Murry, *Between Two Worlds* (Jonathan Cape, London, 1935), p. 194.
3. A letter from Frieda Lawrence to Murry written in the 1950s says 'Lawrence said Katherine had a lot in common with Dickens, you know when the kettle is so alive on the fire and things seem to take on such significance.'
4. K.M. to Sarah Gertrude Millin, [March 1922], unpublished letter in Millin papers, University of Witwatersrand, South Africa.
5. Anthony Trollope, *Australia and New Zealand* (Chapman & Hall, London, 1873), vol. II.
6. R. R. Beauchamp, 'A Family Affair or What Became of Fred?', article held in Alexander Turnbull Library, Wellington, New Zealand (MS 1458).
7. Notes taken in private conversation with Mrs Jeanne Renshaw, 1977.
8. *The Journal of Katherine Mansfield*, November 1906, ed. J.M.M. (Constable, London, 1954), p. 7.
9. ibid., December 1920, p. 234.
10. K.M. to J.M.M., November 1920, *Katherine Mansfield's Letters to John Middleton Murry: 1913–22*, ed. J.M.M. (Constable, London, 1951), p. 605.
11. *Journal*, 12 March 1916, p. 106.
12. ibid.
13. Marion C. Ruddick, 'Incidents in the Childhood of Katherine Mansfield', unpublished TS in the Alexander Turnbull Library.
14. K.M.'s MS notes in the Alexander Turnbull Library.
15. Ruddick, op. cit.
16. ibid.
17. ibid.
18. Notes taken in private conversation with Mrs Jeanne Renshaw, 1977.
19. Antony Alpers, *The Life of Katherine Mansfield* (Jonathan Cape, London, 1980), p. 13.
20. K.M.'s MS notes, transcribed by Margaret Scott and published in the *Turnbull Library Record*, March 1970, p. 8.

21. Ruth Elvish Mantz and J.M.M., *The Life of Katherine Mansfield* (Constable, London, 1933), p. 152.
22. K.M.'s MS notes in Alexander Turnbull Library.
23. Mantz and J.M.M., op. cit., p. 152.
24. *Journal*, March 1916, p. 107.
25. Burney Trapp to his son Joseph Trapp, 4 March 1947, unpublished letter.
26. Mantz and J.M.M., op. cit., p. 152.
27. Burney Trapp to his son Joseph Trapp, 4 March 1947, unpublished letter.
28. Harold Beauchamp, *Reminiscences and Recollections* (Thomas Avery, New Plymouth, New Zealand, 1937), p. 86.

2 QUEEN'S: 'MY *WASTED, WASTED* EARLY GIRLHOOD'

1. K.M. to Harold Beauchamp, 26 June 1922, *The Letters of Katherine Mansfield*, ed. J.M.M. (Constable, London, 1928), vol. II, p. 222.
2. K.M. to Sylvia Payne, 26 December 1904, *The Collected Letters of Katherine Mansfield*, eds. Margaret Scott and Vincent O'Sullivan (Oxford University Press, 1984), vol. I, p. 14.
3. K.M. to Marion Tweed, 16 April 1903, *Collected Letters*, Scott and O'Sullivan, vol. I, p. 5.
4. K.M.'s MS notes, transcribed by Margaret Scott and published in the *Turnbull Library Record*, March 1970, p. 24.
5. K.M. to Sylvia Payne, 10 July 1904, *Collected Letters*, Scott and O'Sullivan, vol. I, p. 14.
6. *Journal*, February 1916, p. 103.
7. Cited in Jeffrey Meyers, *Katherine Mansfield: A Biography* (Hamish Hamilton, London, 1978), p. 15.
8. Elaine Kaye, *A History of Queen's College* (Chatto & Windus, London, 1972), p. 134.
9. K.M. to Sylvia Payne, 24 January 1904, *Collected Letters*, Scott and O'Sullivan, vol. I, p. 10.
10. Mantz and J.M.M., op. cit., p. 198.
11. K.M.'s MS notes, transcribed by Margaret Scott and published in the *Turnbull Library Record*, March 1970, p. 17.
12. ibid., p. 16.
13. ibid., p. 13.
14. J.M.M. to Vere Bartrick-Baker, 2 June 1933, unpublished letter (appears by permission of Navin Sullivan).
15. K.M. to Sylvia Payne, 24 April 1906, *Collected Letters*, Scott and O'Sullivan, vol. I, p. 18.
16. ibid.
17. K.M.'s MS notes, transcribed by Margaret Scott and published in the *Turnbull Library Record*, March 1970, p. 16.
18. ibid., p. 20.
19. Burney Trapp to his son Joseph Trapp, 4 March 1947, unpublished letter.
20. *Journal*, November 1906, p. 6.

21. K.M.'s MS notes, transcribed by Margaret Scott and published in the *Turnbull Library Record*, March 1970, p. 17.
22. *Journal*, November 1906, p. 7.
23. K.M.'s MS notes, transcribed by Margaret Scott and published in the *Turnbull Library Record*, March 1970, p. 25.

3 NEW ZEALAND 1907: 'THE SUITABLE APPROPRIATE EXISTENCE'

1. K.M. to Sylvia Payne, 8 January 1907, *Collected Letters*, Scott and O'Sullivan, vol. I, p. 21.
2. ibid.
3. K.M. to Vera Beauchamp, March 1908, *Collected Letters*, Scott and O'Sullivan, vol. I, p. 42.
4. Burney Trapp to his son Joseph Trapp, 4 March 1947, unpublished letter (appears by permission of Professor Joseph Trapp).
5. Alpers, op. cit., p. 48.
6. K.M. to Sylvia Payne, 4 March 1908, *Collected Letters*, Scott and O'Sullivan, vol. I, p. 41.
7. Cited in Vincent O'Sullivan, *Katherine Mansfield's New Zealand* (Golden Press, Auckland, 1974), p. 6.
8. K.M. to Vera Beauchamp, 19 June 1908, *Collected Letters*, Scott and O'Sullivan, vol. I, p. 45.
9. Burney Trapp to his son Joseph Trapp, 4 March 1947, unpublished letter.
10. Conversation with Mrs Edith Robison, recorded for the author by Bruce Mason in New Zealand, 1977.
11. ibid.
12. *Journal*, June 1907, pp. 12–13.
13. ibid., p. 14.
14. ibid.
15. Conversation with Mrs Edith Robison, recorded for the author by Bruce Mason, 1977.
16. Frieda Lawrence, *Not I, But the Wind* (Heinemann, London, 1935), p. 79.
17. K.M. to Martha Putnam, 22 July 1907, *Collected Letters*, Scott and O'Sullivan, vol. I, p. 23.
18. K.M. to E.J. Brady, 23 September 1907, *Collected Letters*, Scott and O'Sullivan, vol. I, p. 26.
19. *The Stories of Katherine Mansfield*, ed. Antony Alpers (Oxford University Press, 1984), p. 9.
20. K.M. to the Trowell family, 14 November 1907, *Collected Letters*, Scott and O'Sullivan, vol. I, p. 29.
21. *Journal*, 17 December 1907, p. 33.
22. K.M. to Martha Putnam, December 1907, *Collected Letters*, Scott and O'Sullivan, vol. I, p. 35.
23. Cited in *Beltane Book Bureau* (Wellington, 1944), p. 11.

24. K.M. to Martha Putnam, December 1907, *Collected Letters*, Scott and O'Sullivan, vol. I, p. 36.
25. ibid., January 1908, p. 36.
26. K.M. to Vera Beauchamp, spring 1908, *Collected Letters*, Scott and O'Sullivan, vol. I, p. 35.
27. ibid., 17 January 1908, p. 37.
28. ibid., 12 June 1908, p. 47.
29. Beauchamp, op. cit., p. 90.
30. Information from Alison Waley.
31. O'Sullivan, op cit., p. 78.
32. *Journal*, May 1908, p. 37.

4 LONDON 1908: NEW WOMEN

1. Ronald Clark, *The Life of Bertrand Russell* (Cape/Weidenfeld, London, 1975), p. 122.
2. Helen Corke, *In Our Infancy* (Cambridge University Press, 1975), p. 168.
3. Virginia Woolf to Lady Robert Cecil, May 1909, *The Letters of Virginia Woolf: 1882–1912*, ed. Nigel Nicolson (Hogarth Press, London, 1975), vol. I, p. 296.
4. Quentin Bell, *Virginia Woolf: A Biography* (Hogarth Press, London, 1972), vol. I, p. 124.
5. *New Age*, 17 March 1910.
6. Virginia Woolf to Madge Vaughan, May 1909, *The Letters of Virginia Woolf: 1882–1912*, Nicolson, vol. I, p. 395.
7. *Ottoline at Garsington*, ed. Robert Gathorne-Hardy (Faber, London, 1974), p. 281.

5 'MY WONDERFUL, SPLENDID HUSBAND'

1. Ida Baker, *Katherine Mansfield: The Memories of L.M.* (Michael Joseph, London, 1971), p. 31.
2. K.M.'s M S of 'Maata', transcribed by Margaret Scott and published in the *Turnbull Library Record*, May 1979, p. 22.
3. K.M. to Garnet Trowell, 3 October 1908, *Collected Letters*, Scott and O'Sullivan, vol. I, p. 64.
4. Information from Ida Baker to the author, 1977.
5. Karen Usborne, '*Elizabeth*' (Bodley Head, London, 1986), p. 20.
6. K.M. to Garnet Trowell, 21 October 1908, *Collected Letters*, Scott and O'Sullivan, vol. I, p. 75.
7. ibid., 17 September 1908, p. 60.
8. ibid., 12 October 1908, p. 68.
9. ibid., 2 November 1908, p. 84.
10. ibid.
11. ibid., 12 October 1908, p. 69.
12. K.M.'s M S of 'Maata', transcribed by Margaret Scott and published in the *Turnbull Library Record*, May 1979, p. 18.

13. Information from Mrs Dorothy Richards (née Trowell) to the author, 1977.
14. George Bowden, 'Memoir', unpublished T S in Alexander Turnbull Library.
15. K.M., *Poems*, ed. J.M.M. (Constable, London, 1923), p. 28.
16. K.M.'s M S of 'Maata', transcribed by Margaret Scott and published in the *Turnbull Library Record*, May 1979, p. 19.
17. Baker, op. cit., p. 47.
18. K.M.'s draft letter to Garnet Trowell, April 1909, *Collected Letters*, Scott and O'Sullivan, vol. I, p. 90.
19. ibid.
20. ibid.

6 BAVARIA 1909: 'KÄTHE BEAUCHAMP-BOWDEN, *SCHRIFTSTELLERIN*'

1. Vera French to K.M., 12 December 1909, unpublished letter in private collection.
2. Floryan Sobieniowski to K.M., 12 December 1909, unpublished letter in private collection.
3. ibid., 9 January 1910.
4. Beatrice, Lady Glenavy, *Today We Will Only Gossip* (Constable, London, 1964), p. 70.
5. K.M. to S. S. Koteliansky, 10 March 1915, *Collected Letters*, Scott and O'Sullivan, vol. I, p. 154.

The chief sources for this chapter are: C. C. Norris, *Gonorrhea in Women* (W. B. Saunders, Philadelphia and London, 1913); Palmer Findley, *Gonorrhea in Women* (St Louis, 1908); Alfred Keogh, *A Manual of Venereal Disease* (Oxford University Press, 1913); and the *British Medical Journal* between 1890 and 1920, containing a great deal of information about gonorrhoea and with especial reference to a report by Dr Frances Ivens to the Association of Medical Women in 1909.

7 THE *NEW AGE*: 'YOU TAUGHT ME TO WRITE, YOU TAUGHT ME TO THINK'

1. Cited in Philip Mairet, *A.R. Orage: A Memoir* (Dent, London, 1936), p. 59.
2. Mary Gawthorpe, *Up Hill to Holloway* (Traversity Press, Penobscot, Maine, 1962), pp. 191–203.
3. William Orton, *The Last Romantic* (Cassell, London, 1937), p. 269.
4. *Collected Letters*, Scott and O'Sullivan, vol. I, footnote to p. 108.
5. K.M. to William Orton, autumn 1910, *Collected Letters*, Scott and O'Sullivan, vol. I, p. 100.
6. ibid., summer 1910, p. 100.
7. K.M. to Brett, December 1921, *The Letters of K.M.*, J.M.M., vol. II, p. 160.
8. David Arkell, 'The Tigers' Lair in Gray's Inn Road', *Camden History Review*, November 1980.
9. *Journal*, 6 September 1911, p. 46. (Orton printed this passage independently in *The Last Romantic*, p. 281.)

10. J.M.M. to Ida Baker, 29 May 1933, unpublished letter. Murry places the reading and burning of the letters at Runcton Cottage, in the late summer of 1912.

11. K.M. to Anne Drey, probably January 1921, from Isola Bella, cited in *Adam* (no. 300, 1965), p. 93. Murry's letter of 29 May 1933 also asks about K.M.'s friendship with Gwen Otter.

12. Sil-Vara fought in the war of 1914 (against the English, of course) and in the 1920s had some success as a playwright; an English translation of his comedy of sexual manners, *Caprice*, was performed by the Lunts in New York and at the St James's Theatre in London in 1929, and published by Gollancz.

13. K.M. to Edna Smith, September 1911, *Collected Letters*, Scott and O'Sullivan, vol. I, p. 107.

14. End-page of *In a German Pension* (Stephen Swift, London, 1911).

8 'MAKE ME YOUR MISTRESS'

1. J.M.M., 'Life', *Rhythm*, summer 1911.

2. J.M.M., *Between Two Worlds*, p. 194.

3. K.M., *Poems*, p. xiii.

4. J.M.M. to K.M., March 1912, *The Letters of John Middleton Murry to Katherine Mansfield*, ed. C. A. Hankin (Constable, London, 1983), p. 17.

5. Information supplied by Mrs Barbara Barr (née Weekley), who overheard the conversation.

6. J.M.M. to K.M., 26 March 1912, *The Letters of J.M.M. to K.M.*, Hankin, p. 18.

7. K.M. to Frank Harris, summer 1912, *Collected Letters*, Scott and O'Sullivan, vol. I, p. 113.

8. J.M.M., *Between Two Worlds*, p. 179.

9. K.M. to Mrs Beauchamp, 15 December 1914, *Collected Letters*, Scott and O'Sullivan, vol. I, p. 144.

10. Glenavy, op. cit., p. 56.

11. K.M. to Sylvia Payne, 11 September 1912, *Collected Letters*, Scott and O'Sullivan, vol. I, p. 113.

12. D. H. Lawrence to Edward Garnett, 19 December 1912, *The Letters of D.H. Lawrence*, ed. James T. Boulton (Cambridge University Press, 1979), vol. I, p. 489.

13. Jessie Chambers, *D.H. Lawrence: A Personal Record* (Jonathan Cape, London, 1935), p. 82.

14. *Rhythm*, March 1913.

15. D. H. Lawrence to Ernest Collings, 24 February 1913, *The Letters of D.H. Lawrence*, Boulton, vol. I, p. 519.

16. Glenavy, op. cit., p. 58.

9 'ALL I REMEMBER IS SUNSHINE AND GAIETY'

1. K.M. to Edward Garnett, February 1913, *Collected Letters*, Scott and O'Sullivan, vol. I, p. 119.

2. J.M.M. to K.M., 19 May 1913, *The Letters of J.M.M. to K.M.*, Hankin, p. 24.

3. ibid., 12 May 1913, p. 23.

4. K.M. to J.M.M., 13 May 1913, *Collected Letters*, Scott and O'Sullivan, vol. I, p. 122.
5. D. H. Lawrence to Ernest Collings, 13 May 1913, *The Letters of D.H. Lawrence*, Boulton, vol. I, p. 548.
6. J.M.M. to K.M., 6 May 1913, *The Letters of J.M.M. to K.M.*, Hankin, p. 21.
7. D. H. Lawrence to Constance Garnett, 10 July 1917, *The Letters of D.H. Lawrence*, Boulton, vol. I, p. 32.
8. J.M.M., *Reminiscences of D.H. Lawrence* (Jonathan Cape, London, 1933), p. 33.
9. K.M.'s M S of 'Maata', transcribed by Margaret Scott and published in the *Turnbull Library Record*, May 1979.
10. D. H. Lawrence to J.M.M., 27 November 1913, *The Letters of D.H. Lawrence*, Boulton, vol. I I, p. 111.
11. K.M. to Charlotte Perkins (née Beauchamp), 22 December 1913, *Collected Letters*, Scott and O'Sullivan, vol. I, p. 133.
12. *Journal*, 15 November 1914, p. 62.
13. K.M. to Ida Baker, 24 February 1914, *Collected Letters*, Scott and O'Sullivan, vol. I, p. 138.
14. *Journal*, 26 March 1914, p. 56.

10 1914: 'OTHER PEOPLE, OTHER THINGS'

1. J.M.M., *Reminiscences of D.H. Lawrence*, p. 39.
2. J.M.M., *Between Two Worlds*, p. 284.
3. Several accounts of this incident exist, including one by Murry himself and one by Ivy Litvinov, in *Adam* (nos. 370–75, 1972).
4. D. H. Lawrence to Sallie Hopkin, 13 July 1914, *The Letters of D.H. Lawrence*, Boulton, vol. I I, p. 196.
5. J.M.M., *Between Two Worlds*, p. 295.
6. D. H. Lawrence to S. S. Koteliansky, 11 July 1914, *The Letters of D.H. Lawrence*, Boulton, vol. I I, p. 207.
7. D. H. Lawrence to Edward Marsh, 25 August 1914, *The Letters of D.H. Lawrence*, Boulton, vol. I I, p. 212.
8. *Journal*, p. 61.
9. K.M. to Harold Beauchamp, 15 December 1914, *Collected Letters*, Scott and O'Sullivan, vol. I, p. 142.
10. ibid., p. 142.
11. K.M. to Vera Bell (née Beauchamp), 26 February 1916, *Collected Letters*, Scott and O'Sullivan, vol. I, p. 246.
12. *Memoirs and Correspondence of Frieda Lawrence*, ed. E.W. Tedlock (Heinemann, London 1961), p. 64.
13. J.M.M., *Reminiscences of D.H. Lawrence*, p. 40.
14. *Memoirs and Correspondence of Frieda Lawrence*, Tedlock, p. 425.
15. Leonard Woolf, *The Autobiography of Leonard Woolf* (Hogarth Press, London, 1964), vol. I I I, p. 252.
16. S.S. Koteliansky to Sydney Waterlow, 31 June 1927, cited by John Carswell in *Lives and Letters* (Faber, London, 1978), p. 101.

17. D.H. Lawrence to Amy Lowell, 18 December 1918, *The Letters of D.H. Lawrence*, Boulton, vol. I I, p. 244.
18. *The Selected Letters of Mark Gertler*, ed. Noel Carrington (Hart-Davis, London, 1965), introduction, p. 34.
19. ibid., p. 77.
20. *Journal*, 18 December 1914, p. 63.
21. ibid., 1 January 1915, p. 64.
22. ibid., 10 January 1915, p. 67.
23. ibid., 20 January 1915, p. 70.
24. K.M. to Frieda Lawrence, 22 February 1915, *Collected Letters*, Scott and O'Sullivan, vol. I, p. 150.
25. *Journal*, 20 February 1915, p. 78.
26. J.M.M., *Between Two Worlds*, p. 340.
27. K.M. to S.S Koteliansky, 10 March 1915, *Collected Letters*, Scott and O'Sullivan, vol. I, p. 154.
28. ibid., 29 March 1915, p. 173.
29. K.M. to J.M.M, 22 March 1915, *Collected Letters*, Scott and O'Sullivan, vol. I, p. 164.
30. J.M.M. to K.M., 25 March 1915, *The Letters of J.M.M. to K.M.*, Hankin, p. 54.
31. K.M. to J.M.M., 8 May 1915, *Collected Letters*, Scott and O'Sullivan, vol. I, p. 178.
32. ibid., 6–7 May 1915, p. 176.
33. D.H. Lawrence to S.S. Koteliansky, 3 May 1915, *The Letters of D.H. Lawrence*, Boulton, vol. I I, p. 33.
34. J.M.M. to K.M., 11 May 1915, *The Letters of J.M.M. to K.M.*, Hankin, p. 63.
35. K.M. to J.M.M., 14 May 1915, *Collected Letters*, Scott and O'Sullivan, vol. I, p. 187.
36. D.H. Lawrence to Ottoline Morrell, 9 September 1915, *The Letters of D.H. Lawrence*, Boulton, vol. I I, p. 389.
37. J.M.M., *Between Two Worlds*, p. 351.
38. Mark Gertler to Carrington, 14 September 1915. *The Selected Letters of Mark Gertler*, Carrington, p. 102.
39. K.M. to S.S. Koteliansky, 28 November 1915, *Collected Letters*, Scott and O'Sullivan, vol. I. p. 201.
40. K.M. to Anne Drey, 8 December 1915, *Collected Letters*, Scott and O'Sullivan, vol. I, p. 203.
41. J.M.M. to K.M., 20 December 1915, *The Letters of J.M.M. to K.M.*, Hankin, p. 79.
42. ibid., 26 December 1915, p. 88.
43. K.M. to J.M.M., 29 December 1915, *Collected Letters*, Scott and O'Sullivan, vol. I, p. 239.
44. ibid., 30–31 December 1915, p. 244.
45. *Journal*, 22 January 1916, p. 94.
46. ibid., 13 February 1916, p. 96.
47. K.M. to J.M.M., 22 March 1916, *Collected Letters*, Scott and O'Sullivan, vol. I, p. 255.
48. D.H. Lawrence to K.M. and J.M.M., 24 February 1916, *The Letters of D.H. Lawrence*, Boulton, vol. I I, p. 550.

49. Frieda Lawrence to K.M., 8 March 1916, *The Letters of D.H. Lawrence*, Boulton, vol. II, p. 571.

50. K.M. to J.M.M., 22 March 1916, *Collected Letters*, Scott and O'Sullivan, vol. I, p. 254.

11 CORNWALL 1916:'A WHOLE SPRING FULL OF BLUE-BELLS'

1. D.H. Lawrence to J.M.M. and K.M., 5 March 1916, *The Letters of D.H. Lawrence*, Boulton, vol. II, p. 564.

2. ibid., p. 563.

3. K.M. to Virginia Woolf, 26 April 1919, *The Letters of K.M.*, J.M.M., vol. I, p. 228.

4. K.M. to Brett, 26 February 1922, *The Letters of K.M.*, J.M.M., vol. II, p. 189.

5. K.M. to Beatrice Campbell, 4 May 1916, *Collected Letters*, Scott and O'Sullivan, vol. I, p. 261.

6. D.H. Lawrence to J.M.M. and K.M., 24 February 1916, *The Letters of D.H. Lawrence*, Boulton, vol. I, p. 549.

7. K.M. to Beatrice Campbell, 4 May 1916, *Collected Letters*, Scott and O'Sullivan, p. 262.

8. Frieda Lawrence, 'Katherine Mansfield Day by Day', MS in the Humanities Research Center Library, University of Texas at Austin.

9. K.M. to Beatrice Campbell, 4 May 1916, *Collected Letters*, Scott and O'Sullivan, vol. I, p. 261.

10. K.M. to S.S. Koteliansky, 11 May 1916, *Collected Letters*, Scott and O'Sullivan, vol. I, p. 263.

11. ibid., p. 264.

12. D.H. Lawrence to J.M.M. and K.M., 8 March 1916, *The Letters of D.H. Lawrence*, Boulton, vol. II, p. 570.

13. Cited in Paul Delaney, *D.H. Lawrence's Nightmare* (Harvester, Sussex, 1979), p. 222.

14. D.H. Lawrence to Gordon Campbell, 25 January 1917, *The Letters of D.H. Lawrence*, Boulton, vol. III, p. 83.

15. K.M. to S.S. Koteliansky, 24 June 1916, *Collected Letters*, Scott and O'Sullivan, vol. I, p. 269.

16. K.M. to Ottoline Morrell, 27 June 1916, *Collected Letters*, Scott and O'Sullivan, vol. I, p. 269.

17. D.H. Lawrence to S.S. Koteliansky, 7 July 1916, *The Letters of D.H. Lawrence*, Boulton, vol. II, p. 623.

18. *The Selected Letters of Mark Gertler*, Carrington, p. 114.

19. D.H. Lawrence to S.S. Koteliansky, 10 July 1916, *The Letters of D.H. Lawrence*, Boulton, vol. II, p. 628.

20. D.H. Lawrence, *Women in Love* (Martin Secker, London, 1921), chapter 4.

21. ibid., chapter 17.

22. D.H. Lawrence to K.M., 27 March 1919, *The Letters of D.H. Lawrence*, Boulton, vol. III, p. 343.

23. D.H. Lawrence, *Women in Love*, chapter 24.

24. ibid., chapter 29.
25. ibid.
26. ibid., chapter 30.
27. K.M. to S.S. Koteliansky, 3 July 1916, *Collected Letters*, Scott and O'Sullivan, vol. I, p. 270.
28. Delaney, op. cit., p. 252.
29. Brett, *Lawrence and Brett* (Martin Secker, London, 1933), p. 17.
30. *New Age*, 24 May 1917.
31. Leonard Woolf, op. cit., p. 198.
32. Virginia Woolf to Lytton Strachey, 25 July 1916, *The Letters of Virginia Woolf: 1912–22*, Nicolson, vol. II, p. 107.
33. K.M. to Bertrand Russell, 1 December 1916, *Collected Letters*, Scott and O'Sullivan, vol. I, p. 286.
34. ibid., 7 December 1916.
35. *The Autobiography of Bertrand Russell* (Allen & Unwin, London, 1963), vol. II, p. 27.
36. Gerald Brenan, *Personal Record* (Hamish Hamilton, London, 1974), p. 57.
37. K.M. to J.M.M., early January 1917, *Collected Letters*, Scott and O'Sullivan, vol. I, p. 291.
38. ibid., January 1917, p. 290.
39. F.A. Lea, *John Middleton Murry* (Methuen, London, 1959), p. 84.
40. K.M. to Ottoline Morrell, 14 January 1917, *Collected Letters*, Scott and O'Sullivan, vol. I, p. 291.
41. Virginia Woolf to Vanessa Bell, 11 February 1917, *The Letters of Virginia Woolf: 1912–22*, Nicolson, vol. II, p. 144.
42. ibid., 27 June 1917, p. 159.
43. K.M. to Ottoline Morrell, 3 July 1917, *Collected Letters*, Scott and O'Sullivan, vol. I, p. 315.
44. K.M. to Brett, 11 October 1917, *Collected Letters*, Scott and O'Sullivan, vol. I, p. 331.
45. Humanities Research Center Library, University of Texas at Austin.
46. K.M. to Virginia Woolf, December 1917, *Collected Letters*, Scott and O'Sullivan, vol. I, p. 342.
47. K.M. to Anne Drey, 22 December 1917, *Collected Letters*, Scott and O'Sullivan, vol. I, p. 353.
48. K.M. to J.M.M., 23–24 December 1917, *Collected Letters*, Scott and O'Sullivan, vol. I, p. 358.
49. K.M. to Ottoline Morrell, 28 December 1917, *Collected Letters*, Scott and O'Sullivan, vol. I, p. 362.

12 1918: 'A GREAT BLACK BIRD'

1. J.M.M., *God* (Jonathan Cape, London, 1929), p. 19.
2. K.M. to J.M.M., 11 January 1918, *K.M.'s Letters to J.M.M.: 1913–22*, J.M.M., p. 115.
3. ibid., p. 116.

4. ibid., 18 January 1918, p. 124.
5. ibid., 3 February 1918, p. 150.
6. ibid., 19 February 1918, p. 173.
7. Baker, op. cit., p. 113.
8. J.M.M. to K.M., 10 March 1918, *The Letters of J.M.M. to K.M.*, Hankin, p. 137.
9. Virginia Woolf to Vanessa Bell, 1 February 1918, *The Letters of Virginia Woolf: 1912–22*, Nicolson, vol. I I, p. 214.
10. J.M.M. to K.M., 15 February 1918, *The Letters of J.M.M. to K.M.*, Hankin, p. 121.
11. I am indebted to Sophie Tomlin for showing me an unpublished paper on Katherine Mansfield's work which I found helpful in considering '*Je ne parle pas français*', although our conclusions are not identical.
12. K.M. to J.M.M., 1 February 1918, *K.M.'s Letters to J.M.M.: 1913–22*, J.M.M., p. 148.
13. ibid., 26 March 1918, p. 229.
14. Baker, op. cit., p. 112.
15. K.M. to Brett, 30 April 1918, *Collected Letters*, Scott and O'Sullivan, vol. I I, p. 167.
16. J.M.M., *Between Two Worlds*, p. 481.
17. Virginia Woolf to Ottoline Morrell, 24 May 1918, *The Letters of Virginia Woolf: 1912–22*, Nicolson, vol. I I, p. 243.

13 'HE OUGHT NOT TO HAVE MARRIED'

1. K.M. to J.M.M., 19 May 1918, *K.M.'s Letters to J.M.M.: 1913–22*, J.M.M., p. 250.
2. Cut by J.M.M. from letter dated 26 May 1918, in the Alexander Turnbull Library.
3. Baker, op. cit., p. 122.
4. K.M. to J.M.M., 9 June 1918, *K.M.'s Letters to J.M.M.: 1913–22*, J.M.M., p. 292.
5. *The Diary of Virginia Woolf: 1915–19*, 17 June 1918, Bell, vol. I, p. 156.
6. ibid., 12 June 1918, p. 167.
7. Baker, op. cit., p. 122.
8. ibid., p. 135.
9. *Journal*, December 1920, p. 229.
10. *The Diary of Virginia Woolf: 1915–19*, 9 November 1918, Bell, vol. I, p. 216.
11. Leonard Woolf, op. cit., p. 204.
12. *Journal*, May 1919, p. 158.
13. Baker, op. cit., p. 158.
14. *Journal*, 19 May 1919, p. 154.
15. ibid.
16. ibid., June 1919, p. 166.

14 'A BROTHER ONE *LOVES*'

1. Baker, op. cit., p. 133.
2. K.M. to Brett, 27 October 1918, *The Letters of K.M.*, J.M.M., vol. I, p. 215.

3. D. H. Lawrence to Stanley Hocking, 30 October 1918, *The Letters of D.H. Lawrence*, Boulton, vol. I I I, p. 294.
4. J.M.M., *Reminiscences of D.H. Lawrence*, p. 92.
5. *Journal*, October 1918, p. 150.
6. K.M. to J.M.M., 20 November 1919, *K.M.'s Letters to J.M.M.: 1913–22*, J.M.M., p. 399.
7. J.M.M., *Reminiscences of D.H. Lawrence*, p. 93.
8. D. H. Lawrence to K.M., 29 November 1918, *The Letters of D.H. Lawrence*, Boulton, vol. I I I, p. 301.
9. ibid., 10 December 1918, p. 308.
10. ibid., 5 December 1918, p. 302.
11. ibid., 10 December 1918, p. 307.
12. ibid., 27 March 1919, p. 343.
13. ibid.
14. K.M. to S. S. Koteliansky, 17 July 1922, *The Letters of K.M.*, J.M.M., vol. I I, p. 229.
15. *Journal*, p. 185.
16. K.M. to Violet Schiff, January 1922, *The Letters of K.M.*, J.M.M., vol. I I, p. 175.
17. K.M., *Novels and Novelists*, ed. J.M.M. (Constable, London, 1930), p. 308.
18. K.M. to J.M.M., 8 October 1922, *K.M.'s Letters to J.M.M.: 1913–22*, J.M.M., p. 668.
19. ibid., 19 November 1922, p. 688.
20. ibid., 13 October 1922, p. 671.

15 'A SENSE OF BEING LIKE'

1. K.M. to J.M.M., 12 November 1919, *K.M.'s Letters to J.M.M.: 1913–22*, p. 387.
2. ibid., 17 November 1919, p. 395.
3. ibid., 23 November 1919, p. 407.
4. ibid., 12 December 1919, p. 442.
5. K.M. to Anne Drey, May 1920, cited in *Adam* (no. 300, 1965), p. 91.
6. J.M.M. to Brett, 8 March 1920, letter in the Special Collections Department, University of Cincinnati Libraries.
7. K.M. to Violet Schiff, May 1920, British Library Add. M S.
8. K.M., *Novels and Novelists*, pp. 107–11.
9. *The Diary of Virginia Woolf: 1915–19*, 18 February 1919, Bell, vol. I, p. 243.
10. ibid., 22 March 1919, p. 258.
11. *The Diary of Virginia Woolf: 1920–24*, 31 May 1920, Bell, vol. I I, p. 43.
12. ibid., 31 May 1920, p. 44.
13. ibid., p. 45.
14. ibid., 25 August 1920, p. 61.
15. ibid., p. 62.
16. Cited in *Adam* (nos. 370–75, 1972) and dated 27 December 1920.
17. E. M. Forster to Sydney Waterlow, January 1921, *The Letters of E.M. Forster*, eds. Mary Lago and P. N. Furbank (Collins, London, 1983), vol. I, p. 312.
18. British Library Add. M S.

19. *New Statesman*, 15 January 1921.
20. *The Diary of Virginia Woolf: 1920–24*, 25 August 1920, Bell, vol. II, p. 61.
21. ibid., 16 January 1923, pp. 225–7.
22. *The Diary of Virginia Woolf: 1925–30*, 7 December 1925, Bell, vol. III, p. 50.
23. Virginia Woolf to Vita Sackville-West, 8 August 1931, *The Letters of Virginia Woolf: 1926–31*, Nicolson, vol. IV, p. 366.
24. *The Diary of Virginia Woolf: 1920–25*, 17 October 1924, Bell, vol. II, p. 317.
25. *The Diary of Virginia Woolf: 1936–41*, 15 January 1941, Bell, vol. V, p. 352.

16 'I AM A WRITER FIRST'

1. *Journal*, September 1920, p. 216.
2. K.M. to J.M.M., 29 September 1920, *K.M.'s Letters to J.M.M.: 1913–22*, J.M.M., p. 547.
3. ibid., 19 September 1920, p. 539.
4. ibid., 28 November 1920, p. 602.
5. ibid., 16 September, 1920, p. 536.
6. K.M. to J. B. Pinker, 3 May 1922, unpublished letter in the Newberry Library, Chicago.
7. Gilbert Phelps Hutchinson, *The Russian Novel in English Literature* (Hutchinson, London, 1956), pp. 189–90.
8. George Bernard Shaw to Floryan Sobieniowski, 26 September 1924, *The Letters of George Bernard Shaw*, ed. Dan H. Laurence, vol. III, pp. 883–4.
9. K.M. to J.M.M., 31 October 1920, *K.M.'s Letters to J.M.M.: 1913–22*, J.M.M., p. 579.
10. ibid., 10 November 1920, p. 591.
11. ibid., 16 October 1920, p. 563.
12. ibid., 31 October 1920, p. 579.
13. Letter to Ida Baker, which she showed to the author.
14. K.M. to J.M.M., 17 November 1920, *K.M.'s Letters to J.M.M.: 1913–22*, J.M.M., p. 597.
15. ibid., 3 December 1920, p. 610.
16. ibid., 12 December 1920, p. 622.
17. Baker, op. cit., p. 162.
18. Mairet, op. cit., p. 59.
19. Cited in Alpers, op. cit., p. 332.
20. K.M. to J.M.M., 12 December 1920, *K.M.'s Letters to J.M.M.: 1913–22*, J.M.M., p. 622.

17 'READ AS MUCH LOVE AS YOU LIKE INTO THIS LETTER'

1. K.M. to Ottoline Morrell, June 1921, *The Letters of K.M.*, J.M.M., vol. II, p. 118.
2. *Athenaeum*, 4 June 1921.
3. K.M. to Elizabeth (Countess Russell), December 1921, *The Letters of K.M.*, J.M.M., vol. II, p. 163.
4. K.M. to Brett, 29 August 1921, *The Letters of K.M.*, J.M.M., vol. II, p. 131.

5. Baker, op. cit., p. 172.
6. *Journal*, 1 February 1922, p. 293.
7. ibid., 4 February 1922, p. 294.
8. Baker, op. cit., p. 177.
9. ibid., p. 186.
10. K.M. to Brett, 19 March 1922, *The Letters of K.M.*, J.M.M., vol. II, p. 199.
11. Baker, op. cit., p. 197.
12. ibid., p. 203.
13 K M to Brett, 6 June 1922, *The Letters of K.M.*, J.M.M., vol. II, p. 216.
14. Cited in Lea, op. cit., p. 113.

18 'I WANT TO *WORK*'

1. Constance Garnett to Edward Garnett [1922], unpublished letter in possession of Richard Garnett.
2. Cited by Ruth Elvish Mantz, 'In Consequence: Katherine and Kot', *Adam* (nos. 370–75, 1972), pp. 95–106.
3. K.M. to Brett, 3 October 1922, *The Letters of K.M.*, J.M.M., vol. II, p. 247.
4. *Journal*, 14 October 1922, pp. 331–2.
5. ibid., pp. 333–4.
6. Baker, op. cit., p. 213.
7. ibid., p. 218.
8. ibid., p. 226.
9. ibid., p. 234.
10. K.M. to J.M.M., 19 November 1922, *K.M.'s Letters to J.M.M.: 1913–22*, J.M.M., p. 688.
11. *New English Weekly*, 19 May 1932.
12. ibid.
13. ibid.
14. K.M. to J.M.M., 31 December 1922, *K.M.'s Letters to J.M.M.: 1913–22*, J.M.M., p. 699.
15. Murry's narrative, *K.M.'s Letters to J.M.M.: 1913–22*, J.M.M., p. 700.
16. ibid., p. 701.

19 'WHAT IS GOING TO HAPPEN TO US ALL?'

1. D. H. Lawrence to J.M.M., 2 February 1923, *The Letters of D.H. Lawrence*, Boulton, vol. IV, p. 375.
2. ibid., 25 October 1923, p. 520.
3. D. H. Lawrence to Adele Seltzer, 24 September 1923, *The Letters of D.H. Lawrence*, Boulton, vol. IV, p. 503.
4. Testimony of K. S. Crichton in Edward Nehls, *D.H. Lawrence: A Composite Biography* (University of Wisconsin Press, Madison, 1957), vol. II, p. 414.
5. Information from Mrs Valerie Eliot.
6. Information from Moira Lynd.

7. V. S. Pritchett in the *New Statesman*, 1946.
8. *Journal*, 14 October 1921, p. 266.
9. J.M.M., *Katherine Mansfield and Other Literary Portraits* (Constable, London, 1959), p. 72.

APPENDIX 1

'LEVES AMORES'

I can never forget the Thistle Hotel.* I can never forget that strange winter night.

I had asked her to dine with me, and then go to the Opera. My room was opposite hers. She said she would come but – could I lace up her evening bodice, it was hooks at the back. Very well.

It was still daylight when I knocked at the door and entered. In her petticoat bodice and a full silk petticoat she was washing, sponging her face and neck. She said she was finished, and I might sit on the bed and wait for her. So I looked round at the dreary room. The one filthy window faced the street. She could see the choked, dust-grimed window of a wash-house opposite. For furniture, the room contained a low bed, draped with revolting, yellow, vine-patterned curtains, a chair, a wardrobe with a piece of cracked mirror attached, a washstand. But the wallpaper hurt me physically. It hung in tattered strips from the wall. In its less discoloured and faded patches I could trace the pattern of roses – buds and flowers – and the frieze was a conventional design of birds, of what genus the good God alone knows.

And this was where she lived. I watched her curiously. She was pulling on long, thin stockings, and saying 'damn' when she could not find her suspenders. And I felt within me a certainty that nothing beautiful could ever happen in that room, and for her I felt contempt, a little tolerance, a very little pity.

A dull, grey light hovered over everything; it seemed to accentuate the thin tawdriness of her clothes, the squalor of her life, she, too, looked dull and grey and tired. And I sat on the bed, and thought: 'Come, this Old Age. I have forgotten passion, I have been left behind in the beautiful golden procession of Youth. Now I am seeing life in the dressing-room of the theatre.'

So we dined somewhere and went to the Opera. It was late, when we came out into the crowded night street, late and cold. She gathered up her long skirts.

---

* The text has been copied from a typescript lent to me by Navin Sullivan, son of Vere Bartrick-Baker, who left it among her papers.

Silently we walked back to the Thistle Hotel, down the white pathway fringed with beautiful golden lilies, up the amethyst shadowed staircase.

Was Youth dead? ... *Was* Youth dead?

She told me as we walked along the corridor to her room that she was glad the night had come. I did not ask why. I was glad, too. It seemed a secret between us. So I went with her into her room to undo those troublesome hooks. She lit a little candle on an enamel bracket. The light filled the room with darkness. Like a sleepy child she slipped out of her frock and then, suddenly, turned to me and flung her arms round my neck. Every bird upon the bulging frieze broke into song. Every rose upon the tattered paper budded and formed into blossom. Yes, even the green vine upon the bed curtains wreathed itself into strange chaplets and garlands, twined round us in a leafy embrace, held us with a thousand clinging tendrils.

And Youth was not dead.

[Signed] K. Mansfield.

APPENDIX 2

'THE CHILD-WHO-WAS-TIRED': *THE TIMES LITERARY SUPPLEMENT* CORRESPONDENCE

■

19 OCTOBER 1951

Sir – About three years ago Messrs. Constable reprinted the collected edition of Katherine Mansfield's stories. I had never read her before, but, looking through the volume, I got a curious sense of walking through once well-familiar rooms. The feeling was intensified when I came to the end of the volume which contains the stories under the collective title of *In a German Pension* – first published in 1911, and here prefaced by an introductory note by Mr J. Middleton Murry which told me that the sketches and stories composing the volume first appeared in the *New Age* between 1909 and 1911, that the publisher who brought out the book went bankrupt, and that 'Katherine Mansfield was not very disappointed. She quickly became indifferent to the book; then hostile.' Mr Middleton Murry mentions that later offers were made for the reissue of the book, but nothing would induce Katherine Mansfield to have it brought out again. As late as 1920 she wrote, '... I cannot have *The German Pension* reprinted under any circumstances ... I don't even acknowledge it today. I mean I don't hold by it. I can't go on foisting that kind of stuff on the public. *It's not good enough* [the italics are K.M.'s] ... I could not for a moment entertain republishing [it]. ... It's not what I mean, it's a lie ...' But, some time later, Katherine Mansfield yielded to her friends' persuasion and Mr Middleton Murry quotes from her letter expressing consent to have *The German Pension* reprinted: 'But I must write an introduction saying it is early, early work ... because you know ... it's nothing to be proud of. If you didn't advise me, I should drop it overboard ... It makes me simply hang my head ...' Katherine Mansfield never wrote the introduction, and the only living story in the whole book is 'The Child-Who-Was-Tired'. I read it, and the vague sense of familiarity became a disturbing certainty, and, bearing in mind that the Mansfield story was written about 1909, I turned to my Chekhov. The late Prof. Brückner's *Literary History of Russia*, translated by H. Havelock, and published in England in 1908, tells me that by 1905 most of Chekhov's stories had appeared in English.

The particular story I have in mind bears the title '*Spat' khochetsia*'. The tense of the second verb is rather untranslatable in English. It might be rendered as '*I'd like to sleep* ...' It was written by Chekhov in 1888 – *i.e.*, when he was still a young man. It is a terrible picture of a single day in the life of a very small maid-of-all-work in a Moscow cobbler's family. It is a study in black pierced by a single poignant pinpoint of light: the child's desire for sleep. Her past and her present are but stage props. Not a sentence but leads to the inevitable horror of the climax when, half-awake, half-aware, the child realizes (however, falsely, as Chekhov says) that the baby, whose cot she must rock all through the night, is her main enemy, and she comes to a decision to overthrow the enemy by the only means within her reach. In her state of perpetually enforced drowsiness, the child half-dreams about her earlier years, her father's death, her mother's companionship, and the road she must walk to come within the gates of her salvation. The road is sleep, and she can't walk it – because of the cobbler's baby. Chekhov's consummate artistry does not allow him to cumber the background with irrelevancies. There is the child, and the ghostly silhouettes of her parents. There are the brutal cobbler and his wife brought to life within a couple of sentences. But the living people and the ghosts vanish soon enough: nothing is left except her memories of a kindly past, and the crying baby, whose wailing becomes a barrier between the little maid-of-all-work and the desire for sleep. So the shadows deepen unto absolute dark, and the crash comes – all within two or three paragraphs.

Katherine Mansfield's story is laid in Germany. The background is crowded. The mistress and her husband have other children, and another baby is on the way – which, however feebly, is used to explain the climax. A single page of Chekhov's, illustrating the little girl's terribly exhausting day, is here extended to a series of incidents, none of which have much bearing on the climax. Katherine Mansfield begins her story more or less in the middle of Chekhov's version, as will be shown below, and the Mansfield maid-of-all-work, in spite of far more specific biographical details than those given by Chekhov to his child, somehow never comes to life. The attention is distracted by the other children, the gossip of visitors, the irrelevant details, and in the end one is left with a sense of bathos rather than pathos. Did the climax come because of the girl's fear of yet another baby on the way, or because of the actual baby's incessant crying?

What follows are a few parallel passages from the two stories. The translation of the Chekhov passages is my own.

Chekhov
(the middle)

Varka is going through the wood and crying hard, but someone hits her so sharply that she knocks her face against a birch. She raised her eyes and sees the cobbler, her master.

'You – good-for-nothing – you! The child is crying, and you are asleep'; he pulls hard at her ear, and she shakes her head, rocks the cot, and starts crooning her song again.

Mansfield
(the beginning)

She was just beginning to walk along a little white road with tall black trees on either side, a little road that led to nowhere, and where nobody walked at all, when a hand gripped her shoulder, shook her, pulled at her ear: 'Get up, you good-for-nothing brat!'

Chekhov

There come moments when she wants to fall down on the floor and to sleep. The day passes. Looking at the darkening windows, Varka presses her numb temples and smiles for no rhyme or reason. The twilight teases her aching eyes and promises her quick, sound sleep. But guests arrive in the evening.

'Varka, put the samovar on,' shouts the mistress.

The samovar is small, but she must put it on five times before all the guests have had enough tea. The tea finished, she stands for an hour, looking at the company and expecting orders.

'Varka, run and get three bottles of beer.'

She rushes off, trying to run quickly so as to conquer her sleepiness.

'Varka, run and fetch some vodka –'

'Varka, where is the corkscrew?'

'Clean the herring –'

At last, the guests leave; the lights are put out, and her employers go to bed. 'Varka, rock the baby,' comes the last order.

Mansfield

She was afraid to sit down or stand still. When she thought of the nearness of bedtime, she shook all over with excited joy. But as eight o'clock approached, there was the sound of wheels on the road, and presently in came a party of friends to spend the evening.

Then it was:
'Put on the coffee.'
'Bring me the sugar tin.'
'Carry the chairs out of the bedroom.'
'Set the table.'
And, finally, the Frau sent her into the next room to keep the baby quiet.

Chekhov

[Here Chekhov makes Varka get back to her dream. She sees the road, but she feels she can't walk it.]

Something hinders her. She can't understand there must be an enemy who will not let her live or walk. She finds the enemy. It is the child. She laughs. It is wonderful. Why did she not grasp such a simple thing before? ... She gets up from the stool, and, smiling broadly, her eyes unblinking, walks up and down the road. She is pleased and excited at the thought that she will soon be rid of the baby which now chains her whole body. To kill the child, and then to sleep, sleep, sleep ...

Laughing, winking, shaking her finger at a green stain on the ceiling, Varka creeps to the cradle and bends over the child. Having strangled it, she at once tumbles down on the floor, and laughs at the joy of being able to sleep, and within a moment is fast asleep.

Mansfield

And she suddenly had a beautiful, marvellous idea. She laughed for the first time that day and clapped her hands ... And then gently, smiling, on tiptoe, she brought the pink bolster from the Frau's bed and covered the baby's face with it, pressing with all her might as he struggled. Like a duck with its head off, wriggling, she thought. She heaved a long sigh then fell back on to the floor, and was walking along a little white road with tall black trees on either side, a little road that led to nowhere, and where nobody walked at all, nobody at all.

This is the only story of Katherine Mansfield's which I have been able to compare in detail with Chekhov's. There may be others. Unfortunately, I don't possess a complete edition of his stories and plays. Here and there, in the Constable edition of K. Mansfield, I have come across typically Chekhovian 'beginnings' such as, for example 'Eight o'clock in the morning' (*Pictures*, p. 119). If I can ever find a complete edition of Chekhov I might discover further parallels – I can't tell. Mr Middleton Murry attributes her reluctance to have *The German Pension* reprinted to a consciousness of its immaturity, but I am inclined to disagree with him. 'The Child-Who-Was-Tired' in spite of its different setting and far greater length, is merely a copy of Chekhov's story written twenty-one years ago, and not a very good copy either. Chekhov and de Maupassant had few peers in the art of short-story telling, and Katherine Mansfield was certainly not one of them.

E. M. Almedingen

26 OCTOBER 1951

Sir – Miss Almedingen has put a strong *prima facie* case that Katherine Mansfield's youthful story, 'The Child-Who-Was-Tired', was taken substantially from the story by Chekhov, '*Spat' khochetsia*'. But there are difficulties in this supposition, which need to be cleared up.

The first is this. Miss Almedingen *assumes* that an English translation of the Chekhov story was in existence in 1909. She bases this assumption on the statement in a German book published in 1908, that 'by 1905 most of Chekhov's stories had appeared in English'.

I am confident that the German statement is not true. Few of Chekhov's stories had been translated into English in 1905; and still few by 1909. Indeed, I am pretty sure that the story which Katherine Mansfield is alleged to have copied was not available in English then. Has it been translated even now? If it has been, it is very curious that the many students who have written theses on the influence of Chekhov on Katherine Mansfield should have missed this apparently glaring instance.

On the assumption that Chekhov's story was *not* extant in an English translation in 1909 – and I must ask Miss Almedingen to prove that it was – a second difficulty arises. Katherine Mansfield certainly knew no Russian in 1909; in the last months of her life she was painfully learning the rudiments. So that if she did copy Chekhov's story, she must have had access to it in a French or German translation. I very much doubt whether a French version was extant in 1909. Chekhov's popularity came much later in France than in England. A German translation seems to be the only solution. Katherine Mansfield read German easily; she was in Germany in 1909; and I believe 'The Child-Who-Was-Tired' was written there. But if (as is possible) no German translation of Chekhov's story was extant in 1909, there is a real mystery, which needs explanation.

In the interim, I must protest against Miss Almedingen's insinuation that, *if* she possessed a complete edition of Chekhov's, she might be able to discover similar borrowings in other stories of Katherine Mansfield. What she calls 'the typically Chekhovian' opening of *Pictures* amounts to nothing; there is no

· 265 ·

reason to suppose even the influence of Chekhov here; and in any case it is quite different from the kind of borrowing, or copying, which is imputed to her in the case of '*Spat' khochetsia*'. On the face of it, that amounts to plagiarism. Therefore one must be wary of accepting it. It may be true; and it may be that, as Miss Almedingen suggests, this was the real reason why Katherine Mansfield was so extremely reluctant to have *In a German Pension* republished. But, until it is proved that she could have had access to this story in either an English, French or German translation in 1909, judgement must be suspended. It would be very helpful for those ignorant of Russian if Miss Almedingen would direct us to an English translation of the *whole* Chekhov story in order that it may be more diligently compared with 'The Child-Who-Was-Tired'.

J. Middleton Murry

Editor's note: For purposes of comparison the most accessible version of '*Spat' khochetsia*' is Constance Garnett's translation (Sleepy) contained in *Select Tales of Tchekov* (Chatto & Windus, 1927; reprinted 1949).

2 NOVEMBER 1951

Sir – Mr Middleton Murry has asked me for a proof that an English translation of Chekhov's '*Spat' khochetsia*' was extant in 1909, and I can furnish such a proof.

In 1903 and 1908 two volumes of Chekhov's short stories appeared in London. The 1903 collection, translated by R. E. C. Long and published by Duckworth, bore the title *The Black Monk*. It contained twelve stories, and '*Spat' khochetsia*', there rendered as 'Sleepyhead', was among them. That, I think, disposes of the idea that '*Spat' khochetsia*' could not have been available to an English reader in 1909.

E. M. Almedingen

Sir – The extensive space you give, in your issue of 19 October, to Miss E. M. Almedingen's analysis of the likenesses between Chekhov's story 'Sleepyhead' (as the title appears in the published translation) and Katherine Mansfield's 'The Child-Who-Was-Tired' places undue and distorting emphasis upon what is after all a minor matter. The similarities between the two stories have already been examined by Miss Elizabeth Schneider (*Modern Language Notes*, June, 1935), again in the *Mercure de France* (I think in an issue of about 1940; the exact reference is not accessible to me at present). A detailed comparative analysis of several of Katherine Mansfield's stories and Chekhov's appears in *Dead Reckonings in Fiction*, by Dorothy Brewster and Angus Burrell, so that Miss E. M. Almedingen may be spared further research.

Originally 'The Child-Who-Was-Tired' was published by Orage in his journal the *New Age*. I am inclined to think that Katherine Mansfield deliberately adapted the story as a literary exercise, and was careless, rather than devious, about acknowledgement when it appeared in print. It is exceedingly unjust to ascribe her unwillingness to have *In a German Pension* reprinted to the fact that she knew she had 'copied' a Chekhov story a decade before. She took her calling as a writer very seriously. As she matured, her whole consuming endeavour was to attain the greatest possible fidelity to her understanding of life. However one may estimate her achievement (and the stories do persist in being read, in the United States, in France, in Italy, even in England), her sincerity is beyond question. When she writes that she is not proud of her early work, she speaks truthfully; she is referring to attitude, judgement, interpretation of experience, apprehension of truth, the constant preoccupations of her closing years, as one can readily find in her *Journal* and her *Letters*. To impugn her integrity is to impugn the substance of the intense spiritual struggle which culminated in her death at Fontainebleau.

Sylvia Berkman
Via Raimondo da Capua 4, Rome

9 NOVEMBER 1951

Sir – In the course of writing a biography of Katherine Mansfield I have tried to clear up the case of 'The Child-Who-Was-Tired' and '*Spat' khochetsia*', and to determine its bearing on the whole Mansfield–Chekhov question.

I am convinced that Katherine Mansfield did not know the English version of '*Spat' khochetsia*', published in 1903, when she was a schoolgirl in London, in *The Black Monk and Other Stories*. Neither in the copious 'Reading Notes', which she kept at school and later, nor in a collection of letters of the time which I have seen, nor in the recollections of intimate friends with whom she invariably discussed her latest literary 'discoveries' as a girl, is there a single reference to Chekhov.

I believe that her means of access to the story was either a German or even a Polish translation, and that she encountered it in 1909.

'The Child-Who-Was-Tired' was first published by A. R. Orage in the *New Age* in February 1910, immediately after Katherine Mansfield's sojourn in Bavaria. It was the first story of hers that Orage printed. I incline to the belief that she was introduced to '*Spat' khochetsia*' – and to the Russian concept of the short story in general – by one of the enthusiastic literary Poles whom she met in Wörishofen; that she may never have read it for herself but had it read to her (though a direct reading from the German seems more likely); that she tried her hand at recomposing it as an exercise; and that she offered it, rather naughtily, to Orage on her return in the belief that it had not previously appeared in English.

Miss Almedingen's insinuation that the real reason for Katherine Mansfield's reluctance to allow a reprint of *In a German Pension* (which contained the story in question, with others belonging to the Bavarian episode) was a fear of being found out this time will not stand up beside the facts. It implies a furtiveness which had no place in Katherine Mansfield's character, and which her subsequent removal of the prohibition belies. I am sure Miss Almedingen would not have made it had she been familiar with the severe self-criticisms contained in the *Letters* and the *Journal*, and in certain of the *Athenaeum* reviews reprinted in *Novels and Novelists*. She would have known that Katherine Mansfield didn't waste shame on youthful peccadilloes, but did feel deeply about the facile satire of the rest of *In a German Pension*, satire that had been welcomed with anti-German glee in 1912.

As to the larger question of whether Katherine Mansfield imitated Chekhov or derived her method from him, the starting point for that is not, in my opinion, 'The Child-Who-Was-Tired', but an earlier story. 'The Tiredness of Rosabel', written in 1908 when K.M. was nineteen and had not (as I submit) read anything of Chekhov's, embodies, with all its immaturities, all the essential features by which a characteristic Katherine Mansfield story can be recognized. It was a fluke which foreshadowed her later work with perfect originality and remarkable completeness. Coming after it, 'The Child-Who-Was-Tired' was in the nature of an exercise, an *à la manière de Chekhov* by an artist who had already hit upon her personal *métier*.

Antony Alpers

Sir – I apologize for this further trespass on your space, but how does Miss Berkman explain 'undue and distorting' emphasis on what she calls 'a minor matter', and what is, in fact, the whole theme of the story? Katherine Mansfield's self-confessed unwillingness to have the story reprinted is, I believe, a point in her favour rather than otherwise. Miss Berkman is inclined to believe that the story was deliberately adapted 'as a literary exercise'. Even if I were prepared to accept that, I would still maintain that such 'literary exercises', if printed at all, should be accompanied by a frank acknowledgement of the source. Anyone wholly unacquainted with Chekhov's work, either in the original or in a translation, would naturally accept 'The Child-Who-Was-Tired' as an original story, and it is not.

E. M. Almedingen

Sir – May I interpose with a possible explanation of the 'Sleepy' story mystery? Among the snares besetting the pathway of the short-story writer are those kind creatures who insist upon telling you incidents for you to 'write up'. Their episodes are always personally experienced by them, or the participants are their actual acquaintances, it is real life, they vouch for its truth, and so forth. These realities generally fail to arouse any enthusiasm in the writer's bosom, but very very occasionally he may be inspired to use a piece of such material. This kind of thing has happened to me three times – with rather embarrassing results. I can quite well see that this story of 'Sleepy' came to Katherine Mansfield in such a way, was told to her by a person who claimed to know the participants personally in a real-life story.

My own first instance was presented to me in a country inn near Oxford where an old thatcher related an excellent yarn about a friend of his 'dead these thirty year, can see his gravestone over there in churchyard,' etc., and so on. I wrote up the story, published it, got paid for it, gave the old thatcher a present, and a few years later came across the undoubted origin of my thatcher's yarn in *The Hundred Merry Tales* referred to by Shakespeare in *Much Ado About Nothing*. My second example was a clear case of appropriation by a reader from one of Stephen McKenna's novels. Fortunately I was made aware of it in time and destroyed the manuscript. The third case likewise was told me as a true tale, not fiction. I wrote it and published it in the usual way. Some time later I read a story in the *Cornhill* which was obviously based on my tale. I kicked up a fuss about such 'blatant plagiarism', but was soon convinced that the *Cornhill* writer had never heard of me, but had derived his material from a source which if not identical with mine was closely related!

I have no doubt at all that some similar circumstance betrayed Katherine Mansfield, that someone who had read or heard of Chekhov's tale told it to her as original material, and that the questions of whether she understood Russian or had access to early German or French translations of Chekhov, and the dates thereof, are of no importance. Incidentally, I must say that Miss Almedingen's 'discovery' was common knowledge twenty years ago.

Although I neither knew Katherine Mansfield nor corresponded with her, I am as convinced of her artistic integrity as Miss Berkman and Mr Alpers; nobody who has read her sympathetically, as well as delightedly, could have any possible doubt of that, while you have only to read *In a German Pension* to understand her later reluctance to republish such minor work.

As to whether she was influenced by Chekhov – why of course she was! The writer who has not been has still a lot to learn in the art on which she conferred so much distinction.

A. E. Coppard

Sir – Writing as one of the few surviving members of the staff of the *New Age* under Orage's editorship, who also knew Katherine Mansfield, there can be no question about the derivative character of her stories. At that time (1906–8), I had read many of Chekhov's short stories, which were available in several volumes in English translations.

The theme of '*Spat' khochetsia*' reappeared in Katherine Mansfield's moving story 'A Day in the Life of Ma Parker'. The derivative nature of her stories was the subject of several mild protests from me to Orage; but they were without effect as Orage was a close friend of Katherine Mansfield, he being with her at Fontainebleau at her death.

Some other books from which Katherine Mansfield derived the basis of her stories were Hubert Crackanthorpe's remarkable volumes of short stories, *Wreckage* and *Sentimental Studies*, many of which first appeared in the *Yellow Book*. Others were Henry Harland's *Grey Roses* and *Mademoiselle Miss*, and George Egerton's *Keynotes* and *Discords*. Two French authors she apparently knew well were Villiers de Lisle Adam, whose *Contes cruels* is perhaps the most borrowed from collection of short stories (except E. A. Poe) in literature, and Barbey D'Aurevilly. I had happened to have read these authors with some attention, so I could trace many of the themes of Katherine Mansfield's stories back to their origins. Orage's reply to my remonstrance was that all writers of fiction, other than the rare genius like Poe, were derivative, and he quoted many examples from leading figures in the history of literature in support of his action in publishing Katherine Mansfield's stories. Yet he was very critical of other forms of literary borrowing then and now indulged in by some of the leading figures in literature.

C. H. Norman

Sir – Miss Almedingen has asked me to explain the phrases 'undue and distorting emphasis' and 'a minor matter' in my earlier letter in the Chekhov–Katherine Mansfield exchange. To isolate the ambiguous origin of 'The Child-Who-Was-Tired', written in 1910, drawing from it a damaging insinuation against Katherine Mansfield's integrity a decade later, places an emphasis upon the matter which throws it out of proper focus (distorts). It may be worth remarking that at the very time Katherine Mansfield rejected *In a German Pension* as 'too immature', 'not good enough', for the same reasons she rigorously excluded all the stories she had written before 1914 from the collection she was preparing for *Bliss*. In its relationship to her development as a woman and a writer, the whole '*Spat' khochetsia*' incident is of distinctly subsidiary (minor) importance.

Sylvia Berkman

Sir – Will you allow me to sum up the question? Of the correspondents who have written on this subject, Mr Middleton Murry thought that the Chekhov story could not have been accessible to Katherine Mansfield. Miss Berkman thought it to have been 'a deliberately adapted literary exercise'. Mr Alpers had an idea that the Chekhov story may have come to Katherine Mansfield via some Poles met in Germany. Mr Coppard dismissed all the findings as irrelevant, and Mr Norman recorded his own impression of the derivative character of Katherine Mansfield's stories – (incidentally I do not, *pace* one of the correspondents, claim to have made any 'discovery') – but nobody, except Mr Norman, seemed prepared to admit that a story written by Chekhov in 1888 came to be used by Katherine Mansfield in a manner far beyond the scope allowed by mere influence. Bernard Shaw was indebted to Chekhov and, incidentally, in an article in *Pravda* he said that the idea of *Heartbreak House* had come to him after studying Chekhov, but Shaw's play is no echo of Chekhov's.

Katherine Mansfield tried to find her way, and very likely she would have found it, had she been allowed more time, but it is a pity that a writer so gifted never acknowledged her debt to one of the greatest masters of the short story, and I still hold that it was a debt which cannot be explained by mere 'influence', at least, to anyone really familiar with Chekhov's work. I came to read Katherine Mansfield with an open mind – certainly with no intention of 'damaging' her integrity, but I did not see why such a curious example of unacknowledged imitation should pass without comment.

E. M. Almedingen

Sir – Katherine Mansfield has been left so bedraggled by the animus of this belated attack upon her, which she, being dead, is unable to meet, that I beg to be allowed a comment on Miss Almedingen's summing up.

The point at issue is how did Katherine Mansfield come to write that particular story 'The Child-Who-Was-Tired', for nobody could be so stupid as to deny that its origin is Chekhov's story 'Sleepy' – the evidence glares at you. I have not dismissed Miss Almedingen's findings as irrelevant, but I certainly reject her interpretation of the evidence and have cited three examples from my own experience as a short-story writer which indicate a far more probable solution of the little mystery. Furthermore, if Katherine Mansfield was 'merely copying' Chekhov's tale, as Miss Almedingen contends, why did she alter it so calamitously? Her version contains only three items actually paralleled in 'Sleepy', the impact of the visitors, the bright idea, and the murder, the latter being, of course, the dominating intention of both tales. Apart from this, as Miss Almedingen herself insists, the Mansfield version is very different, and inferior, both in structure and décor, Chekhov's marvellously adjusted pre-history of the sad little Varka being replaced by the ineffectual intrusion of three other children, one of whom, Miss Almedingen may care to note, is rather startlingly named Anton!

Mr C. H. Norman, appearing for the prosecution, is altogether summary. 'Writing as one of the few surviving members of the staff of the *New Age* ... there can be no question about the derivative character of her stories.' I may be dull, but this seems to me to be a complete *non sequitur*. He goes on to assert that Katherine Mansfield derived the bases of her stories from many other writers besides Chekhov; he names five of these but omits to give any instances of such derivations beyond the extraordinary assertion that the theme of 'Sleepy' reappears in 'A Day in the Life of Ma Parker'. This piles such a ramshackle Pelion on Miss Almedingen's doubtful Ossa that one obtains quite a clue to the process whereby that wretched sheep-stealing Shakespeare reft all the glamour from high-souled Francis Bacon, de Vere, Uncle Tom Cobley and all.

A. E. Coppard

BIBLIOGRAPHY

∎

I. WORKS BY KATHERINE MANSFIELD

Stories and articles are found in the *New Age*, 1910, 1911, 1917, *Rhythm*, 1912–13, the *Blue Review*, 1913 and *Signature*, 1915.

In a German Pension, Stephen Swift, London, 1911; Knopf, New York, 1922; Constable, London, 1926.

Prelude, Hogarth Press, London, 1918.

Je ne parle pas français, Heron Press, London, 1920.

Bliss and Other Stories, Constable, London, 1920; Knopf, New York, 1921.

The Garden Party and Other Stories, Constable, London, 1922; Knopf, New York, 1922.

The Doves' Nest and Other Stories, Constable, London, 1923; Knopf, New York, 1924.

Poems edited by J. M. Murry, Constable, London, 1923; Knopf, New York, 1924.

Something Childish and Other Stories, Constable, London, 1924; Knopf, New York, 1924.

The Aloe, Constable, London, 1930; Knopf, New York, 1930.

Novels and Novelists edited by J. M. Murry, Constable, 1930. These are the reviews she wrote for the *Athenaeum*.

Stories by Katherine Mansfield, Knopf, New York, 1930. Approximately in chronological order.

Collected Stories of Katherine Mansfield, Knopf, New York, 1937; Constable, London, 1945. This edition, which contains all the stories from *In a German Pension, Bliss, The Garden Party, The Doves' Nest* and *Something Childish*, is still available in hardback.

'Brave Love', a story written in 1905 and never published, was printed by Margaret Scott in *Landfall*, the New Zealand quarterly, 1972.

Undiscovered Country edited by Ian Gordon, Longman, London, 1974, contains all the New Zealand stories, including some omitted by Alpers.

Katherine Mansfield: Publications in Australia 1907–9 edited by Jean Stone, Sydney, 1977. Includes some early material not available elsewhere.

The Stories of Katherine Mansfield edited by Antony Alpers, Oxford University Press, 1984, has useful notes, but, although it is described as the 'definitive edition', omits several stories and some, but not all, fragmentary stories.

Among the many paperback editions in print are a Penguin *Collected Stories* (same text as the Constable hardback); separate Penguin editions of *In a German Pension, Bliss* and *The Garden Party*; a *Selected Stories* chosen by D. M. Davin (Oxford University Press) and an Everyman Classics *Selected Stories* chosen by the present author. *The Aloe* is also available from Virago.

2. LETTERS

The Letters of Katherine Mansfield edited by J. M. Murry, Constable, London, 1928, 2 vols.; Knopf, New York, 1929, 1 vol.

Katherine Mansfield's Letters to John Middleton Murry 1913–22 edited by J. M. Murry, Constable, London, 1951; Knopf, New York, 1951.

Extracts from letters appear in *The Letters and Journals of Katherine Mansfield: A Selection* edited by C. K. Stead, Penguin, 1977.

None of the editions listed above is indexed. Now at last this situation is being remedied with the admirable *The Collected Letters of Katherine Mansfield* edited by Margaret Scott and Vincent O'Sullivan, Oxford University Press. Two volumes have so far appeared, in 1984 and 1987, taking the letters up to 1919.

3. JOURNALS

The Journal of Katherine Mansfield edited by J. M. Murry, Constable, London, 1927; Knopf, New York, 1927.

The Scrapbook of Katherine Mansfield edited by J. M. Murry, Constable, London, 1939.

Both these consisted of material culled in somewhat arbitrary fashion from a mass of papers. Murry reassembled the material into what he called the 'definitive edition' of *The Journal of Katherine Mansfield*, Constable, London, 1954. Currently available in a Constable paperback edition.

The Urewera Notebook edited by Ian Gordon, Oxford University Press, 1980. The notes she kept during her camping trip in 1907.

Many interesting fragments of her journals have been published in Margaret Scott's transcriptions in the *Turnbull Library Record*, Wellington, New Zealand, between 1970 and 1979.

The Life of Katherine Mansfield by Ruth Elvish Mantz and J.M. Murry, Constable, London, 1933.

Reminiscences and Recollections by Sir Harold Beauchamp, New Plymouth, New Zealand, 1937. Very guarded on the subject of his famous daughter; in fact, the chapter on her is written by a tactful 'literary expert', not by Sir Harold.

Katherine Mansfield: A Biography by Antony Alpers, Jonathan Cape, London, 1953. This has been massively enlarged and altered to make Alpers's second version, *The Life of Katherine Mansfield*, Jonathan Cape, London, 1980; Viking, New York, 1980. Also available in paperback, Oxford University Press. Everyone who writes about K.M. is indebted to Antony Alpers, who researched for decades and maintained an impressive equilibrium when dealing with rival authorities and rival versions of the truth.

Katherine Mansfield: The Memories of L.M. by Ida Baker, Michael Joseph, London, 1971. Contains letters and information found nowhere else; but it is sad that Miss Baker did not write her account until she was too old to have reliable recall. Now available as a Virago paperback.

Katherine Mansfield's New Zealand by Vincent O'Sullivan, Golden Press, Auckland, New Zealand, 1974. Fascinating picture and caption material.

Katherine Mansfield: A Biography by Jeffrey Meyers, Hamish Hamilton, London, 1978. Excellent research, less good on interpretation.

Lives and Letters by John Carswell, Faber, London, 1978. Very good on Orage and Koteliansky friendships, but avowedly hostile to K.M. herself.

5 . OTHER WORKS

John Middleton Murry

The Problem of Style, Oxford University Press, 1922. His 1921 Oxford lectures, in which he alludes to K.M.

God, Cape, London, 1925. Contains anecdote about K.M.

Son of Woman: The Story of D.H. Lawrence, Jonathan Cape, London, 1931.

Reminiscences of D.H. Lawrence, Jonathan Cape, London, 1933.

Between Two Worlds, Jonathan Cape, London, 1935; Messner, New York, 1936. Autobiography up to K.M.'s death.

Katherine Mansfield and Other Literary Portraits, Peter Nevill, London, 1949.

Katherine Mansfield and Other Literary Studies, Constable, London, 1959. A posthumous publication, with foreword by T. S. Eliot.

The Letters of John Middleton Murry to Katherine Mansfield selected and edited by C. A. Hankin, Constable, London, 1983.

John Middleton Murry by F.A. Lea, Methuen, London, 1959; Oxford

University Press, New York, 1960. A kindly account by a personal friend and admirer.

To Keep Faith by Mary Middleton Murry (fourth wife and widow), Constable, London, 1959.

One Hand Clapping by Colin Middleton Murry, Gollancz, London, 1975; and *Beloved Quixote* by Katherine Middleton Murry, Souvenir Press, London, 1986. Murry's son and daughter by his second wife fill out the picture of his character.

D. H. Lawrence

Sons and Lovers, Duckworth, London, 1913; Mitchell Kennedy, New York, 1913.

The Rainbow, Methuen, London, 1915; B. W. Huebsch, New York, 1916.

Women in Love (privately printed for subscribers only), New York, 1920; Martin Secker, London, 1921.

Touch and Go, C. W. Daniel, London, 1920.

The Lost Girl, Martin Secker, London, 1920; Seltzer, New York, 1922.

Aaron's Rod, Martin Secker, London, 1922; Seltzer, New York, 1922.

The Tales of D.H. Lawrence, Martin Secker, London, 1934.

D.H. Lawrence: l'homme et la genèse de son œuvre by Emile Delavenay, Klinckseck, Paris, 1969, 2 vols.; in English *D.H. Lawrence: The Man and His Work*, Heinemann, London, 1972, 1 vol.; Southern Illinois University Press, 1972.

D.H. Lawrence and Edward Carpenter by Emile Delavenay, Heinemann, London, 1971.

D.H. Lawrence's Nightmare by Paul Delaney, New York, 1978; Harvester, Sussex, 1979.

D.H. Lawrence: A Composite Biography edited by Edward Nehls Madison, University of Wisconsin Press, Madison, 1957–9, 3 vols.

The Letters of D.H. Lawrence under the general editorship of James T. Boulton, Cambridge University Press, 1979. Four volumes have been issued so far, taking us up to 1924. They supersede Aldous Huxley's 1932 edition and the two volumes edited by Harry T. Moore in 1962.

Not I, But the Wind by Frieda Lawrence, Viking, New York, 1934; Heinemann, London, 1935.

The Memoirs and Correspondence of Frieda Lawrence edited by E. W. Tedlock, Heinemann, London, 1961; Knopf, New York, 1964.

Frieda Lawrence by Robert Lucas, Secker & Warburg, London, 1973.

Virginia Woolf

The Voyage Out, Duckworth, London, 1915.
The Mark on the Wall, Hogarth Press, London, 1917.
Kew Gardens, Hogarth Press, London, 1919.
Night and Day, Duckworth, London, 1919.
Monday or Tuesday, Hogarth Press, London, 1921.
Jacob's Room, Hogarth Press, London, 1922.
The Waves, Hogarth Press, London, 1931.

Virginia Woolf: A Biography by Quentin Bell, Hogarth Press, London, 1972;
    Harcourt Brace Jovanovich, New York, 1972, 2 vols.
The Letters of Virginia Woolf edited by Nigel Nicolson, Hogarth Press, London,
    1975–80, 6 vols.; Harcourt Brace Jovanovich, New York, 1975–80.
The Diaries of Virginia Woolf edited by Anne Olivier Bell, Hogarth Press,
    London 1977–84, 5 vols.; Harcourt Brace Jovanovich, New York, 1977–84.
Virginia Woolf: A Writer's Life by Lyndall Gordon, Oxford University Press,
    1984.

The Autobiography of Leonard Woolf, Hogarth Press, London, 1964 and 1967,
    5 vols.; Harcourt Brace Jovanovich, New York, 1964 and 1967. See especially
    vols. I I I and I V, *Beginning Again* and *Downhill All the Way*.

Lady Ottoline Morrell

Ottoline: The Early Memoirs and *Ottoline at Garsington* edited by Robert
    Gathorne-Hardy, Faber, London, 1963 and 1974; vol. I only, Knopf, New
    York, 1964.
Ottoline: The Life of Lady Ottoline Morrell by Sandra Jobson Darroch, Chatto
    & Windus, London, 1976; Coward, McCann, New York, 1975.

A. R. Orage

Friedrich Nietzsche: The Dionysian Spirit of the Age, Foulis, Edinburgh, 1906.
Nietzsche in Outline and Aphorism, Foulis, Edinburgh, 1907.

The Old New Age: Orage and Others by Beatrice Hastings, Blue Moon Press,
    London, 1935.
A. R. Orage: A Memoir by Philip Mairet, Dent, London, 1936.
Orage and the New Age Circle by Paul Selver, Allen & Unwin, London, 1959.
The New Age Under Orage by Wallace Martin, Manchester University Press,
    1967.

Rooms in the Darwin Hotel by Tom Gibbons, University of Western Australia Press, 1973.

Lives and Letters by John Carswell, Faber, London, 1978.

Miscellaneous

The Journal of Marie Bashkirtseff, Cassell, London, 1890. Now a Virago paperback.

Savage Messiah (life of Gaudier-Brzeska) by H. S. Ede, Heinemann, London, 1931.

The Last Romantic by William Orton, Cassell, London, 1937.

The Autobiography of Bertrand Russell, Allen & Unwin, London, 1963, 2 vols. See especially vol. II.

Today We Will Only Gossip by Beatrice, Lady Glenavy, Constable, London, 1964.

The Selected Letters of Mark Gertler edited by Noel Carrington, Hart-Davis, London, 1965.

Lytton Strachey by Michael Holroyd, Heinemann, London, 1967 and 1968, 2 vols.; Holt, Rinehart & Winston, New York, 1967 and 1968.

The Rise and Fall of the Man of Letters by John Gross, Weidenfeld, London, 1969.

The Life of Bertrand Russell by Ronald Clark, Cape/Weidenfeld, London, 1975.

Gurdjieff by Fritz Peters, Wildwood House, London, 1976.

The First Fabians by Norman and Jean MacKenzie, Weidenfeld, London, 1977.

Gilbert Cannan by Diana Farr, Chatto & Windus, London, 1978.

Gurdjieff and Mansfield by James Moore, Routledge, London, 1980.

Brett by Sean Hignett, Hodder & Stoughton, London, 1984.

T.S. Eliot by Peter Ackroyd, Hamish Hamilton, London, 1984.

'Elizabeth' by Karen Usborne, Bodley Head, London, 1986.

INDEX

■

Murray, John Middleton – *cont*
Harris, 105, 106; hatred of plagiarism, 106;
moves with K.M. to Runcton, 110;
friendship with Gaudier-Brzeska, 107;
financial problems, 110; living in Chancery
Lane, 110, 113; takes 'The Gables', 116; first
meeting with D. H. Lawrence and Frieda,
117–18; failure of *Blue Review* and move to
Chaucer Mansions, 118; moves with K.M.
to Paris, 123; failure to find work and
declared bankrupt, 124; living with K.M. in
Chelsea, 124, 125, 127; witness at wedding
of D.H.L. and Frieda, 128; reaction to
outbreak of war, 129; holiday in Cornwall,
129–30; at 'Rose Tree Cottage', 130;
difficulties with K.M., 132, 133; goes to stay
with Lawrences in Sussex, 134; meets K.M.
on her return from France, 135; takes rooms
in Elgin Crescent, 136; letters to K.M. in
Paris, 136–7; takes house in Acacia Road,
138; brings out *Signature* with D.H.L., 138,
139; goes to France with K.M., 140; spends
Christmas at Garsington, 141; rejoins K.M.
at Villa Pauline, writing book on Dostoevsky,
142; goes with K.M. to Zennor to join
Lawrences, 145; relations with D.H.L., 149;
abuses D.H.L. in letters to Ottoline Morrell,
149; finds cottage at Mylor, 150; gets job in
war office, 154; moves into 'The Ark', 157;
leaves letters on pillows of Ottoline and Brett
(Christmas 1916), 158; lives separately from
K.M. (1917), 159; ill, goes to Garsington to
convalesce, 163; correspondence with K.M.
winter 1917–18, 164–6, 167, 168; reaction to
'*Je ne parle pas français*' and other work, 169,
170; reaction to K.M.'s return, 173; wedding,
173; visits K.M. at Looe, 178; offered
editorship of *Athenaeum*, 182; K.M.'s
feelings for, 182; rejection of D.H.L.'s
articles for *Athenaeum*, 182; relations with
K.M.'s family, 183; jealousy of D.H.L., 185;
travels to San Remo with K.M., 192; returns
to London, 192; Christmas visit to K.M. in
Ospedaletti, 194; plans for holiday with
K.M. summer 1920, 196; flirtations with
Brett and Elizabeth Bibesco, 196–7, 211;
observed by Virginia Woolf with K.M. at
Portland Villas, 198–9; attitude to blackmail
by Floryan Sobieniowski, 207–8; visits K.M.
at Isola Bella, 214; lectures at Oxford, 214;

218; in Switzerland with K.M., 218–19, 222;
reluctant to go to Paris, 223; in Paris, 223–
4; returns to Switzerland with K.M., 225;
separation from K.M., 226–7; travels to
London with her, 228; visits her at Le
Prieuré, 236; present at her death and
funeral, 237, 238; subsequent behaviour,
238, 239, 240, 241–2; letter about 'The-
Child-Who-Was-Tired', 265–6
Works: Aspects of Literature, 208; *Between Two
Worlds*, 97; *Cinnamon and Angelica*, 199; *Son
of Woman: The Story of D H. Lawrence*, 240;
Still Life, 126, 136
Murry, Mary Middleton (fourth wife of
J.M.M.), 77n
Murry, Mr (J.M.M.'s father), 96
Murry, Richard (J.M.M.'s brother, known as
'Arthur', 1902–1984), 180, 229
Mylor (Cornwall), 150, 153

Napier (New Zealand), 39, 41
Nation, 204
Native Companion, 39, 40, 42
Nesbit, Edith (1858–1924): writes to *New Age*,
objecting to Beatrice Hastings's article, 86
New Age, 47–8, 50, 59, 80, 81–2, 84–6, 88–9,
91, 93, 95, 101, 103, 112, 127, 159–60, 170,
259, 265, 266, 268, 270
New Statesman, 84
New Zealand, 8, 10, 35, 124, 126
Newhaven, 58
Nietzsche, Friedrich Wilhelm: admired by
Orage, and subject of two books by him, 83
Nitsch, Rosa, 71
Niwaru, 18, 19
Norman, Clarence, 84, 268, 269, 270
Nottingham, 53, 54

Old Church Street, Chelsea (London), 159
Open Window, 89
Orage, A. R. (1875–1934), 153; editor of *New
Age*, 47, 84; association with Beatrice
Hastings, 47, 84, 136; first meeting with
K.M., 80; encouragement of K.M., 81; her
view of him, 81; his view of her, 81, 91;
family background, early life, 82; education,
82; first marriage, 82; character, 82; in Leeds,
82; ambition, 83; attractiveness to women,
83; comes to London, 83; in Fabian Arts
Group, 83; supports suffragettes at first, 84;

READ MORE IN PENGUIN

In every corner of the world, on every subject under the sun, Penguin represents quality and variety – the very best in publishing today.

For complete information about books available from Penguin – including Puffins, Penguin Classics and Arkana – and how to order them, write to us at the appropriate address below. Please note that for copyright reasons the selection of books varies from country to country.

In the United Kingdom: Please write to *Dept. EP, Penguin Books Ltd, Bath Road, Harmondsworth, West Drayton, Middlesex UB7 0DA*

In the United States: Please write to *Consumer Sales, Penguin Putnam Inc., P.O. Box 999, Dept. 17109, Bergenfield, New Jersey 07621-0120.* VISA and MasterCard holders call 1-800-253-6476 to order Penguin titles

In Canada: Please write to *Penguin Books Canada Ltd, 10 Alcorn Avenue, Suite 300, Toronto, Ontario M4V 3B2*

In Australia: Please write to *Penguin Books Australia Ltd, P.O. Box 257, Ringwood, Victoria 3134*

In New Zealand: Please write to *Penguin Books (NZ) Ltd, Private Bag 102902, North Shore Mail Centre, Auckland 10*

In India: Please write to *Penguin Books India Pvt Ltd, 210 Chiranjiv Tower, 43 Nehru Place, New Delhi 110 019*

In the Netherlands: Please write to *Penguin Books Netherlands bv, Postbus 3507, NL-1001 AH Amsterdam*

In Germany: Please write to *Penguin Books Deutschland GmbH, Metzlerstrasse 26, 60594 Frankfurt am Main*

In Spain: Please write to *Penguin Books S. A., Bravo Murillo 19, 1° B, 28015 Madrid*

In Italy: Please write to *Penguin Italia s.r.l., Via Benedetto Croce 2, 20094 Corsico, Milano*

In France: Please write to *Penguin France, Le Carré Wilson, 62 rue Benjamin Baillaud, 31500 Toulouse*

In Japan: Please write to *Penguin Books Japan Ltd, Kaneko Building, 2-3-25 Koraku, Bunkyo-Ku, Tokyo 112*

In South Africa: Please write to *Penguin Books South Africa (Pty) Ltd, Private Bag X14, Parkview, 2122 Johannesburg*

BY THE SAME AUTHOR

The Invisible Woman
The Story of Nelly Ternan and Charles Dickens

WINNER OF THE NCR BOOK AWARD, THE HAWTHORNDEN PRIZE AND THE
JAMES TAIT BLACK MEMORIAL PRIZE

'A biography of high scholarship and compelling dectective work.
Made visible is Nelly Ternan, and, in the process, Tomalin gives us the
world of a nineteenth-century actress and, most importantly, the real
world of Charles Dickens, whose passions for her – at last proved –
changed his life, his career and his work' Melvyn Bragg, *Independent*

'A masterpiece of sympathetic detection' Richard Holmes

'She tells with great clarity and with much sympathy and
understanding the story that Dickens would never have cared, or
indeed dared, to write' John Mortimer, *Spectator*

The Life and Death of Mary Wollstonecraft

One of the most controversial figures of the late eighteenth century,
Mary Wollstonecraft had travelled to France; lived through the
Terror and the destruction of the incipient French feminist movement;
produced an illegitimate daughter; published *Vindication of the Rights
of Women* (1792); and married William Godwin before dying in
childbirth at the age of thirty-eight. Witty and courageous, yet often
embattled and disappointed, she never gave up her radical ideals or
her belief that courage and good intentions would triumph over dead
convention.

'Wide, penetrating, sympathetic . . . there is no better book on Mary
Wollstonecraft, nor is there likely to be . . . The author brings a deep
understanding to a remarkably complex woman . . . but it is more than
a biography: it illuminates the radical world of the 1780s and 1790s as
few others do' J. H. Plumb, *New Statesman*

'She makes Mary Wollstonecraft unforgettable' Mary Kenny, *Evening
Standard*

BY THE SAME AUTHOR

Her latest, much acclaimed biography

Jane Austen: A Life

'A perfect biography: detailed, witty, warm ... Claire Tomalin involves us so deeply that Austen's final illness and death come almost as a personal tragedy to the reader' Dirk Bogarde, *Daily Telegraph*

'Tomalin is one of our greatest biographers, and her genius is to capture in the story of Austen's life the shifts of tenor, the alternating play of light and shade, comedy and tragic undertone, which characterize the novels ... [Tomalin] enriches and makes brighter our perception of Austen's life and work' Jackie Wullschlager, *Financial Times*

'Tomalin, with scrupulous research and inspired conjecture, offers us a brave, sharp-tongued character who fairly bounces off the page ... This wonderful biography makes you avid to reread and relish Austen's six great novels' Val Hennessy, *Woman's Journal*

Mrs Jordan's Profession

'Claire Tomalin's intelligent, finely made and wonderfully readable new biography not only brings to life a remarkable character and unusual talent, but also provides us with a whole rich background of English life and society ... a story of great poignancy and great romance ... certainly as gripping as the best fiction' Jan Dalley, *Independent on Sunday*

'Claire Tomalin brilliantly animates her lead character, the actress Dora Jordan, the thirteen Jordan children, her weak royal partner (later King William IV), the theatre itself. Meticulous biography at its creative best' Naomi Lewis, *Observer*

'An admirable biography ... it is one her subject would have esteemed, for its technique, brio and warmth' Pat Rogers, *The Times Literary Supplement*